The History of

Sorn

Village & Parish

(Excluding Catrine)

Other books by Dane Love:

Scottish Kirkyards	Robert Hale
The History of Auchinleck – Village & Parish	Carn Publishing
Pictorial History of Cumnock	Alloway Publishing
Pictorial History of Ayr	Alloway Publishing
Scottish Ghosts	Robert Hale
Scottish Ghosts	Barnes & Noble
The Auld Inns of Scotland	Robert Hale
Guide to Scottish Castles	Lomond Books
Tales of the Clan Chiefs	Robert Hale
Scottish Covenanter Stories	Neil Wilson
Ayr Stories	Fort Publishing
Ayrshire Coast	Fort Publishing
Scottish Spectres	Robert Hale
Scottish Spectres	Ulverston Large Print
Ayrshire: Discovering a County	Fort Publishing
Ayr Past and Present	Sutton Publishing
Lost Ayrshire	Birlinn
The River Ayr Way	Carn Publishing
Ayr – the way we were	Fort Publishing
The Man who sold Nelson's Column	Birlinn
Jacobite Stories	Neil Wilson

www.dane-love.co.uk

THE HISTORY OF

SORN

VILLAGE & PARISH

(EXCLUDING CATRINE)

DANE LOVE

CARN PUBLISHING

© Dane Love, 2008.
First Published in Great Britain, 2008.

ISBN - 978 0 9518128 5 3

Published by Carn Publishing,
Lochnoran House,
Auchinleck, Ayrshire, KA18 3JW.

Printed by Bell & Bain Ltd,
Glasgow, G46 7UQ.

Contents

List of Illustrations

Introduction

It is over one hundred years since Helen Steven's *Sorn Parish – its History and Associations* was published and, apart from a number of small booklets and pictorial books with old postcards or photographs, no real history of the parish has been written. And yet the history of Sorn is as interesting as any other parish in Ayrshire, having associations with almost every aspect of Ayrshire history, from the feuds of the sixteenth century, through Covenanting struggles, coal mining, and other industries.

Although this book purports to be a history of the parish of Sorn, I have omitted the history of Catrine from it. The mill-village of Catrine lies within Sorn parish, but to include it would have skewed the history too much away from the village of Sorn and its associations that I have decided to leave Catrine out. Perhaps it will be the subject of a future volume, either by myself or some other local historian.

During the writing of this book I have come across many strange facts and tales associated with the parish, some of which I am sure were not generally known in the parish. Who would have thought, for example, that the ancestors of 'Banjo' Paterson, who wrote 'Waltzing Matilda', came from Sorn, or that if it wasn't for Joseph Train, a son of the parish, many of Sir Walter Scott's works would perhaps not have seen the light of day. It is amazing what turns up with a little digging through the annals of history!

In writing this book I have had considerable assistance from a number of people, all of whom have been keen to supply information for a new history of Sorn parish. Many locals have simply answered questions, whereas others, often from far corners of the world, have supplied more detailed information on various subjects, as well as welcome cups of tea during my visits! I must acknowledge the assistance of Ayrshire Archives, Ayr; Baird Institute Museum, Cumnock; David Bone, formerly of Auchencloigh; Maureen Borland, Kilmarnock; Angus L. Campbell in Manila, Philippines; Lindsay Clark in Daldilling; Bill Frew of Barrshouse; David Frew; Donna Hamilton; Elizabeth Johnstone; The Countess of Lindsey and Abingdon, Gilmilnscroft; Jamie McIntyre of Sorn; Henry Norreys, Lord Norreys of Rycote, Gilmilnscroft; David Shaw of Crofthead; John Sinclair of Glenlogan; and Judy Wardlaw in Melbourne, Australia. There are many others, each of whom have supplied individual nuggets that, when added together, make up a bigger account of the parish.

Dane Love
Auchinleck, 2008.

CHAPTER ONE

EARLY TIMES

DESCRIPTION OF PARISH

The village and parish of Sorn probably get their name from Gaelic, *Sron*, which means nose, snout, projection, or perhaps rough visage, and is descriptive of the headland on which Sorn Castle was built. The *Statistical Account* written in 1796 states that the name Sorn may also mean 'a rising ground of a frowning or unpleasant aspect'. The parish only dates from 1692, when it was disjoined from Mauchline. Initially the parish appears to have been called Dalgain, but at some time this was changed to Sorn, apparently at the wish of the owners of the castle who were to purchase Dalgain estate. Writing in 1852, James Paterson notes that Dalgain Church was 'occasionally called the Church of Sorn ... and ultimately the designation of Sorn altogether supplanted that of Dalgain.' Dalgain is said to mean the 'field of sand' or 'gravel field'.

The parish extends to 19,303 acres (or around 30 square miles), most of it productive farmland, although there are extensive areas of moorland on the eastern edge of the parish, incorporating parts of Airds Moss and the hill of Blackside. It has been calculated that there are also 116½ acres of water. The lowest point of the parish is where the River Ayr leaves it below the old Howford Bridge, where the water is 297 feet above sea level. The highest point of the parish is 1404 feet above sea level, at Blackside. In the *New Statistical Account* of the parish it is stated that some folk claim that sixteen counties are visible from the summit of Blacksidend, but this seems unlikely.

The parish is bounded by the parishes of Mauchline to the west, Galston to the north, Auchinleck to the south and Muirkirk to the east. At a remote spot on Blackside the parish also bounds with Avondale parish in Lanarkshire. At one time part of the farm of Garfield, an enclave within Mauchline parish, extending to 11 acres, formed part of the parish, but this was removed and added to Mauchline in 1891 by the Boundary Commissioners. Part of Sorn parish was designated a *quoad sacra* parish of Catrine in 1871.

The population of the village and parish (which includes the village of Catrine) has varied little over the years, being as follows:

Year	Village	Parish	Year	Village	Parish
1755		1,494	1881	354	4,255
1791		2,800	1891	302	3,919
1796	191	2,779	1901		3,607
1801		2,606	1911		3,758
1811		3,348	1921		3,465
1821		3,865	1931		3,369
1831		4,253	1951	300	3,506
1841		4,054	1961		3,537
1851		4,174	1971	326	3365
1861	363	4,042	1981		3044
1871	393	4,032	1991		2803

The parish populations (from 1801) are taken from the Census returns and include the village of Catrine. The population figures for the village are less precise, and indicate the approximate population of Sorn village at various times over the years.

THE STONE AGE

The writer of the entry for Sorn in the first *Statistical Account of Scotland* wrote that, apart from Sorn Castle, 'there is nothing particularly worthy of being noticed' concerning antiquities in the parish. There are no major relics of the Stone Age in Sorn parish, any that may have existed being long-since removed, and no tradition of there having been stone circles or monoliths survives. However, during ploughing and other disturbances of the ground, a number of Stone Age artefacts have been uncovered at times, many of which have been transferred to the National Museum of Antiquities in Edinburgh, now the National Museum of Scotland.

Sometime prior to 1886 a partially perforated Stone Age axe-hammer head was found in the ground at Blindburn, on what was Dalgain estate. This head is made from the local whinstone, which was in 1988 petrologically identified as being porphyritic olivine basalt. In size, this hammer head measures 9½ inches by 3½ inches by 2½ inches. On one side the half hole is partially perforated, reaching to a depth of ½ inch, and on the opposite side it is 1½ inches deep. The hammer head was donated to the National Museum of Antiquaries in Edinburgh in March 1886 by James Gall in Montgarswood through John Borland, FSA Scot.

Another axe that was found at Montgarswood was also donated to the National Museum in 1894. This axe head was of clay ironstone, which had been polished to make it smooth. The head was six inches in length, and was three inches across at the cutting face.

In 1871 a finely-crafted flint arrow-head was found on the moors east of Newhouse farm, at the northern end of the parish, by Mr MacGavin of Newhouse.

The arrow-head was barb-shaped, with an edge as sharp as a knife all round it. It was reckoned to be one of the finest examples of stone-age arrow-heads found in the district.

The location of a flint scraper found at Carleith farm, on the northern edge of the parish, is lost. This scraper was made from a grey, slightly mottled, flint stone. It measured $3^3/_8$ inches in length, and was 2 inches wide at its widest point. Other ancient stone artefacts found at Carleith include two spindle whorls. One of these had ornamentation on one side; the other appears to have a screw thread in the hole through it. Both were found by John Main in the nineteenth century.

1.1 Scraper found at Carleith
(Author's Collection)

An ancient quern stone, possibly dating from the Stone Age, was found at Auchmannoch farm. This was the upper quern stone from a set, and measured 20 inches in diameter. In the centre was a hole which tapered from 4 inches to 1½ inches, through which the grain would have been fed. To one side was a second, but blind, hole into which a wooden handle would have been placed. The stone, which weighed 67 lb, comprised a quartz conglomerate.

There was probably a stone circle dating from the Stone Age at Auchencloigh farm, at the northern end of the parish. The name Auchencloigh comes from the Gaelic, *Achadh na Cloich*, which means field of stones. Some of the stones were located near to the present steading, but many of them were removed by David William Bone, the farmer at the time, to the edge of the fields. Others, which were too large to move, were blown up. One of the stones was a conglomerate stone, which was alien to the immediate area, indicating that it had been brought some distance to the circle. The surviving stones from the circle were later relocated to Beechcroft cottage, the house erected by David Bone in 2003.

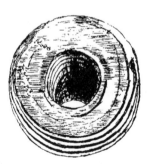

1.2 Spindle whorls found at Carleith *(Author's Collection)*

Writing in *Homes, Haunts and Battlefields of the Covenanters*, in 1888, A. B. Todd makes reference to the stones:

> …it is somewhat remarkable that, fully ninety years ago, a small field near to the house [Auchencloigh] was then thickly covered over with

flat, broad stones, on most of which strange figures were carved, and characters like rough, illegible inscriptions – memorials, doubtless, of the dead, and records, perhaps, of some long-forgotten battle. From, and after the year 1789, the writer's mother passed five years of her girlhood there, and used, in the warm summer days, to rub these strange old stones over with dry, sandy turf, and thus clear them of the lichen, or moss-fog, and then trace, with childish wonderment, the unknown and mysterious characters with which they were covered over. It is unfortunate that they were soon after taken up, broken, and built into the wall of the new houses which were then being erected by or for the then farmer, whose name was William Richmond, and who, it is evident, possessed none of the antiquarian likings and tastes of the Johnathan Oldbuck of Scott's celebrated novel, 'The Antiquary', for when the old houses were taken down, some swords were found hidden away in a hitherto unknown recess in the wall, of which so little care was taken, that they were soon after lost, or taken away.

It is reckoned that the swords may have belonged to supporters of the Covenanters, and had been hidden to prevent them from being found by the dragoons.

THE BRONZE AGE

Bronze Age relics in the parish include the burial cairns that stand on the summits of Blacksidend and Glen Garr. The cairn on Blacksidend has been greatly altered by visiting walkers over the years but is now scheduled as an ancient monument. John Smith, writing in *Prehistoric Man in Ayrshire* in 1895, noted that it 'has been a large one, and is 30 paces in diameter, being surrounded by a thick, dry stone dyke, as if it had been fortified. There are some large stones lying in the centre of it, which probably formed parts of cists. The view from here embraces the greater part of Ayrshire, the height of the hill on which it stands being 1,360 feet.' Recent Ordnance Survey maps indicate that this cairn is located 1349 feet above sea level. Part of the cairn, which was generally elliptical in plan, was destroyed when the Ordnance Survey triangulation station was erected at the site. Today the cairn measures around 90 feet on an east-west axis by 75 feet on a north-south axis, and rises to a maximum height, at the north western end, of five feet. Within the cairn, which comprises large and small stones, which are partially grass covered, modern visitors have carved out two small dry-stone shelters.

The second Bronze Age cairn on this hill range can be found on the summit of Glengarr Hill, or 'Glengyron or Glengaur Hill' according to John Smith. This cairn is located 1404 feet above sea level and is also a scheduled ancient monument. Smith noted that it was 67 paces in diameter and rose seven feet in height. More recent measurements have indicated that the cairn is 80 feet in diameter at its base, but the stone mound is around 55 feet across and rises six feet in height. The cairn comprises sandstone boulders. At one time a stone-built triangulation pillar was erected in the middle of the cairn, but this was later demolished. Although never properly excavated, there are signs that some folk in the past have dug into the mound. From the cairn views can be had of Loudoun Hill and Main Castle fort to the north and north-east.

A third burial cairn existed somewhere on the southern base of Blacksidend Hill. John Smith wrote that it had been 'a large cairn, which has been removed'. Where this was cannot be more accurately determined, and the stone was probably robbed when new stone dikes were erected in the eighteenth century.

Bronze Age cairns of this type are fairly common on the high hills of eastern Ayrshire, there being others on Cairn Table and Wardlaw, near Muirkirk, and elsewhere. Bronze Age man carried their dead chieftains to the hill-tops and laid out the bodies, often enclosing them within chambers formed by large stones, or cists. Over these cists large cairns of either earth or stone were raised, becoming prominent landmarks in the locality.

On Brown's Muir, at Meadowhead of Auchmannoch, near to a modern duck pond at Todhills, is a small knoll known as Keekie Fawr, the old Scots for 'gaze afar'. This knoll affords a wide panorama around the Ayrshire countryside and it has been speculated that it may be an ancient burial cairn or other mound. For many years locals traditionally went here for a picnic, and the women often gathered moss from the surroundings, used for dressing wounds.

1.3 Bronze flagon found at Carleith
(Author's Collection)

A very rare Bronze Age flagon, or tripod ewer, was discovered on the farm of Carleith in the nineteenth century. It has three short legs and a kettle of around 6½ inches in height on top. A fine handle is located to one side, and an elongated spout, supported by a tie, on the other. As Carleith was part of Lanfine estate at that time, the flagon was passed to the owner and remained in the possession of the Browns of Lanfine for many years. It was later passed over to the National Museum of Antiquities in Edinburgh.

OTHER ANTIQUITIES

An ancient enclosure can be found on a low knoll at Reoch Hill, on Auchmannoch Muir, 926 feet above sea level. This measures approximately 45 feet in diameter, though the boundary rim is currently only around three feet in height at most. The enclosure is surrounded by a ditch that measures from six to nine feet across and which is around eight inches deep in places. There may be remains of a causeway at the south-west side. On the south-eastern side are traces of a second, outer bank, which is around six feet wide. In the middle of the enclosure is a sizeable stone. It is difficult to ascertain what the earthwork was, as it is now overgrown with peat and moss, and appears to have been considerably eroded. It may have been a funerary site. Four other old enclosures of indeterminable date are located to the south of Reoch Hill. The westmost is around 40 feet square. Just east of it is a rectangular enclosure measuring around 55 feet by 40 feet. East again is a third enclosure 25 feet in diameter, and to the south of these is a fourth enclosure measuring approximately 60 feet by 65 feet. These four enclosures were probably early cattle folds or small field plots.

During the Norman period a motte and bailey were constructed on an elevated position above the River Ayr, almost two miles upstream from Sorn. It is known today as the Castle Hill but due to the growth of bushes and trees it is difficult to make out on the ground. The site is an ideally defensive one, being located high on a promontory between the River Ayr to the south and the Wyndy or Hole Burn to the west. The motte is a circular knoll, measuring 46 feet in diameter and standing 68 feet in height. In front of the motte is a smaller mound, and beyond this is an enclosure, measuring 66 feet square. The western side of this is defended by a strong parapet constructed of earth and boulders. The opposite side has lost its parapet, and it has been speculated that it collapsed into the River Ayr at some time. This enclosure was probably the bailey associated with the motte hill. A narrow neck of land joins the motte hill with the adjoining land, a causeway lined with stones being noted. Archibald Fairbairn carried out some minor excavations on site sometime around 1913-27, and on the flat summit of the motte hill he found a very dark soil indicative of occupation. Two feet under this soil he found a clay floor. As part of the western side of the motte had collapsed into the Hole Burn, located steeply below, he was able to unearth a mass of red burnt ash, charcoal, pieces of slag, teeth, bones, and other items typical of a dumping ground.

A second old castle site exists at the northern end of the parish, near to Little Carleith. Castle Daffin, as it is named, is today a low mound located on the rising slopes of the ground about 500 feet to the south east of Little Carleith. The land rises a few feet above the level of the surrounding field, and the earthworks are about one quarter of an acre in extent. The castle was also known as Carleith Tower. Little is known of the history of this castle, or timber motte as it may have been, but locals claim that it had connections with Sir William Wallace. Tradition claims that in the thirteenth century Castle Daffin was owned by the Cunninghame family, but that one of their sons was held prisoner in England, as a bond over the Cunninghames in order that they would keep the peace. However, this son escaped, resulting in the English soldiers from Ayr barracks attacking the castle, killing all the occupants – traditionally fourteen people in all. William Wallace is said to have arrived at Castle Daffin soon after, for the Cunninghames were relatives, and found the slaughtered household. It was this deed that is claimed to have given him the drive to fight for Scottish freedom, and he set off for Lanark, where he found out that Sir John Fenwick, one of the English leaders, was responsible for the murders. Wallace and his men were to attack the English at the Battle of Loudoun Hill in 1296, where he killed Fenwick with a single blow from his longsword. The story may be apocryphal, however.

A celt made from ironstone, measuring around six inches in length, was found prior to 1895 within a wood at Montgarswood. A celt was a stone hatchet, adze or chisel, from the Latin *celtis*, meaning chisel.

On 24 June 1837, when a new footpath was being constructed through a wood in the Cleuch Glen, which was built to link Sorn Castle with Dykeneuk farm, a hoard of ancient coins was discovered. It was located only three inches below the level of the ground and was disturbed by the shovel of one of the workmen. The hoard comprised of around 500 coins, mainly silver and copper coins dating from the reigns of James IV and James VI (1488-1513 and 1567-1625, respectively), though some were dated to the reign of Robert III (1390-1406). The denomination of the coins was small, and some of them appeared to have had some of their edges clipped, as though parts of them were removed in order to get the silver. The coins were handed over to the Exchequer, as treasure trove, but around 50 of them were returned to the area and kept at Sorn Castle. The find is noted in J. Lindsay's *Coinage of Scotland*, published in 1845.

CHAPTER TWO

PARISH LIFE

PRE-1656

The parish of Sorn, as it was to become, was originally part of the larger Mauchline parish, and as such was for centuries owned by the monks of Melrose Abbey in the Borders. During the time of King William the Lion, these lands were granted by him to the monks, and they ran the estate of Kylesmure, as it was known, from the castle at Mauchline. From the records of Melrose Abbey we can glean a few early records associated with Sorn parish, which at that time would have been very different to what it is today.

In 1430 the lands of Kylesmure were erected into a regality, which meant that the abbot and monks had the power of law over their tenants. These powers were extended in 1510 when Mauchline was created a burgh. The bailies for the barony were the Campbells of Loudoun, whose family was later to acquire much of the parish when the abbey estates were broken up.

During the period when the parish was owned by Melrose Abbey, there were numerous small ferm-touns, or groupings of cottages across the parish. These would operate a rotating run-rig system of agriculture. The lands were occupied by rentallers, who held their holdings for their lifetime, paying their rent twice yearly. This could either be paid in cash or, in many cases, in kind. When some repair work was being done to Mauchline Castle between January and May 1528 some of the timber used was taken from the woods of Daldilling, east of Sorn.

The names of some of the tenants from Sorn parish recorded in the rental of arrears of mail (or rent) for 1527-29 have been transcribed from the Melrose Abbey rental books by Margaret H. B. Sanderson:

> *Clews:* Adam Aird, Esplan Aird, Richard Aird, Andrew Boyd, David Campbell, James Campbell, Hugh Crawford, Bessie Douglas, John Dugald, Bernard Farar, John Heateth, Sandy MacQuail, George Mitchell, John Patrickson, Downie Weddail, James Wilson, Matthew Wilson and William Wilson.
>
> *Logan:* John Campbell, James Coltherd and Bessie Douglas.
>
> *Heateth:* John Allan, James Coltherd, Hugh Crawford, Bessie Douglas

in Catrine and John Sym.

Holehouse: Andrew Wood.

Carleith: John Holm, Gib Reid and William Reid.

Auchmannoch: Robert Barnochan, Adam Burnet, John Campbell, the laird of Cessnock, Widow James, John Keir, John Reid, Hobe Wachman, John Wachman and Thomas Willock.

Daldilling: Widow Aird, Alexander Farar, Andrew Mitchell, Lowre Mitchell, William Mitchell, John Reid and Thomas Reid in Heilar.

Dalgain: John Aird, Widow Aird, Andrew Mitchell and William Mitchell.

Over Muir: Thomas Finlay.

Over Sorn: Adam Boyd, laird of Gadgirth.

During the mid sixteenth century there was much feuding going on between various families across Ayrshire, and the local lairds seem to have become involved in these. George Reid of Daldilling was one of many Ayrshiremen who was accused of taking part in the murder of Gilbert Kennedy, 2nd Earl of Cassillis, who was killed at Prestwick around Whitsunday, 1527. It was also he, if not, then a son of the same name, who barricaded the church at Mauchline to prevent Rev George Wishart from preaching in Mauchline kirk in 1544, the Kennedys being devout Catholics. Wishart was due to preach, but the Sheriff of Ayr and other armed men, including Reid, the Campbells of Brownside and Montgarswood and the laird of Templand, closed the doors and prevented access to the building. The reformer's supporters wished to take the church by force, but Wishart persuaded them against this, and instead he preached for three hours on Mauchline Muir.

Another, more significant example, as it took place locally, was James Reid in Mid Heilar, who was convicted of the murder of John Reid in Cronberry on 24 April 1539. James Reid was the son of William Reid in Clare, which may have been an older name for Nether Heilar, and he feuded with Reid of Cronberry, who may have been a relation. James Reid had been in attendance at the wappenschaw, a regular meeting to practise arms, in Ayr but when all his neighbours and friends decided to leave their 'jakkis' behind, he refused, claiming that he had need for his jack, or defensive coat, and weapons at home. An attempt on John Reid's life on Whitsunday 1539 had been unsuccessful, as he had managed to escape. In Robert Pitcairn's *Ancient Criminal Trials in Scotland*, the murder is reported as follows:

On the Sounday before the committing of the said slachter zour father fader cumand fra the Kirk of Machlyne said to Johne Vdart, that he could get na way dressit betuix him and the said vmqle. Johne, for the heicht of his sonnis: and thairefter ze and zour said complices lay continewlie on the Moss of Darndougall, awaiting the said Johne for his slauchter, fra the Monunday quhill Furisday, that ze slew him: and on the day befoir, ze slew his servandis doggis that skeyit [detected] zou quhare ze lay: and when ze saw him cumand, ze, the said James, and zour bruther, ranne befoir zour fader and slew him; and ze war hurt and woundit in the meyntyme, and had fled with the remanent, war nocht ze war hurt, and passit to ane bank [strip of grass between tilled land], and was fundin be James Logane, sheref-depute of Are.

It was reported that there were nine accomplices of Reid at the murder. Reid's supplication in defence gives further details:

Laitlie, I wes gangand vpone my said faderis maling of Clare, pertening to my Lord of Melros, liand in the lordschip of Kilismure, within the scherefdome of Air, vesyand [inspecting] the samen, and my said faderis gudis [livestock] gangand thairon, traisting na trouball of ony personis, bot to have livit vnder Goddis pease and the Kingis: Neuirtheless, Johnne Reid in Cogertoune, his wife, sonnies, and complices, to the nowmir of ten personis, bodin in feir of weir, come iij mylis [3 miles] fra thair avne houssis, vponne auld feid and forthocht felony, and be way of Hamesukkin, inuaidit and persewit me and my said fader and his seruandis for his slauchter, and chaceit him and his catale and ws of [off] his said maling: and in the chaceing

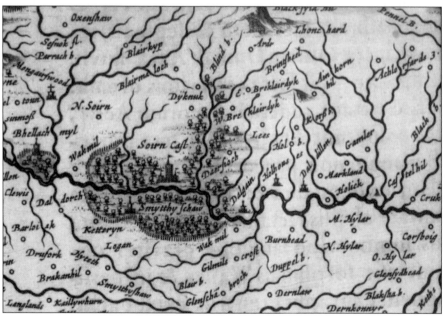

2.1 Sorn district from Blaeu's Map of 1654 *(Author's Collection)*

of ws tha hurt me in my bak: and quhenne we turnit agane to defend
ws, the said Johnne, in his awin defalt, and our pure defence, happynit
to get ane straik, my vnwitting; threw the quilk he is deid.

Reid's defence was unsuccessful, for he was later beheaded. The spot where the
murder took place is known as the Moss of Darndougall, on the boundary between
Sorn and Auchinleck parishes, near to Templandshaw Loch.

At the time of the Reformation, the extensive estates and properties of the
abbeys were broken up and in many cases acquired by the previous tenants. Thus
the grip of the monks of Melrose Abbey was lost, and the all-powerful Campbell
family became the new owners of the bulk of what was to become Sorn parish. This
was just a small part of their extensive holdings in Ayrshire, which were centred on
Loudoun Castle, in the parish of the same name, near Galston.

It is said that the great reformer, Rev John Knox, came to Sorn parish and
preached at Glenlogan House, at that time known as Burnhead. He stood below a
great oak tree that once existed there and preached to a gathered congregation. This
may have taken place in 1566, when he spent some time travelling through the
western part of Scotland. No other record is known of Knox's visit, but he certainly
visited John Lockhart of Barr Castle (Galston), Hew Wallace at Carnell Castle
(Craigie), Andrew Stewart, Lord Ochiltree, at Ochiltree Castle, James Chalmers at
Gadgirth Castle (Coylton), and Robert Campbell of Kingencleugh Castle, near
Mauchline, and held communion at the last-named.

John Bleau compiled an atlas of Scotland in 1654, based on earlier work by
Timothy Pont. In the page depicting *Coila Provincia*, or the province of Kyle, Sorn
district is shown in reasonable detail. Marked with some importance, with
woodland around it, is 'Soirn' castle. Other small lairdships indicated are 'Smytthy
Schaw', Dalgain, 'Holhouses' and 'Daldillen'. Farm names that we still recognise
today include Logan, Daldorch, 'Ketteryn', 'Glenschabrock', Nether, Mid and Over
'Hylar', 'Corsboig', 'Cruk', 'Markland', Lees, 'Breklairdyk', 'Brintsheel', 'Dyknuk',
'Blairmaloch', 'Blairkyp', 'Oxenshae', and 'Achmunnoch'. It is quite significant to note
that 'Mongairswood' is marked with the symbol for a church or chapel, though no
indication of this having existed is known today. A number of place names on
Blaeu's map are lost to us, such as 'Gamler', located near to Merkland, 'Daersioch',
which would have been located north of Sornbank Plantation, and 'Ardr', located on
the south side of 'Black Syid Hil'.

COVENANTERS

From 1638, when the National Covenant was signed, until 1688, when the last
Covenanter was martyred and the Presbyterian church was restored as the
established church of Scotland, there were numerous religious struggles when the
Covenanters were persecuted by the government dragoons. Although Sorn parish

was at that time still part of the larger parish of Mauchline, there are known to have been a number of locals involved in the struggles.

One of these was Robert Farquhar of Over Catrine, or Townhead of Catrine. He is thought to have been a descendent of the Gilmilnscroft Farquhars. Although he supported the Covenant, he was at length forced into taking the test, by which he swore his allegiance to the king and accepted him as head of the Episcopal church. When the Episcopal church was overturned and Presbyterianism was restored, Farquhar was extremely repentant of his actions, and was able to be re-elected as an elder of the church when Rev Mungo Lindsay was inducted in 1693.

Another noted Covenanter was one of the Craufurds of Smiddyshaw. The Craufurds of Smiddyshaw were an old family, Hugh Craufurd being one of those cited on suspicion of murdering the Earl of Cassillis in 1527. The Craufurd of Smiddyshaw who was a Covenanter was listed by John, 1st Earl of Middleton, as one of those who were fined for their non-compliance with the religious regulations of the time. He was perhaps removed from his property, for soon after this the lands were owned by the Campbells of Cessnock and by 1702 were owned by Patrick Boyle.

George Campbell of Auchmannoch was a supporter of the Covenant and fought with General Alexander Leslie (later 1st Earl of Leven) in 1639. His son, Arthur Campbell of Auchmannoch, was also a supporter of the Covenant, and it is known that Lord Middleton fined him in 1662. He was later captured and held prisoner in Avondale Castle, at Strathaven in Lanarkshire, at that time used as a garrison by the redcoats.

Ministers in Scotland were, in 1662, obliged to swear an oath of allegiance to the king and to accept him as head of the Church of Scotland. Covenanting ministers could not agree with this, as they felt that only Jesus Christ could be the head of the church and that the king should not control them. Those ministers who refused to accept this were 'outed' from their charges, and deprived of their living. In Scotland around 262 ministers were forced to leave. In their place, ministers who accepted the king's Episcopal demands were given these vacant charges. To the supporters of the Covenant these ministers were often known as 'curates', and in many cases they were of questionable moral standing. Many refused to attend their services, but the curates could and often did send a list of defaulters to the local garrison, so that the soldiers could search for supporters of the Covenant. In this way they again lost the faith of their parishioners. When the Glorious Revolution took place and Presbyterianism was restored, almost all the curates were removed from their charges, often forcibly. This happened in many local parishes, and Sorn was no exception. A number of locals went to the manse and forced Rev William Anderson out of the house. In fear of his life, he ran as fast as he was able down to the foot of the Cleuch Burn, next to the River Ayr, and jumped across the water to the far side. From there he was able to reach the safety of the castle. Ever since that time this spot at the foot of the Cleuch Glen has been known as the Curate's Steps.

At Auchencloigh farm, on the northern extremity of the parish, the famous Covenanter, Alexander Peden, was born around 1626. There is considerable doubt about his ancestry, there being many families of the name Peden at this time, though it has been claimed that all the Pedens were branches of the Auchenlongford family. He was trained for the ministry and initially became a teacher, precentor and session clerk in Tarbolton. He was ordained to the church of New Luce in Wigtownshire in 1659, but in 1663 he was 'outed' from his charge for failing to accept the authority of the Episcopal Bishop of Galloway. From that time onward he became a celebrated Covenanting minister, preaching to congregations on the wild moors of southern Scotland, and even as far as Northern Ireland and northern England. He was captured in 1673 and held prisoner for a time in Edinburgh, and also on the Bass Rock in the Firth of Forth for four years, but was later released. In December 1678 he was sentenced to banishment to Virginia in North America, but when the slave ship taking him there docked at London, he was able to escape, prior to the ship leaving Britain. He became infirm from the privations he had suffered from living rough for so long, and eventually had to live with his brother at Tenshillingside, on Auchinleck estate, where he died on 26 January 1686. His family buried him in secret within the Peden burial plot in Auchinleck kirkyard, but within six weeks the soldiers discovered that he had been buried and, incensed that they had failed to capture him, decided to disinter his body. The corpse was dug up and carried by them into Cumnock, where they proposed hanging it from the gallows tree on Barr Hill. However, the lady of Leifnoreis Castle intervened, so they buried him at the gallows foot 'out of contempt' according to his gravestone. In 1891 a large memorial of Aberdeen granite was erected over his grave.

In the woods above Glenlogan House is an ancient holly tree known as Peden's Tree. It is claimed that the minister hid here at some time during the persecutions. At one time within Glenlogan House was a small staircase known as Peden's Stair. It has been claimed that he used this stair to reach a hideout within Glenlogan House. However, the dates of the present house and when Peden lived don't tie up. The old staircase was destroyed in the 1980s.

During the time of the Covenanters, around 1665, Sorn Castle was requisitioned as a garrison of the soldiers used to track down the Covenanters. This was a common outcome for those lairds who were supporters of the Covenanters, and at the time Sorn was owned by Sir James Campbell, 2nd Earl of Loudoun, who had escaped to Leyden to avoid the troubles.

The infamous persecutor of the Covenanters, John Graham of Claverhouse, certainly passed through the parish on more than one occasion. In a letter written by him from East Kilbride, 15 June 1684, to that other notable persecutor, Sir Thomas Dalyell of the Binns, he describes his route taken in trying to track down Covenanters:

…I sent immediately to the Glenkens, to Captain Strachan, to march to Dalmellington, and to the Sorn, and to leave Mauchlin on the left hand, and Newmilns and Loudoun-hill on the right, and so to this place, scouring all the suspected places as he came along.

Similarly, on 16 June 1684, he wrote to the Archbishop of Glasgow from Paisley:

I sent on Friday night for my troop from Dumfries, and ordered them to march by the Sanquhar to the Muirkirk, to the Ploughlands, and so to Streven. I sent for Captain Strachan's troop from the Glenkens, and ordered him to march to the old castle of Cumlock [*sic*], down to the Sorne, and through the country to Kilbryde, leaving Mauchlin and Newmills on his left, and Loudon-hill on his right.

The garrison in Sorn Castle was under the command of Lieutenant Lewis Lauder. He is known to have killed a number of Covenanters himself, including William Shillilaw, or Shiringlaw, who was shot at Woodhead of Tarbolton in July 1685 or, according to Rev Robert Wodrow, July 1684. Shillilaw was only eighteen years of age and worked at the farm of Stairhead. His name had been supplied to the garrison by the curate of Tarbolton. Lauder's men asked him a few questions, and his replies being regarded as unsatisfactory, he was shot on the spot. The soldiers then went to his employers and questioned the laird and two friends. They were threatened with instant death, Lauder ordering them to kneel and cover their eyes, but the soldiers refused to carry out the deed, claiming that one martyr per day was sufficient.

Lieutenant Lauder issued at least one document to an individual in which he confirmed that the person bearing the 'pass' had subscribed their allegiance to the king. Long-owned by the Campbells of Auchmannoch, but now lost, this is known to have read as follows:

I, Lewis Lauder, Governour of Sorn Castle, dow heirby certifie and declare, viz. ---- Kirkwood, servitor to Arthour Campbell of Auchmannoch, in the parish of Sorne, did compeir before me, on solemn oath before Almightie God, did abjure and renounce the late tratours appollogeticall declaration, in so far as it declares war against his Ma[jes]ttie, and asserts that it is lawful to kill all such as serve his Ma[jes]ttie in church, state, armie, or contrie, conform to his Majestie's late proclamation of the 30 daye of Decr. last.
Given at Sorne, the aught day of February 1685 ziers.
Lewis Lauder.

The Battle of Airds Moss, between the supporters of Covenanter Rev Richard

Cameron and the government dragoons under Captain Andrew Bruce of Earlshall, took place on Thursday 22 July 1680. The night before this battle Richard Cameron spent at the farm of Meadowhead, in Sorn parish, at that time tenanted by William Mitchell. With Cameron were about 23 horse and 40 foot soldiers, who were camped near to the farm. They determined that on the following day it would be safer to head for the wilder hills around Muirkirk. On the morning of battle, Cameron washed his face in a stone trough at Meadowhead farm. When asked by the farmer's wife what he was doing, he replied, 'This is their last washing, I have need to make them clean, for there are many to see them!' The woman's mother burst into tears when she heard this, but Cameron told her, 'Weep not for me, but for yourself and yours, and for the sins of a sinful land, for ye have many melancholy, sorrowful, and weary days before you.' The stone trough was a relic that was long revered at the steading, being noted as still there in 1913. It no longer exists, sadly. Cameron was not to reach Muirkirk, being killed in battle along with eight of his men, including his brother, Michael, and his head and hands were cut from his body in order to carry them to Edinburgh to claim the bounty of £500 Sterling that had been offered.

The only Covenanter known to have been shot in the parish was George Wood of Tincornhill. The story behind his murder starts with the Preaching Societies of the Covenanters deciding to invite Rev David Houston over from Ireland to become one of their ministers. He was called to be a minister in June 1687 and he appears to have preached a number of times to the Covenanters. However, in January 1688 he was apprehended back in Ireland and held in prison for some months. In June he was to be transported to Edinburgh for trial, and the Covenanters of the district decided to spring his release as he was being taken through the Bello Path, two

2.2 Detail of original gravestone of George Wood, Covenanter *(Dane Love)*

miles east of Cumnock. This took place on 20 June. A couple of soldiers were killed in the affray, and John MacGeachan, a Covenanter, was seriously injured, dying four weeks later and being buried at Stonepark, east of Cumnock. Though Houston was freed, he suffered some injuries to his head, as his legs had been tied below the horse's stomach on which he was being carried, and the horse was frightened by the gunshot and bolted, causing Houston to turn upside down.

A proclamation was issued on 22 June against the rebels who had freed Houston. The soldiers from the garrison at Sorn Castle were given the task of tracking down those responsible for the incident. The troopers left the castle and made their way towards Cumnock. They then headed north-east towards Muirkirk, but turned back and followed the roadway back to Sorn. It was now evening. Near to Tincornhill farm they came upon a boy of sixteen years, George Wood, who was in the fields looking after the cattle. It is said that he had been noted as having attended conventicles, or field-preachings, and as such had been reported by someone to the garrison of soldiers at Daldilling, home of John Reid. Reid was a near-neighbour of Wood's, and on spotting him decided that he should be shot on sight. This was carried out, and it is stated that Reid did not even ask him any questions. When one of his men questioned Reid, he responded by saying that he knew him to be one of the Whigs, and that they ought to be shot wherever they were found.

Old and detailed Ordnance Survey maps indicate the place of martyrdom as being on the southern slopes of Tincorn Hill at national grid reference NS 578274. However, other folk reckon that the martyrdom took place on the moss to the north of Tincorn Hill, ever since known as the Blood Moss.

The body of Wood was taken under cover to the kirkyard of Sorn and interred there. George Wood has the distinction of being the last ever martyr killed during the years of persecution of the Covenanters. A stone was erected over his grave, inscribed:

HeRE LYeS GORG
WOOD WHO WAS SHOT
AT TINKHORNHILL BY BL
OODY JOHN ReID TRVPeR
FOR HIS ADHeRANCE TO
THE WORD OF GOD AND
THE COVeNANTeD VORK
OF ReFORMATION 1688

A public subscription took place in the first half of the nineteenth century and a second memorial was erected to Wood, mainly through the exertions of Miss Jane Ranken of Glenlogan (1795-1852). The original stone was lifted and located on the wall of the church, below the second memorial. The new stone reads:

2.3 Covenanter George Wood's memorial
(Dane Love)

TO
PRESERVE FROM OBLIVION
THE FATE OF
GEORGE WOOD
WHO WAS SHOT AT TINKHORNHILL
MDCLXXXVIII
FOR HIS ADHERENCE TO THE WORD
OF GOD
AND THE COVENANTED WORK OF
REFORMATION
AND TO MANIFEST GRATITUDE
FOR THE INVALUABLE
RELIGIOUS PRIVILEGES
NOW ENJOYED.
[THIS STONE WAS
ERECTED BY SUBSCRIPTION, 1828.]

The last two lines appear to have been obliterated at some time. The original stone had its inscription recut around 1890 by George Cameron, a mason who lived in Sorn.

The Covenanters made a number of banners which were carried in battle, principally at the battles of Drumclog and Bothwell Bridge. The banner made for the parish of Sorn survives, and currently hangs on the wall of Sorn Castle. It bears the inscription:

*DALGAIN W.R. FOR
GOD THE
COVENANTED
PRESBYTERIAN
REFORMATION
CROUN AND
COUNTRIE 1689.*

2.4 Dalgain parish Covenanters' standard *(Dane Love)*

The flag was flown again in 1689 to mark the accession of William III and Mary to

28

the throne, hence the date. The flag had been in the possession of the Sorn Curling Club since 1798 when it was presented to them by Mrs Jane Gray Farquhar of Gilmilnscroft. Around 1840 the flag was in a very poor condition, the silk in danger of rotting away. The curlers arranged to have it repaired with a backing of new silk, inscribing this information on it. The flag was presented to Sir Henry Farquhar of Gilmilnscroft, 4th Baronet, by the members of Sorn Curling Club for safe keeping on St Andrew's Day, 30 November 1907, prior to the sale of Sorn Castle, where it had been preserved

2.5 Drum, reputedly from Covenanting times, Sorn Castle *(Dane Love)*

in a mahogany chest within a quaint old cupboard in the library. In return, Sir Henry presented the club with a silver salver for competition.

1656-1780

The parish of Sorn was created in 1656 when almost 20,000 acres were disjoined from the parish of Mauchline. Initially the parish was to be named Dalgain, after the estate on which a church was to be erected, but this took time to follow through, due to the religious upheavals of the time. The church was built in 1658 but the parish did not become totally separated from Mauchline until 1692.

This was not the first attempt at establishing a separate parish. The Presbytery of Ayr, according to the records, approved the erection of a 'new kirk' on 15 August 1649 to serve the proposed parish, which appears from the minutes to have been called 'New Mauchline'. Sites for New Mauchline church, kirkyard, manse and glebe were decided upon according to the minutes of 7 November 1649, and this appears to have been located on ground that belonged to the Farquhars of Gilmilnscroft. This would imply that New Mauchline was to have been established on the south side of the river, perhaps somewhere between Bridgend and Linthouse, and Wheelhouse and Holmhead, where a number of old cottages and mills were located, although this is pure speculation. It could have been quite as easily built elsewhere on Gilmilnscoft's lands.

New Mauchline had its own minister appointed to it, Rev John Blair, though he appears to have been the first and last minister of the church, if one was ever built. Rev Blair was educated at the University of Glasgow and became minister of New Mauchline in 1649. At the time of the 'Act for the Restitution and Re-establishment of the Antient Government of the Church' he was removed from the charge in 1662. He was accused of turbulent and seditious conduct with a number of others on 14 July 1663 and confessing his part in this disturbance was prohibited from acting as a minister and banished to north of the River Ness before 1 October

1663, 'under the highest peril'. Rev Blair appears to have ignored this banishment, for he is noted as having preached at a conventicle at Inverkeithing in Fife at the end of 1679 or beginning of 1680. The last mention of New Mauchline parish takes place in the Privy Council Register of 1672. Attempts by early factors of Gilmilnscroft to determine the location of the proposed church and manse proved fruitless.

In 1690 a Hearth Tax was imposed on the people of Scotland with the intention of raising funds to repay the debts of the army. This was a one-off tax of 14 shillings, payable at Candlemas (2 February) 1691. The tax applied to all, owner or tenant, but the poor registered with the parish were exempt. The Hearth Tax for Sorn lists the households at that time, though there is little more information that can be derived from them. According to the tax return, there were 309 hearths taxed in the parish. A further 28 hearths belonged to the poor and thus were exempt. Five parishioners had failed to pay the tax, namely Alexander Fleming, Mistress Mitchell in Catrine (2 hearths), James Willsone in Breckhole (2 hearths), John Gilbert in Simberhill (2 hearths) and John Willock in Carleith.

From the tax returns we can get an idea of the scale of certain properties from the number of hearths within them. Hew Mitchell in Dalgain had 6 hearths; Robert Farquhar had 5 hearths; Adam Andrew had 6 hearths; Robert Farquhar had 8 hearths; 'The Main House of Daldilling' had 6 hearths; Patrick Ewing of Greenfoot Inn had 4 hearths. The largest house in the parish was the Earl of Loudoun's house (Sorn Castle) which had 11 hearths. The tax lists people, rather than places, so it is impossible to determine where some folk lived from it, however, we can tell that Woodenhead had one hearth, South Limmerhaugh had three hearths, William Aird of Holl had one hearth, Hector Paton in Mains had one hearth, Andrew Allan in Murehead had one hearth, Merkland had two hearths, and John Smith in Bogend had two hearths.

The first detailed maps of the country were compiled in 1747-55 by General William Roy, who had been commissioned to survey Scotland following the Jacobite rising. These maps are large enough to show the country in some detail, and from them we find that Sorn parish had only one road in it – from the castle by way of Montgarswood and Welton to Mauchline.

In 1775 Captain Andrew Armstrong published a *Map of Ayrshire*, which was a fairly detailed plan of the county. Sorn is shown in some detail on the map, though at this time the village had not been created in its present form. The road from Machline [sic] to Sorn is shown making its way up the valley, passing Sorn Castle and the few houses that were located in the village at that time. The road passes by 'Bank' and 'Degan' (Dalgain), before heading east past 'Daldellin' and 'Hollis' (Holehouse) and out onto the moor past 'Lamrough'. Other farms and placenames listed on the map in the parish at that time include 'Heliar' (at that time a sizeable house surrounded by improved farmland and trees), Holm (located north of Heliar at Laigh Crook), Henerystoun, and Burnhead (the old name for Glenlogan).

Gilmilscroft (without the 'n') is shown within an extensive wooded policy, as is Catrin and Whitlet (Whiteflat). Halfmark and Lindsayhill are also shown to the south, both places no longer surviving.

To the north of the main route through Sorn Armstrong's map depicts the roadway from Sorn Castle heading towards Galston, though it appears unfinished, petering out at Wealth of Waters. It also shows the farms of Merkland, Branchill, Pluck, Rodenhead, Blindburn, Hill (Hillhead of Sorn), Crofts (Crofthead and Croftfoot), Redgate, Barnallach (Blairmulloch), Clonfords (Auchenlongford – it is still often pronounced this way), Auchenmonach (Auchmannoch) and Auchenclosh (Auchencloigh).

1780-1900

The village of Dalgain was laid out as a planned village in 1780, or thereabouts, by Dr Alexander Stevenson of Dalgain. Planned villages were very common in Scotland at that time, and were distinguished by their straight lines and grid pattern. Local examples include Catrine and Auchinleck, and no doubt Stevenson had intentions of emulating their success. Sorn was not as large as either of these villages, but undoubtedly Dr Stevenson had plans to create a sizeable community. The old roadway, which took a gentle curve and passed nearer to the river, was straightened off, between the Coal Ford and the Smiddy. Along the northern side of the new street, named Dalgain Street, were laid out feus, let to the tenants at fourpence per fall of annual feu duty. By 1796 it was noted that the village had 24 houses, occupied

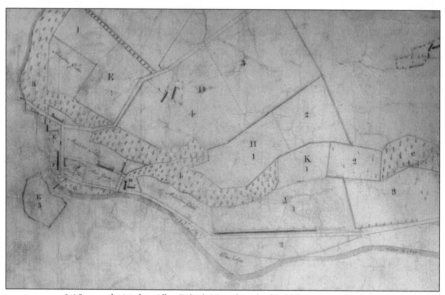

2.6 Sorn as depicted on Allan Fisher's *Map of Lands of Daldillan*, surveyed in 1782.
The letters refer to the following: D – Dalyearnoch; E – Greenfoot; F – Coal Houses and Yards; H – Damside; J – Sandbedholm. *(Jamie McIntyre)*

by 43 families. In addition there were seven further families occupying houses that were older than the planned village. Many of the new houses were taken up by residents of the parish, and it was noted that many of the cot-houses that they left behind soon fell into ruins.

A plan of Dalgain, or 'Daldillan', estate was surveyed by Allan Fisher for Alexander Stevenson in 1782. As well as detailing the various farms on the estate and their acreages, the plan also shows the new village of Sorn as it was at that time. In addition to the new street of houses erected at first along the north side of what was known as Dalgain Street, the plan also shows a row of houses that existed between Greenfoot Inn and Dalgain Mill. This row was known as the 'Coal Houses and yards', indicating that at this early time there were some miners' homes in the village.

A number of businesses and places of work had established themselves by the end of the eighteenth century. At the time of the *Statistical Account* of 1796, there were 3 shopkeepers in the village, 3 innkeepers, 3 masons, 7 shoemakers, 5 weavers, 5 tailors, 4 seamstresses and 7 colliers, or miners. In addition there were a number of labourers and widows.

Unlike many neighbouring parishes, in the eighteenth century Sorn had no annual fair. However, since around 1740 there had been an annual race, held in March, to which most of the villagers attended. Many of these people carried on business as if it was a fair, however. The race was run by the village children. They started at one end of the street when a man struck the village drum, and the children turned around at the opposite end of the village, once they had reached the man bearing the halberd. The race appears to have died out at the start of the twentieth century and the drum and halberd, which date from Covenanting times, were thereafter kept in Sorn Castle. A separate horse race used to take place in a field adjacent to the village, where a variety of horses and ponies battled it out. At the end of the horse-race day, a meal was had comprising veal and oatmeal.

The health of the parishioners in the late eighteenth century is reported on by the compiler of the *Statistical Account*. He notes that in 1796 there were no fewer that six children, aged from 1 to 12 years, who were to die of smallpox, and that some older residents suffered blindness, deafness and were dumb as a result of the disease. Nevertheless, he went on to recount that a number of parishioners survived to in excess of 80 or 90 years. A shoemaker in the village, still living in the house where he was born, was 90, the church-officer was 85, a small farmer was 97 and a gardener and his wife were 95 and 94, having been married for 68 years.

Body-snatching was a major problem in the first half of the nineteenth century. Recently-buried corpses were often dug up at night by unscrupulous persons who took them to the universities of Glasgow and Edinburgh where professors bought them from them, allowing them to carry out experiments on the bodies. Naturally, this caused great distress across Scotland, and in most parishes organisations were set up to allow watches to be made over fresh graves.

On a few occasions the stolen corpse was rescued by surviving members of the family. An unusual case was that of a young girl who had died and was buried in the kirkyard at Sorn. According to the *Glasgow Herald* of 27 February 1824, the body of the girl

> ... was traced to Glasgow, and the robbers discovered by the afflicted father. Finding themselves detected, they agreed to restore the body; but before doing so they imposed on the father the strongest obligations of secrecy, and exacted a solemn promise from him not to prosecute for the offence. The distraction of the family induced him to comply, and he was then directed to call at a certain house in a closs in the Gallowgate, at a particular hour, where he would find the corpse. He went accordingly, and found the body, which he easily recognised, enclosed in a box. It has since been re-interred in Sorn Church-yard. The Sheriff and Fiscal took a precognition on the subject at Sorn on Thursday last, at the close of which a warrant was issued for the apprehension of the three students at the Glasgow College, who it is reported, have since left the country.

The Sorn Parish Mort-Safe Society was instituted in 1827, members being allowed the used of a steel mort-safe, or iron clamp, that protected the coffin in the ground until such times as the body had decayed sufficiently to be of no use to the dissectionists. Members had to pay five shillings to join, rising to ten shillings soon after the formation of the society. The committee met quarterly, in Catrine then Sorn at alternate meetings. The mortsafes were hired out to members and they were placed in the ground for four weeks after the burial. The number of mort-safes increased, and it was determined that should no mortsafe be available for members, then a watch over the newly-dug grave would be arranged to prevent body-snatching.

In May 1830 the Sorn and Catrine Mort-Cloth Society was founded. A mort-cloth was used to drape the coffin as it was being taken to the kirkyard, the quality of this being in relation to the amount paid. However, Sorn Kirk Session insisted that parishioners used their cloth, which was regarded as being too dear by many villagers. The Session even insisted that mourners paid the fee even if they used the mort-cloth or not. Robert Howie disputed the right of the kirk session to enforce the use of its cloth on all parties, and to compel payment for it. At court he lost his case, but he appealed, losing once more. As a result, the mort-cloth society was founded at the instigation of Henry Shanks More, an ecclesiastical and civil lawyer. The society was still in existence in 1883, when there were proposals made to merge it with the Catrine Funeral Society, but both organisations remained separate for a number of years thereafter.

In 1837, according to Pigot's *Directory of Ayrshire*, we find that Hugh Howat was in business as a cattle dealer in Sorn. James Kay had a more unusual occupation - that of 'portrait painter'.

John Nicholson Brown was born in Sorn and became a professor in Paris. Brown, according to his gravestone, erected in 1861 by some friends, was 'a self-taught man [who] supported himself from the age of eight. Attended Sorn School only 18 months, devoted his leisure hours from daily toil to the pursuit of self-acquired knowledge. Became, in Paris, at 21 years of age teacher of English in some of the first families of France, and was appointed Professor in the College of St Barbe, Paris. He died at 34 years of age.'

The European wars of the early nineteenth century affected a number of people in the parish, and it is said that the laird of Montgarswood celebrated the victory of the Battle of Waterloo on 18 June 1815 by laying out a plantation in the format of the battle. This pattern of trees has now been obliterated.

In 1861 *The Persecuted Family – a tale of the village of Sorn and the Covenanters* was published by H. S. Nisbet of Mauchline. This tells the story of Rev James Bruce and his family. The book was the work of poet and author, Robert Pollok (1798-

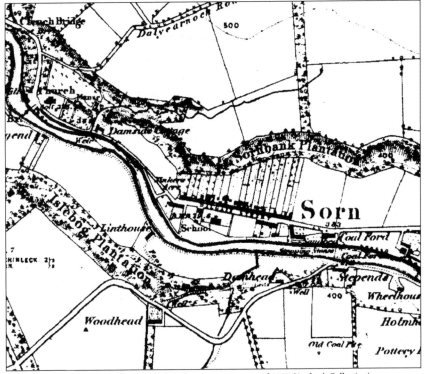

2.7 Sorn as shown on the 6" Ordnance Survey map of 1867 (*Author's Collection*)

1827), author of the best-selling *The Course of Time* and *Ralph Gemmill*. Pollok is commemorated by a memorial located in the junction of the roads at Loganswell, south of Newton Mearns.

A few sons of the parish have gone on to become ministers of religion in other places. Rev Hugh Baird was born in the parish and was ordained to Cumbernauld U. P. Church on 5 December 1837. He died on 10 December 1879. During his time as minister he wrote a number of books, including *Words in Season, Beaten Oil for the Light of Life* and a local history for the Cumbernauld area, *Castlecary and the Great Roman Wall.*

Another minister son was Rev Alexander McCarlie. He emigrated to Western Australia under the auspices of the Free Church of Scotland and was ordained at Perth in that province in 1896. In September 1898 he moved to take up a position at Cottesloe, also in Western Australia.

Rev James Aird B.D. was born in Sorn and became minister of Peterculter Church in Aberdeenshire. He died on 18 May 1905.

Rev Alexander Clark M.A. was to be minister of Wick Parish Church in Caithness. He was born in Sorn in 1832 and died on 17 November 1908.

Rev John Watson M.A. B.D. (1848-1921) was the son of Hugh Watson of Barboigh farm. He became minister of South Yell, Shetland, in 1876, serving for 38 years. He is also credited with introducing the first modern plough into Shetland.

Rev James Clark MA (1852-1921) was the son of William Clark of East Auchenlongford. He was educated at Sorn, Glasgow University and the Divinity Halls, Edinburgh. He became minister of Milton of Balgonie Parish Church, where he served for almost 40 years. He never married. Another son of the same family was Rev Gilbert Clark, who was born at Auchenlongford. He was educated at Sorn and at Catrine, and spent some time as a pupil teacher in Sorn school. He trained to become a minister at Scottish and continental universities, and served as an assistant minister for a number of years before being called to Haywood Church at Carnwath, Lanarkshire. He was to published *Home, and Other Poems* in 1888.

A number of accidents have occurred over the years resulting in tragic deaths. On 17 December 1851 Archibald Mair was killed at Auchmannoch at the age of 8½ years. More recently, William Cameron died as a result of an accident on 7 October 1940 aged 28.

The *Catrine and Sorn Almanac* for 1882, published by John Hunter of Catrine, gives a list of tradesmen in the village at that time. These include John Andrew, tailor; James Baird, shoemaker at Montgarswood Bridgend; Mrs Dalglish, postmistress and grocer; John Gibson, baker; Peter Johnston, tailor; Joseph Johnston, tailor; William Mitchell, grocer; Robert Watson, shoemaker and Registrar of Births and Collector for Catrine Funeral Society in the village of Sorn.

Around 1885 George MacMichael, in *Notes on the Way*, describes Sorn as being 'much composed of one-storey houses, and lies, with the River Ayr on its south side, in a beautiful holm all but enclosed in a frame of woods, impressing the visitor with a sense of blissful peace.'

In 1886-7 the valuation of the parish was set at £19,607 8s 0d. The census of 1881 indicated that the whole parish had a population of 4,255, of which 2,573 lived in Catrine. The village of Sorn had 294 inhabitants, Glenlogan village had 122, Gilmilnscroft village had 104 and Montgarswood Bridgend had 76.

The Kilmarnock District Committee of Ayrshire County Council established a water works in the parish which supplied fresh water to many of the homes at the end of the nineteenth century. On 5 October 1878 a piped water supply was introduced into Sorn at the same time as Catrine Water Scheme was augmented. Water was gathered on the southern slopes of Blacksidend, at East Auchinlongford and Nether Whitehaugh, and was piped down through Sorn and into Catrine. Chairman of the Water Supply Committee was Graham Somervell of Sorn, and his wife was responsible for turning the supply on. A branch pipe allowed a public water supply to be introduced to Meadowside at the same time. Sorn was made into a water supply district under the Public Health Act in 1899. In 1906 Kilmarnock District Committee took James Somervell of Sorn to court over his failure to adhere to the regulations. Prior to the arrival of piped water, supplies had to be obtained from wells located adjacent to farms and cottages, or else at wells in the village. The public had to collect their water from cast iron water pumps in the street, these being manufactured in Kilmarnock by Glenfield & Kennedy. Among the old wells was one located at the back of the school playground, against the riverside wall. Beyond this, adjacent to the River Ayr bank, was the Beggars' Well. The water scheme was extended and revamped in 1922, and in 1930 a gravitation water supply was piped to Auchencloigh schoolhouse and surrounding areas.

1900-1945

During the First World War a number of parishioners served abroad in various regiments. A poem, *On the Sorn Soldiers*, named many of the locals who took part. Written by John S. Gall of Bridgend, it was inspired by a letter written by Archibald Muir of Sorn to the local lads serving with the troops at Gallipoli in November 1916:

> Weel, Baldie, in answer tae your letter,
> Aboot the Sorn chaps noo oot fightin'.
> Altho' there's plenty hav'na gane,
> I'm sure it's no theirsels tae blame,
> For here we're trainin' every day
> The treacherous Germans for to slay.
> But plenty o' oor kind ha'e gane
> An' steeped their bluid on foreign plain.

There's Sanny Watson frae Barboigh,
He mourns a gallant nephew twice;
An Gordon, gairdener frae the Castle,
Lost a brave son in the battle.
An' Sanny frae the Brocklar ferm,
A better never lifted airms;
An' Sergeant Clark frae Nether Shiel,
A truer never pointed steel,
An Louie, whom we kent gey weel,
Five Big Turks, he made them squeal,
But a sniper got him on the heid
Alas! Puir Louie, noo is deid.
The Bishop, tae, altho' short-sichtit,
He showed us a' he wisna frichtit;
There's Willie, Andy, and Jock Piper,
I'm sure they'll a' mak' richt guid fighters;
The Harrisons a' are guid cheuch stuff,
They'll show their country what they're worth.
The Tamsons, tae, they a' ha'e gane,
Scarce ane o' them is left at hame,
Jamie, he has done his bit,
Lang Syne, when he was feeling fit,
But noo rheumatic pains he's ta'en-
I hope he'll sune be right again.
An' Johnnie Harper frae West-toun,
He'll mak' a right guid sodger sune;
An' Jock, the Plumber, frae Coal Ford,
He wisna sweart tae draw his sword.
Then Birkie, Rab the grocer's son,
I'm sure some laurels he will win;
The twa wee Wolfs scarce left the scule,
They're awa', some Germans for tae kill;
An' Tam McKerrow frae Croftfoot,
He's awa' again some mair tae shoot;
An' Andra Alston the sturdy blacksmith,
An' Burley Sloan, juist scarcely age yet,
Amang them a' the young Sorn Laird,
The woes o' Battle he has shared,
May he guide them safely back again
Tae Sorn, their guid auld ancient hame.
An' plenty mair I'll ha'e omitted,

But some ither time, if I'm permitted,
I'll write tae them a line or twa
Tae show they're freens o' Johnnie Gaw.
An' before I close my wee bit rhyme
I want you just tae bear in min'
That when oor fecht on earth is dune
I hope we'll a' meet up abune.

As related in the verses, a number of those serving abroad lost their lives. These include:

Sergeant Robert Anderson, Ayr and Lanark Yeomanry, 12th Royal Scots Fusiliers, killed at Ploegsteert, 8 September 1918 aged 23.
Private Robert Baillie, 9th Royal Scots, killed in France, 11 June 1917, head gardener at Gilmilnscroft.
Private John Bell.
Sergeant John Bennie served with the 1st/5th Battalion Royal Scots Fusiliers. He was the son of James and Martha Bennie, of 1 Roundshaw Cottage, Auchinleck. He was killed on 6 September 1918 at the age of 23 years and is buried in Ligny-sur-Canche British Cemetery.
Private David Black, Seaforth Highlanders, 4 November 1914, formerly of Meadowside Cottages.
Corporal Joseph Black, Seaforth Highlanders, killed 26 October 1914, formerly of Glenlogan village.
Lieutenant Colonel Francis Douglas Farquhar DSO, Coldstream Guards, killed at St Eloi in Flanders, 20 March 1915 aged 40.
Sergeant John Fleming, 1st/5th Battalion Royal Scots Fusiliers, died of wounds received at the Dardanelles, 2 July 1915, of Burnside Cottages.
Private James Gordon, Royal Defence Corps, killed 12 February 1919 aged 22.
Private John Gordon, 1st/5th Battalion Royal Scots Fusiliers, killed by a piece of shrapnel at the Dardanelles, 12 July 1915, aged 28, of Sorn village.
Private John Harvey, Royal Fusiliers (Banker's Battalion) attached to 12th Middlesex Regiment, killed 24 October 1916 aged 21, son of Gilbert Harvey, Redgate farm.
Private, James C. Lees, 36th CCS, 2nd Royal Scots Fusiliers, died of pneumonia, France, 1 November 1918, from Woolmill, aged 19.
Private Archibald MacDougall, Gordon Highlanders, near La Bassee

in France, 17 June 1915, formerly of Glenlogan village.

Private Colin MacIntyre, 6/7th Battalion, Royal Scots Fusiliers, died of wounds, France, 1 February 1917, formerly of Holmhead, Sorn.

William MacNee, R.A.M.C., killed at the Dardanelles, 12 July 1915, formerly of Dalgain Mill.

Private Thomas Mitchell, Seaforth Highlanders, killed 1 July 1916, of Sorn village.

Private Joseph Moffat, Royals Scots Fusiliers, Salonika Forces, died of wounds, 2 October 1918, formerly of Auchencloigh.

Lance Corporal Hugh Muir, 1st Royal Scots Fusiliers, killed in France, 28 March 1918 aged 22.

Private Archibald James Perry, Worcester Regiment, killed 16 August 1917.

Private William Piper, Camel Gun Corps, died in Beirut, 1919.

Private James Randall, 5th Battalion Royal Scots Fusiliers, killed in action on 30 December 1915 at the age of 22. He was the son of James and Barbara Randall of Meadowside. His grave is located in Twelve Tree Copse Cemetery, Turkey.

Sergeant John Randall.

Private John Retson, Cameron Highlanders, killed in France, 4 June 1916, aged 19.

Private Hugh Reynolds, 20th Australian Force, died on board the hospital ship HMS *Caledonia*, of wounds received on 10 October 1915 at Dardanelles, eldest son of William Reynolds of Dalgain Cottage.

Sergeant Louis Somervell Robertson, New Zealand Expeditionary Force, 8 June 1915, son of Edward Robertson, formerly schoolmaster, Sorn.

Ordinary Seaman Neil Robertson A.B., who served with the Royal Navy on board HMS *Victory*, died on 12 May 1918 in Haslar Naval Hospital, Gosport, at the age of 19 years. He was the son of James Robertson and nephew of Thomas MacKinna, formerly of Sandbed, Sorn. His grave is in Haslar Royal Naval Cemetery.

Private Harry Telfer, Ayr and Lanark Yeomanry, 12th Royal Scots Fusiliers, killed in action on 20 September 1918.

Private Samuel Thomson, Seaforth Highlanders, killed July 1916, aged 26.

Private William Thomson, 12th Royal Scots Fusiliers, died of wounds in France, 27 March 1918, aged 33.

Sergeant Robert Winder, Ayr and Lanark Yeomanry, 12th Royal Scots Fusiliers, killed in action on 20 September 1918.

Many of the parish men served with distinction during the war, and the 'young laird' of Sorn Castle, Captain J. G. McIntyre was awarded the Military Cross and Bar, as well as the French Croix de Guerre, for his bravery. Another son of the parish, Lieutenant Gilbert Clark, of Nethershield, who served with the Ayrshire Yeomanry and who was attached to the 1st/4th Battalion Royal Scots Fusiliers, was also awarded the Military Cross for 'conspicuous gallatry and initiative ... His action greatly helped the success of the attack in the evening.' Sergeant James Steven, of the

2.8 Aeroplane crash, 1917 *(William Frew)*

Royals Scots Fusiliers, was awarded the Military Medal for his part in the Battle of Augi, near Jaffa, and was fêted at his home at Meadowside when he returned home in July 1918.

Sorn Castle was requisitioned and used as a military hospital for invalided soldiers for the duration of the war. Most of the furnishings were removed and stored elsewhere on the estate. Gilmilnscroft policies were used as a depot for the storage of tanks and other military vehicles.

The Sorn Woman's Guild Work Party commenced a collection of goods for the troops, sending numerous parcels containing socks, shirts, scarves, etc. to the men of the parish serving abroad. A number of Belgian refugees arrived at Sorn in 1914, residing at Hillhead of Sorn and Kilknowe on Sorn Castle estate. Numerous fêtes and socials were organised by other groups to raise funds for the Prince of Wales' Fund and Lord Eglinton's Fund. The local Red Cross unit raised considerable funds, encouraged by Mrs McIntyre of Sorn Castle.

On the Duke of Portland's estate, at the northern end of the parish, many of the old beech trees were cut down and converted at a sawmill near Auchencloigh into props used in the trenches in Europe.

On the Sunday afternoon of 9 September 1917 an aeroplane was to land on fields at Smiddyshaw farm, to the south of the village. The two pilots, who were members of the Army Flying Corps, from Turnberry aerodrome, had come to Sorn to meet Rev Henry Begg, and landed their aeroplane as close as they could to the manse. As soon as they had landed, their aeroplane became an object of considerable curiosity in the district, with many folk making their way from Catrine and Sorn to look at it. By the time the two pilots returned in the early evening it was

2.9 First World War Military Grave – Private J. Gordon *(Dane Love)*

reckoned that there were around two or three hundred spectators awaiting the take off. Unfortunately, this failed to be as simple as the pilots planned, for shortly after leaving the ground they discovered that there was a fault in their aeroplane and they were unable to control it. The aircraft gradually descended and crashed through a hawthorn hedge at North Logan farm. Fortunately the two pilots escaped unharmed, but the aircraft was beyond use. On the following day the remains of the aeroplane were removed from North Logan and taken back to Turnberry on the back of a lorry.

News of the armistice reached Sorn on Monday 11 November 1918, whereupon the church bell was rung. On Saturday 16 November Mr T. W. McIntyre treated the children of the parish to tea and a treat to the cinema, and on Sunday 17 November a service of thanksgiving was held in the church. Proposals for a war memorial were made in the parish church in 1919, and fundraising for this commenced. The plaque erected was unveiled by Captain J. Gordon McIntyre in Sorn Parish Church on 30 January 1921.

2.10 War Memorial Plaque, Sorn Church
(Dane Love)

The oldest pictures of Sorn depict the houses in the village as being single storey in height, with thatched roofs. As the years passed many of these houses were enlarged, with the addition of a second storey, and roofed over with slates. The long Main Street, or Dalgain Street as it was originally known, had a line of houses along the north side, the front doors opening directly onto the street. The south side of the street did not develop in the same manner, and was more random in its layout.

A police station was established in the village in the nineteenth century, at first in a cottage owned by Mrs Marion Clark of Sandbed. In 1900 the village constable was William Morris. A second constabulary office was located in Main Street, in 1940 occupied by Constable Malcolm Allan. When the new council houses were erected in Fir Park in the village, Number 1 included a police station at the side, the constable in 1937 being Robert Bell. The police station was eventually closed, and the village was served by police constables from elsewhere.

In 1920 proposals were made to turn Sorn into a 'dry' parish, legislation at that time – the Local Option Act – allowing a referendum amongst parishioners to decide whether the parish should have any licensed premises in it or not. To promote the 'dry' proposal, Rev Mr Craig from America preached in Catrine and Sorn in 1920 on the benefits of prohibition as it was there. The vote took place on 7 December but there was insufficient support to change the status of the parish from 'wet'.

In 1920-1 Sorn was in the grip of a major strike amongst the coal-workers,

2.11 Red Cross at Sorn Castle *(Baird Institute)*

who demanded an increase in their wages of two shillings. The strike lasted for some months, and by July 1921 a soup kitchen was established in Sorn, seeking donations from non-miners. The soup kitchen committee also decided to raise funds themselves, and were even able to establish a small mine to dig coal which could be sold. Gordon McIntyre of Sorn agreed that a small mine could be sunk on the estate, for the benefit of the parish. This was hewn from the ground at the 'Coal Craig', located well up the River Ayr from the village, Archibald Muir being appointed as manager. Care was to be taken to avoid damage to the estate, and all coal excavated was to be sold within the parish - within the first few weeks £40 worth of coal had been sold.

In the early 1920s Sorn had its own fire-engine, little more than a hand-operated apparatus for putting out fires. The Fire Brigade in the village consisted of James Gibson, joiner, and James Alston, blacksmith, the fire extinguishing appliance being kept at the smithy.

Many of the older houses in the Main Street were demolished prior to the Second World War, resulting in a few gap sites in the Main Street for a few years. A number of modern council houses were to be erected on these sites. Other houses remained empty and were uninhabited for the duration of the war. The new houses were often located further back from the street, allowing the creation of a front garden, and thus breaking up the rather dense layout of the street. A number of houses were erected by Ayr County Council in the mid twentieth century, redeveloping a number of gap sites. Prior to the Second World War twelve council houses were built in a cul-de-sac to form Anderson Crescent at the west end of the village, and twenty houses in Woodlands Road.

The Second World War (1939-45) saw more sons of the parish die in battle. Captain David Eugene Strachan was killed in India on 18 July 1944 at the age of 29. Tel. James C. Stewart, son of James Stewart in Over Heilar, was lost at sea when the escort carrier H.M.S. *Avenger* was sunk in the Mediterranean in November 1942. Private George R. Leggat was killed in action in Madagascar on 6 May 1942. A Fusilier with the Royal Scots Fusiliers 1st Battalion, he was active at the seizure of the large naval base and harbour of Diego Suarez in Operation 'Ironclad'. Leggat was killed in this campaign, and his grave is located in the Diego Suarez War Cemetery in the town of Antsiranana.

The village was set to receive a number of evacuees, and on 31 August 1939 the school was closed to local children to allow it to be used for the distribution of evacuees from Glasgow. Once the pupils were dismissed the staff were to make up rations that would last for two days, so that they could be given to the 112 children expected to arrive on 1 September. A cottage owned by William Cook in Main Street, a few doors along from the Sorn Inn, was leased by Mrs Ross of Gilmilnscroft to allow evacuees to stay there. A further 50 evacuees were expected from Glasgow in April 1941. Evacuees continued to arrive in small numbers for the following few years, for the school log books make reference to six evacuees being enrolled in 1941, one more in 1942, and one from London in 1944. In 1940 it was noted by the headmaster that the evacuees had perfect attendance at school, there being 22 at that time. However, the roll at the school had dropped from 108 in 1941 to 59 in 1942 as a result of most evacuees returning home.

A platoon of the Home Guard was established in Sorn, carrying out exercises in the district and ensuring the safety of the locals. A cadet branch was also in existence for the younger boys of the district. The Home Guard was instrumental in raising funds for the War Comforts Work Party and in 1944 held a large open-air fete in aid of the Sorn Home Guard Service Fund. This was opened by Major and Mrs Ross of Gilmilnscroft and raised £323.

Rationing was introduced across the country due to shortages during the war, and Sorn was no exception. The school drill room was taken over by the Food Office officials on 26 May 1943 in order to allow them to distribute identity cards and ration books to the locals. New ration books were issued on 26 May 1944 at the school, and at the same time 'Salute the Soldier Week' raised £60 amongst the pupils. As the target had been £25, the children were given a half day off school for their efforts.

In 1944 a Lancaster Bomber crashed near to Auchencloigh at the north end of the parish. The aeroplane was being flown by Royal Air Force personnel, who had been in training in Canada. However, they were to miss landing at Prestwick airport and the aeroplane was to crash on the fields near to Auchencloigh. The plane careered through a number of large beech trees on the drive into the farm, and crashed into the Stony Green field. The crew were all killed. Their bodies were found and were buried at Prestwick. The remains of the fuselage was pulled to the side of the field and remained there for many years.

During the war the hills and moors around Sorn were used for military practise. The old shepherd's cottage of Grange, located on Weitshaw Muir, was used by the army as target training. Shells were fired from the Muirkirk road, near to Auchenlongford, blowing the building into bits. Around the present ruins are circular hollows filled with mossy grass – these are the remains of craters left by other bombs.

Victory in Europe was celebrated in the village, and when the brothers, Corporal Jim Jamieson and Guardsman Robert Jamieson, returned to Sorn in June 1945, after having been held Prisoners of War, more rejoicing took place. The men had been captured at the Battle of Salerno and held in a German camp for some time.

1945-PRESENT

After peace was resumed, sixteen houses and a police station were erected by Ayr County Council at Fir Park in the centre of the village, and a further six houses were added to the north end of Woodlands Road. In later years six old folks' houses were added to Fir Park, and in the 1990s four new private houses were built in what was the garden of the Sorn Inn.

In more recent years private housing has been built in Sorn, such as the cul-de-sac of Dalgain Drive at the eastern end of the village, and the houses lining the road to Catrine at Damhead. The first three there were located in a small field on the north side of the road - Glenside in 1962, Olive Lodge in 1963 and Shangri in 1964. On the south side of the road houses were erected in 1972, 1973 and 1975 (Torlinn). The block of houses known as Riverside, in Main Street, was erected in 1991, and other private bungalows were erected in various spots in the village. Sixteen new houses were erected at Woolmill Place in 2006-8.

Between 10.30 pm and 11.00 pm on Monday 13 August 1956 an A26 Douglas Invader aeroplane crashed on the high moorland on the edge of the parish, midway

2.12 Aeroplane Crash – 1956 *(Baird Institute)*

between Distinkhorn and Glen Garr Hill. The aeroplane exploded and burst into flames on contact with the ground, but the fire was soon extinguished by itself. The aeroplane was a former American (U.S.A.F.) one, and the two airmen on board were killed. They were Edgar Joseph Flanagan, aged 38, who was the pilot, belonging to Collingswood, New Jersey, and Wayne Archer Taylor, aged 32, the navigator, from Lamissa, California. The aircraft was originally a twin-engined bomber belonging to the American air force, but it had been sold to the French air force and was being transported across the Atlantic Ocean to France when it crashed. Having left Iceland, it was being ferried to France by two members of Fleetways Incorporated, a civilian air ferry firm. The last contact with the aeroplane was with Prestwick airport at 10.30 pm after which there was silence. An emergency search was then instigated, from both the Sorn and Darvel sides of the moor, but the flames having gone out, it was difficult to locate the wreck. As morning light arrived, the burned out wreck was found. One of the pilots was severely burned but both men were found dead. The bodies were removed by a helicopter scrambled from Prestwick. Remains of the aircraft are still to be found at the location.

Innkeepers in Sorn recorded in 1837 were Robert Kirkland and John Retson, though it is not known which inn they operated. Similarly, in 1867 innkeepers in Sorn were William MacMillan and John Somerville. The Sorn Inn was erected in the late eighteenth century. In 1882 the innkeeper was Robert Aird, who also operated a carriage to Kilmarnock every Friday. The Sorn Inn was later owned by James Kirkland of Kirkbean, Kirkcudbrightshire, but was operated by William Hendry, innkeeper in 1900.

2.13 Sorn Inn *(Dane Love)*

In the 1900s the inn was owned by Alexander Aird and his family, and by 1919 by his trustees. In 1925 the owner was Elizabeth Duncan. In 1934 the tenant was

Thomas Muir. In 1941 the innkeeper was Thomas Muir Junior. The Sorn Inn was owned by Toni and Tony Smith in the 1990s followed by Karen MacFadzean. The inn was seriously damaged in a fire on 9 December 1998. The building was subsequently restored, but at this time the upper floor was converted to flats. It was then acquired by George Smith. In September 2002 the inn was purchased by Craig Grant, who has won numerous awards as a chef. These include Egonay Ronay one star, Michelin Bib Gourmand (2007) and Chef Medaille d'Or (2008). The inn now currently has a main restaurant, smaller chop-house and four bedrooms.

The Greyhound Inn was established in 1782. The innkeeper at one time was William Mackie, who died at the inn in 1897 aged 64. The inn was then operated by his widow, Mrs Isabella Mackie (nee Kennedy) who was still there in 1919. In the 1920s through to the early 1940s the owner and mine host was Thomas Brodie. Around 1954 the Constitutional Club Hall next door was closed and it was taken over and redeveloped as part of the Greyhound Inn, allowing larger functions to be held. The hall was rebuilt considerably, with large windows on the upper floor. By 1987 the proprietors were Hugh and Dorothy Moorhead. The inn was closed in 1991 and redeveloped as houses, the incongruous windows of the former hall being reduced to their eighteenth century Scots Georgian appearance.

The Greenfoot Inn was located at the west end of the village, near to the Cleuch Bridge. It was perhaps the oldest inn in the village, and was located on the west side of the road facing the foot of Dalyearnoch Road. The inn was listed in 1691 in the poll tax returns of the time, Patrick Ewing being liable for the tax on the inn's four hearths. In 1823 the elders and lesser heritors of the parish held a special dinner here to mark the ordination of Rev James Stewart. Around this time it was kept by an elderly man named Hugh Baird, who also ran a small farm. When attendance at Sorn church's Communion services often meant taking in two services on a Sunday, the Greenfoot Inn was a common location for parishioners to eat and drink prior to returning to the church. However, according to Helen Steven, writing in 1898, when things became too rowdy in church because of the alcohol consumed, attendance at the inn between services was stopped. According to A. B. Todd, Greenfoot Inn was then 'the cleanliest, tidiest looking country inn I have set eyes upon.' The inn appears to have been demolished before 1865, the ground where it stood being planted as part of the policies of Sorn Castle, and a footpath from the church to the footbridge at the mouth of the Cleuch Burn passing through where it stood.

Many societies have come and gone over the years. Still in existence is Sorn Women's Rural Institute, which was founded in 1921 following a meeting at Bridgend Cottage, home of Mrs James Gibson. The institute was only established nationally in 1917. The first president was Jeanie McIntyre, mother of Lord Sorn, who held the position until 1941. Meetings have been held in the church hall, the Constitutional Hall, the school and, since its opening in 1954, in the Village Hall.

2.14 Sorn Village Hall *(Dane Love)*

The institute have been responsible for running the baking classes at Catrine Show since 1946. Membership has fluctuated from 123 in 1976/77 to 46 in 2005.

Auchencloigh Women's Rural Institute was also founded on 10 August 1921, the first president being Miss Moir, teacher at the school. Meetings were held in the school to start with, but the institute outgrew this and were active in getting the Auchencloigh Hall erected in 1924. In that year the membership stood at 67, the highest recorded. In the 1920s and 1930s membership varied in the fifties, and in the seventies and eighties in the forties.

The village hall was opened in autumn 1954 as a result of a number of years' fund-raising by the Village Hall Committee. The chairman of the committee was J. G. Stephen of Glenlogan and the honorary president of the committee was Lord Sorn. The first function organised by the committee was held in the school on 21 December 1945 when a series of sketches and plays were performed by Catrine Gordon Memorial Church Woman's Guild Players. At Sorn Castle a garden fete was held in June 1946, opened by Group Captain D. F. McIntyre, the pilot who was the first to fly over Mount Everest. By January 1948 almost £2,200 had been raised by a variety of concerts, whist drives, and soirees. The hall was erected by builders named Brown, from Muirkirk. When the hall was opened there was still some debt, and fund-raising events continued to be organised, the village's first Midsummer Fair being arranged for June 1956, raising £300. Within the hall film shows were often held, films reels being projected onto a large screen.

In recent years the community in Sorn has taken an active part in the Beautiful Scotland in Bloom competition, winning the title in 1986. At the church hall a small garden area was created by members of the community with assistance from BBC Scotland's *Beechgrove Garden* 'Hit Squad' in 1997. This garden was to win various awards at the time.

2.15 English Civil War re-enactment at Sorn, 1986 *(Sheila Love)*

On 23-24 August 1986 a large re-enactment of a battle took place on the Kilnknowe Park, opposite Sorn Castle. Attracting large crowds of almost 5,000 over two days, the English Civil War Society demonstrated their skills in dressing up in period costume and taking part in armed combat in a mock battle. The event was organised by the Ayrshire Valleys Tourist Board.

A small hamlet existed at Bridgend of Montgarswood. This village was created sometime between 1766, when the new turnpike road was created, and 1787. It was established by the laird of East Montgarswood as a weaving community, but it never grew to be any more than thirteen houses, no doubt the larger and more prosperous milling village of Catrine attracting the weavers. According to A. B. Todd, the weavers at Bridgend produced everyday goods, including 'blankets, druggets, and such like fabrics for the farmers' wives of the district.' A sweep of houses made their way from Bridgend Bridge up the brae towards East Montgarswood. Many of these houses were also occupied by workers at Bridgend Tile Works. Although established as a weaving community, by 1900 it seems to have had more than its fair share of shoemakers, four houses being occupied by them – James Baird, James Baird, James Cunninghame and James Johnstone. Three of the houses were empty or in ruins at this time. In 1903 the remaining houses were noted as being damp and past their best, the others being roofless and beginning to decay. And yet by 1940 seven remained in occupation, only number 7 being empty and condemned. The occupied cottages had Loudon MacAuslan, David Purdie, James MacGregor, Henry Kilmurray (pedlar), James Cummings, Mrs Smith and William Murdoch (labourer)

2.16 Bridgend of Montgarswood from the north *(Baird Institute)*

as tenants. The houses were owned by the trustees of the late John Kerr at that time, apart from Number 1, which was owned by James Wilson, joiner, of Auchmillan, and Number 8, which was owned by Sorn estate. One of the cottages at Bridgend appears to have been a small shop, for in 1919 it was noted that the houses in the hamlet were all occupied, but that the shop was empty. Some of the houses remained occupied during the Second World War, and when peace resumed they were demolished and the residents re-housed in Catrine.

CHAPTER THREE

ROADS AND TRANSPORT

Before the second half of the eighteenth century there were no proper roads in the parish, people just making their way along rough unfenced tracks from one place to another. With the improvement of agriculture, and the enclosing of fields, these trackways were fenced off and as time passed were developed into what we would recognise as a roadway.

One of the oldest roadways through Sorn parish linked Cessnock Castle and Galston with Sorn Castle, the castle at Sorn being the property of the Keiths of Galston. This old roadway followed a route further to the east of the present Galston-Sorn road, on average half a mile to one mile further uphill. From Galston the route took a more direct approach through the grounds of Cessnock Castle to Threepwood, then across country to Langside, March House, Bogend, and Auchencloigh to Auchmannoch. From Auchmannoch the route made its way to Sorn by a way now totally lost.

It is claimed that following her defeat at the Battle of Langside, on 13 May 1568, Mary Queen of Scots followed this old road on her escape from Scotland. Local tradition claims that she stopped at Auchmannoch to allow her horses time to drink at a well located near to the roadway. This spot is now known as the Lady's Well and was later marked by a tall stone cross. This well

3.1 Lady's Well *(Dane Love)*

51

traditionally had curative powers, and locals would make their way to it to take the waters in hope of curing some ailment or other. It was the tradition to tie a ribbon of cloth to the trees nearby, in the same way as there are a number of 'clootie' wells in Inverness-shire, but this practise seems to have died out around the time of the Second World War. The well may have existed centuries prior to Mary Queen of Scots' visit, for the stone cross has the date 'A.D. 1250' inscribed on it, but this may just be someone's flight of imagination.

In the nearby vicinity, 2,600 yards up the Stra Burn, is a spot known as the Queen's Dyke, which reputedly had connections with Mary, but the traditional tale seems to have been forgotten. Known also as the 'Queen's Kype' this was a dry stretch of ground, or low ridge, surrounded by wet marshland. Kype is the old Scots word to describe a pointed knoll. Mary Queen of Scots may have camped here on her route south.

South of Sorn this old roadway may have continued to Auchinleck and Cumnock. A possible route it may have followed at the village is from Blairmulloch by way of Laigh Brocklar to Laigh Holhouse. The River Ayr may have been forded to Waterside of Glenlogan, and then a roadway up through the wood to Shiel farm. From here an old Drove Road appears on some maps heading south to Roundshaw farm. The route from Roundshaw Cottage south to Cumnock has been lost, but may have passed near to Birnieknowe farm and between Blackston and Dykes farm to the roadway down past the railway at Templand into Cumnock.

Reference to the droving of cattle in this area is found in the letters of the Marquis of Titchfield. Writing to him on 21 September 1796, his factor, George Douglas, writes of cattle passing from Cessnock to Cumnock:

> My Lord, on Friday 9th ... the bullocks from the Falkirk market arrived. As they have been far drove and had still a long way to go I thought it proper to give them a few days rest here. They left again on Wednesday ... and joined the bullocks from Galloway that evening at Cumnock and proceeded next morning to Welbeck ... They are under the care of Andrew Campbell, who is one of your workers upon your Lordship's estate of Cessnock ... He had two Highlandmen alongst with him.

This drove road from Galston to Cumnock was probably used up until the countryside was divided into fields, blocking the route. This may have taken place in the second half of the eighteenth century. Between Newhouse of Auchencloigh and Meadowhead of Auchmannoch was an area of ground used as a drove stance, a spot where drovers traditionally rested for the night, the cattle getting time to graze. It was claimed that this stance was common ground, and therefore did not belong to anyone, but around 1900 David Bone of Auchencloigh was caught

3.2 Sorn Old Bridge *(Jamie McIntyre)*

shooting on it. Despite his protestations that the land was common ground, he was taken to court and fined thirty shillings.

The first major improvement in roads within the parish took place sometime between 1739 and 1751, at the time Rev William Steel was minister of the parish. Many parishioners on the south side of the River Ayr had difficulty in attending church when the river was swollen, it being dangerous to try to cross. Tradition claims that someone was drowned in the swollen waters of the river whilst trying to reach the church and the minister vowed that it should never happen again. Rev Steel decided to collect subscriptions from local landowners and others and with the money raised was able to erect the Sorn Old Bridge. This is a rather fine old hump-backed structure, crossing the river by means of two arches. The carriageway is only 9 feet 6 inches in width, which was sufficient at the time for foot passengers and the odd horse and cart which went its way through the glen.

In 1767 the Ayrshire Commissioners of Supply met to consider the establishment of a turnpike act which would allow them to build new roads through the county, and to charge the users a toll for their use. An Act of Parliament was received allowing the trustees to commence work on 24 roads across the county, two of which traversed Sorn parish. These roads were to be 30 feet wide, from fence to fence (where they existed) with 15 feet of surfaced roadway in the middle, comprising stones 16 inches thick. This was later reduced to 24 feet between fences or ditches, the 15 feet of surfaced road being 14 inches thick in the middle, tapering outward to 9 inches thick at the side.

The most important of these new routes was the roadway from Ayr by way of Mauchline and Sorn towards Muirkirk, and thence by Douglas to link with the roads to Edinburgh. This was originally the main road from the county town of Ayr to the capital city of Edinburgh, the route by Cumnock to Muirkirk not being created until a second act of 1774. Previously the roadway used took a more direct route from Bridgend of Montgarswood to Mauchline, passing the Welton farms, but most of this route is in Mauchline parish. The bridge over the Burn o' Need at Bridgend of Montgarswood was erected around 1768. Other bridges in the locality include Glenlogan Bridge, erected in 1778 and at one time inscribed *Jean Smith Mahon 1778*.

According to the account books of the *Mauchline and Sorn Conversion Money Accounts*, £216 7s ½d was paid in cash to Alexander Pedine for making the roadway from Sorn to Muirkirk. The payments were made between 22 December 1780 and 6 May 1783.

The second turnpike road created by the 1767 Act was laid from Galston south through Sorn to Auchinleck. This replaced the ancient roadway located further to the east, along which Mary Queen of Scots is supposed to have travelled. Permission

3.3 Bridgend of Montgarswood, showing bridge of 1768 *(Baird Institute)*

was granted for the Galston to Cumnock road committee to have toll bars erected and commence charging tolls at a meeting of the trustees on 8 September 1772, which indicates that this roadway was not started until then. The road seems to have taken a number of years to construct, for in November 1783 it is noted as still being under construction.

Tolls were established at intervals along these routes, and a toll house with gate was located at Sorn. The tollhouse stood on the west side of the road, between the Dalgain Mill and the Greenfoot Inn. This building appears to have been demolished prior to 1865. The location of this toll was ideally placed, for it actually covered both roadways, both sharing the same route from Sorn Castle gatehouse across the foot of the Cleuch Glen to Sorn Bridge.

Tolls payable at Sorn in 1767 on the Edinburgh road were as follows:

Coach, Chariot, Berlin, Landau, Calash, Chaise, Chair or Hearse drawn by Six Horses, Mares, Geldings or Mules:	4s 0d
Drawn by four:	3s 0d
Drawn by three:	2s 6d
Drawn by two:	1s 6d
Drawn by one:	0s 9d
For every Wagon, Wain, Cart or other Wheel Carriages, drawn by Six Horses, Oxen, or other Beasts of Draught:	6s 0d
Drawn by five:	5s 0d
Drawn by four:	4s 0d
Drawn by three:	2s 0d
Drawn by two:	1s 0d
Drawn by one:	0s 6d
For every Sledge without Wheels	0s 6d
For every Horse, Mare, Gelding, Mule, or Ass, laden or unladen, and not drawing:	0s 3d
For every drove of Oxen or Neat Cattle, per score, and so in proportion for any greater or less number:	0s 10d
For every drove of Horses or Fillies unshod, per Score:	1s 8d
For every Drove of Calves, Sheep, Lambs, Hogs or Goats, per Score:	0s 5d.

The Galston to Cumnock road through Sorn was charged at a lower levy for coaches, wagons, sledges and horses, only Droves being charged the same. For comparison purposes, a coach drawn by six horses paid 2s 8d at this time. The tolls on the Edinburgh route were doubled in 1774, a coach and six horses being charged 8s 0d at that time. Tolls were not payable by those travelling to church on a Sunday, by soldiers on the march, or by cattle and horses being taken to pasture.

A check bar, with toll gate was established at Mossfoot Cottage, located at Gilmilnscroft Cottages. Known as the South Logan Check Bar, this controlled traffic on the roadway created from Mossfoot to Birnieknowe. Tolls were eventually abolished on 31 May 1883, with considerable rejoicing by the carters.

On Friday 8 November 1782 James Boswell of Auchinleck (1740-95) was in

3.4 Damhead Cottage *(William Frew)*

the area to assist in laying out a new roadway from Sorn towards Auchinleck. What road this was is not known, for the current roadway from Sorn Old Bridge to Auchinleck was laid out as part of the original Turnpike Act.

The road from Sorn to Muirkirk was discovered in the 1790s to be rather steep in places, particularly at the Dalgain Brae, and it was proposed that a new line for the road should be found, nearer to the River Ayr. The first attempts at building this road failed for lack of funds, and again in 1796 proposals were made for building it, but these came to nought.

By 1796 local estate owners had created around six private roads for themselves, many of which have now become public roads.

The Sorn New Bridge was erected of sandstone in 1871 on the downstream side of the Coal Ford. It was built by George Reid and Son of Catrine and the foundation stone was laid with Masonic honours on 24 June 1871 by Andrew Ranken of Glenlogan. Previously the roadway here passed through a narrow lane between houses at Coalford and down to the riverside. The ford allowed travellers to pass to the south side of the river, adjacent to Stepends Cottage, before climbing westwards past Damhead to Woodhead. The new bridge was erected between Coalford and Sandbed. Constructed of red sandstone, the bridge crosses the river by means of two arches, supported on pointed buttments. The carriageway from parapet to parapet is 21 feet 6 inches in width, much more spacious than the old bridge. The walls of the bridge comprise rustic masonry, with a rounded string course at carriageway level, the parapets of dressed masonry.

Carriages or buses could be hired at the start of the twentieth century from James Murdoch, who operated from Sorn and Catrine. He also ran omnibuses from Sorn to Catrine and Mauchline to tie in with the trains.

3.5 Main Street, Sorn *(Baird Institute)*

The railway had little effect on Sorn parish, although the main Glasgow-Dumfries line passed through the south western edge of the parish. This line was opened from Kilmarnock as far south as Auchinleck on 17 July 1848. Construction of the railway meant that fields at Clews and Brackenhill were divided and bridges had to be built over the road between High and Low Clews and under the road at Brackenhill, in addition to over the Dippol Burn on the southern edge of the parish. This line still remains in use today.

The only other railway created in the parish was the branch line that linked Brackenhill Junction with the station at Catrine, opened on 31 August 1903. This line was created to allow goods from Catrine mills to be transported more easily, but passenger trains were also operated. The line was closed to passengers on 3 May 1943 and for goods on 6 July 1964. The line was subsequently lifted.

In addition to these two railways, there were a number of proposals for other lines through the parish. One of the most significant would have been the Caledonian Western Extension Railway which was to pass through the parish from west to east, linking Mauchline with Muirkirk, and thus to the homeland of the Caledonian Railway Company in Lanarkshire and Clydeside. Maps of the proposed route through the parish survive and, if built, this line would have entered the parish at Montgarswood, skirted Sorn Castle and passed along the top of Sornbank Plantation, above the village, and continued by way of Holhouse and Hole, leaving the parish at Limmerhaugh. No doubt a station would have been established at Sorn, but the plans do not show one.

These proposals for a new railway were opposed by the local landowners, and an alternative route was suggested by the owners of Sorn estate. The original proposal would have had the railway passing through the Sauch Park, above the castle, which would have destroyed the views from the castle. The alternative route proposed by the landowners had the line of the railway further up the hill, passing

3.6 Townhead, Sorn *(Baird Institute)*

from near Sorn Mains along the edge of the Sauch Park woods, crossing the Cleuch Glen by means of a viaduct and rejoining the original proposed route near to Laigh Holhouse.

As part of this alternative scheme, the landowners intended moving the public roadway away from Sorn Castle. The route would have left the Mauchline road to the west of the Kilnpark Plantation, crossed the Galston Road above the 'S' bend and followed the northern side of the Sauch Park wood before turning to the south-east, following the line of the proposed railway to the Blindburn road. On the east side of the Cleuch Glen wood a new road was to be constructed alongside the edge of the wood and winding down to the village, passing along the back of the manse glebe and joining the present road on the east side of Damside Cottage. Dalyearnoch Road would also have been upgraded, and it would have been extended with a new roadway along the southern edge of the Gillhead shelterbelt before swinging down to join the Muirkirk road near to Holehouse-hillhead. This would have provided an alternative route into the village without having to traverse the steep Dalgain Brae. None of these proposals was ever to come to fruition.

CHAPTER FOUR

ESTATES AND LANDOWNERS

SORN CASTLE

When the first fortified castle was erected at Sorn is unknown, but it is reckoned that the present castle has as its oldest part the original tower of the fifteenth century, or possibly earlier. The earliest known owners of the Barony of Sorn were the Keiths of Galston, and it is thought that it was them who built the old keep. Tradition claims that the masons employed in building the castle were given a choice of being paid either one peck of meal (8¾ lb) or 1½d per day. Early accounts of the owners are difficult to tie down to Sorn parish, for the castle was at this time only a secondary tower house on a larger estate. It was not until 1782 that Sorn estate became a separate entity in its own right.

Sir William Keith of Galston had an only daughter, Janet Keith, the heiress of the family, who was married to Sir David Hamilton, 3rd of Cadzow Castle, the ancestor of the ducal houses of Hamilton and Abercorn. Sir David is reckoned by family historians as being the first member of the family to adopt the surname Hamilton. They had at least five sons, Sir John Hamilton, who succeeded to Cadzow,

4.1 Sorn Castle – H. E. Clifford's drawing *(Dane Love)*

George Hamilton, Andrew Hamilton, Sir William Hamilton, John *(secundus)* Hamilton and Elizabeth Hamilton, who married Sir Alexander Fraser of Cowie. George Hamilton acquired Borland Castle in Old Cumnock parish. Andrew Hamilton was gifted lands in Ayrshire by his mother on 11 December 1406, and became the ancestor of the Hamiltons of Udston. Sir William was granted lands in Bathgate, West Lothian, by his mother, and was the ancestor of the Hamiltons of Bathgate. John *Secundus* acquired the lands of Bardowie, Stirlingshire

Sir David Hamilton died before May 1392. Janet Keith married a second time, to Sir Alexander Stewart of Darnley, by whom she appears to have had other issue.

Around the year 1406 the castle was acquired by Sir Andrew Hamilton, third son of Sir David Hamilton and Janet Keith, as part of the greater lands of Galston. The charter by which this transfer was made is recorded in the *Registrum Magni Sigilli Regum Scotorum* or the *Register of the Great Seal of Scotland*. Written in Latin, this only makes reference to the 'terras de Sorne', or lands of Sorn, from which nothing about the extent of the lands can be made.

Andrew Hamilton married Agnes, daughter of Sir Hugh Campbell of Loudoun, which family were the hereditary Sheriffs of Ayr. Sir Hugh (d. *ante* 1430), however, appears not to have been a Sheriff, for on the charter dated 11 December 1406 he is listed as a witness, and the charter also makes reference to William of Conyngham as Sheriff at that time. Andrew and Agnes Campbell had a son, Sir Robert Hamilton, who inherited the castles of Sorn and Sanquhar (better known as Newton Castle, at Newton-upon-Ayr). He was married to a daughter of Sir William Craufurd of Leifnoreis Castle, in the parish of Old Cumnock. They had a son, Sir William Hamilton, who succeeded.

Sir William Hamilton of Sorn and Sanquhar was one of the Senators of the College of Justice and held the position of Lord Treasurer to King James V. Sir William, the Lord Treasurer, was married to a daughter of the Kennedys of Cassillis, by whom he had an heiress, Isobel Hamilton. He probably did not spend much time at either Sorn or Newton Castle, most of his time being employed in work in Edinburgh. He was quickly promoted through the royal service, from servitor at the court of James IV in 1512, to a Gentleman of the Royal Household, becoming Depute Master of the Royal Household in 1526. He was sent on foreign missions, one of which was to try to find a bride for James V in 1528. From 1542-43 he was active in negotiating the marriage of Prince Edward of England with Mary Queen of Scots, which resulted in the Treaty of Greenwich. He was appointed one of the judges of the Court of Session in 1546 and had a lease of the Edinburgh Mint from 1547-9. From 1548-53 he was Keeper of Edinburgh Castle and in 1553-4 he was Provost of Edinburgh. Hamilton had also been Provost of Ayr from 1539-60 and a Member of Parliament for Ayr. He had extensive landholdings throughout Ayrshire, for as well as owning Sorn (which was purchased from the monks of Melrose by March 1533), he also held land at Auchendrane near Ayr, Barbieston at Dalrymple,

MacNairston near Ayr, Newton Castle, Kingcase near Prestwick, Symington, Barnweill near Craigie, Mossgiel near Mauchline, Auchinruglen near Galston, Glenmuir in Auchinleck parish and Glencop near Straiton. He died in 1560.

An old rhyme supposedly spoken by James VI that referred to Sir William Hamilton was recounted by James Boswell in his journal of 1777:

> Sir William Hamilton, I bid you good morn,
> Laird of Newton and Laird of the Sorn,
> Sheriff of [unknown] and Sheriff of Ayr,
> And what the de'il wad ye ha'e mair?

Sir William had a natural son, also William, who died before 1572, but who had a family of his own. His eldest son, also William, appears to have occupied Sorn. He was married to Annabell Wallace (d. 1620), daughter of John Wallace of Craigie, and they had three sons and three daughters, William (alive in 1605), Henry, Hugh, Jane (alive in 1614), Margaret and Elizabeth. Sir William's grandson, William Hamilton, was styled as 'of Sorn' in some accounts. In the 1570s and 1580s, William Hamilton sold off many of the Hamilton lands, mainly to the Regent Arran, another Hamilton. He attempted to regain possession of Newton Castle in Ayr in November 1587 but was unsuccessful in this, the castle being confirmed as the property of the Wallace family. William Hamilton seems to have lived at Mossgiel for a time, and sold most of the remaining Hamilton lands to the Wallaces of Craigie. He died in 1589. Nothing more is known of him.

Sir William Hamilton was succeeded in Sorn by his daughter, Isobel Hamilton (c. 1529-1604) of Sorn and Sanquhar. She was married to George, 5th Lord Seton (1531-1586), on 5 August 1550. George was educated in France and was Provost of Edinburgh from 1557-9. They had six children, George, the eldest son and Master of Seton, but who died as a boy in March 1562; Robert, who succeeded his father as 6th Lord Seton and who was created 1st Earl of Winton in 1600; Sir John, who was Scottish Ambassador to the Court of Spain, and who died in May 1594; Alexander, who was created 1st Earl of Dunfermline in 1605; Sir William of Kylesmure (1562-1635), who became Postmaster General of Scotland; and Margaret (d. 1616), who married Claud Hamilton, Lord Paisley, and who was the mother of the 1st Earl of Abercorn.

The 5th Lord Seton was a very important person in the Scottish royal household. He was selected by parliament to be present at Mary Queen of Scots' wedding to the Dauphin of France on 24 April 1558. Henry II, king of France, gifted him with some silver plate and a yearly pension of 1200 francs. When Queen Mary returned to Scotland he was appointed as Master of Her Majesty's Household and entertained her at his home at Seton Castle, or palace, which he had rebuilt. Following the murder of Lord Darnley, he looked after Mary and Bothwell and was present when their wedding contract was signed. He was involved in her escape from Lochleven Castle in 1568, after which he hid her at his castle of Niddry, at Winchburgh in West Lothian. He spent time in Europe supporting Mary in exile, and returned on royal business on a few occasions. He died in January 1586, aged around 55, and was buried in Seton Church, East Lothian.

Isobel Seton, Lady Seton, died on 13 November 1604, aged around 75 years. She was interred at Seton Church alongside her husband. Her son and heir, Robert, who had been created 1st Earl of Winton on 16 November 1600, predeceased her (on 22 March 1603), so the estate of Sorn, as part of the larger Seton estates, went to her grandson, Robert Seton, 2nd Earl of Winton. Robert, 1st Earl, was married in 1582 to Lady Margaret Montgomerie (d. 1624), daughter of the 3rd Earl of Eglinton.

It was during the time of the ownership of the Earls of Winton, in 1598, that King James VI visited Sorn Castle. He was there to attend the marriage of Isobel, the only daughter of the 1st Earl of Winton, to James Drummond, 4th Lord Drummond, who was created 1st Earl of Perth in 1605. An old tale recounts how the king was making his way south to Sorn from Glasgow. The route across the Fenwick Moor was at that time little more than a rough track, and at one point the king's horse sank into a deep peat bog. From that time onward the spot became known as the King's Stable. In the same vicinity he quenched his thirst at a spring, now known as Kingswell. King James was later to announce that if he should ever wish to play a trick on the Devil then he would send him to a bridal at Sorn in the middle of winter!

According to Sir Richard Maitland in *Historie of the House of Setoune*, 'the union [of Isabel Hamilton and George Seton] was devised to bring about an alliance betwixt the Setounes and the Governor Arran, to whose house Sir William belonged, and was of such political importance that a medal commemorating it

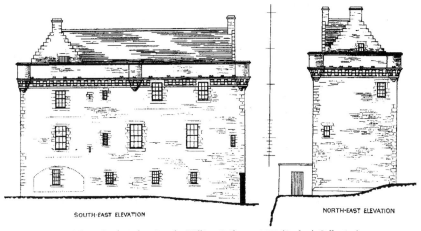

4.2 Sorn Castle – elevations by William Railton, c.1880 *(Author's Collection)*

was struck, bearing the initials of the bride and bridegroom, I.H. and G.S., and the motto *Ung loy, ung foy, ung roy.*' For many years the special chair that was used by the king was kept at Sorn Castle, but when the castle was sold in 1782 it was transferred to Loudoun Castle where it remained an object of antiquarian interest for many years. This chair was made from oak, had curious carvings over it, and on the rear bore the arms of Sir William Hamilton.

Robert Seton, 2nd Earl of Winton, was married on 1 February 1603 to Anna Maitland, daughter of the 1st Lord Thirlestane. This marriage was something of a disaster, for 'he showed symptoms of mental aberration on his wedding night, was separated from his bride, and was thereafter kept in restraint at Seton Palace till he died. The lady sued for divorce on the ground of impotency. She died 6 July 1609, aged nineteen.' On their wedding night Seton apparently lifted a chamber pot and emptied it down his wife's cleavage. Robert, 2nd Earl of Winton, signed over the titles and lands of Seton and Winton in 1606 to his next brother, George Seton, who became 3rd Earl of Winton. This was ratified in a crown charter dated 12 May 1607. George Seton appears to have still been alive in 1636.

The 3rd Earl of Winton extended his east coast estates, and in 1620 built the new mansion of Winton, located three miles east of Tranent in East Lothian. In 1630 he extended Seton Palace considerably. During this time he decided to sell off his Ayrshire lands, and he sold the estate and castle of Sorn to Sir John Campbell of Lawers (1598-1663) in 1620. The 3rd Earl of Winton died on 17 December 1650 and was buried at Seton Church.

Sir John Campbell of Lawers was knighted by King James VI and in 1620 married a distant cousin, Margaret Campbell, Baroness of Loudoun in her own right. They received a charter to the lands of Sorn on 2 March 1620. Written in Latin, it lists the estates as covering the:

> 10 librat. terrarium de Sorne, Blairmalloche et Blairkip, cum fortalicio, maeriei loco, piscariis, molendino, lie Sorne-mylne, ejus terris, etc.

Sir John's father-in-law resigned the title of Lord Loudoun to him in December 1622, and as Lord Loudoun he was given a charter to the lands of Kylesmuir on 4 September 1630, this being re-issued on 15 March 1634 to him and his wife. In 1641 he was created Earl of Loudoun, Lord Terrinzean and Lord Mauchline, but with a precedency of 1633, when he was first offered the titles, but which were withdrawn on his opposition to the crown. Lord Loudoun was a supporter of Charles II, and assisted in his reclamation of the crown. He died in Edinburgh on 15 March 1663 and was buried in Loudoun Kirk.

The 1st Earl of Loudoun was succeeded by his eldest son, James, who was married to Margaret Montgomerie, daughter of the 7th Earl of Eglinton. He did not support Charles II at the time of the Covenanters and escaped abroad for most of the troubles, dying at Leyden, now Leiden, in the Netherlands, in 1684. It was during his absence that Sorn Castle was requisitioned around 1665 by the government forces and used as a garrison to suppress the Covenanters.

Hugh Campbell, 3rd Earl of Loudoun (1667-1731), succeeded. He was active in parliament from 1696 and was Commissioner of the Treasury from 1702-4 and Secretary of State in 1705. He obtained a new charter to his earldom in 1707. He fought against the Jacobites at the Battle of Sheriffmuir in 1715 and was Lord High Commissioner to the Church of Scotland on six occasions. He died at Loudoun Castle on 20 November 1731.

On 28 February 1668 Sir Hugh Campbell received a charter under the Great Seal confirming his ownership of Loudoun estate and other lands. At the time Sorn was included in these lands, and the references to places within the parish mentioned in the charter are as follows:

> ... Over and Nether Sornes, with manor-place, woods, salmon and other fishings, grain and walk-mill and multures; Blairkip, Blairmulloch ... Mungerswood, Clutersland, with manor-place and pertinents ... Blacksyde ...Burntsheill, and salmon fishing on the water of Air, within the bounds thereof ... Smiddieshaw and Daldorch, Hielach [Heilar?] ... Holhouse, Daldilling, Brocklairdyke, Sands ...Oxinshaw, ---haugh, Cowieland, Hoill in Nethermeiklewood, and pertinents; Hoill, Nether Meiklewood, and pertinents, commonly called Redinghead....

Although John Campbell succeeded as 4th Earl of Loudoun, the widow of Hugh, 3rd Earl, was still alive, and she settled in Sorn Castle following her husband's death, although many accounts state that she lived at Sorn from 1727. She was to remain there for the rest of her life.

Margaret Dalrymple, the Dowager Countess of Loudoun, is said to have been born on 4 February 1677, only daughter of John Dalrymple, 1st Earl of Stair and Elizabeth Dundas, daughter of Sir John Dundas of Newliston. However, records show that she was baptised on 25 August 1684 at Kirkliston, West Lothian, and thus the story that she lived to be 100 years of age is unfounded. She died on 3 April 1779, at the age of 94. Margaret married Sir Hugh Campbell, 3rd Earl of Loudoun (1667-20 November 1731), at Kirkliston in West Lothian, on 6 April 1700 and had three children, Sir John Campbell, 4th Earl of Loudoun (6 May 1705-27 September 1782), Lady Elizabeth Campbell (died unmarried at Sorn Castle, 19 April 1771) and Lady Margaret Campbell (married John Campbell of Shawfield and died without issue at Edinburgh on 7 October 1733, being buried in St Giles' High Kirk, Edinburgh). Lady Loudoun lived for some time at the Courts of Queen Anne and George I.

At the time the Dowager Countess of Loudoun lived at Sorn Castle the countryside around the castle was wild and open, with hardly a road, hedge or tree. Lady Loudoun was determined that she would transform the appearance of the estate and convert it to something that was more to her liking. In the immediate policies of the castle she enlarged and improved the gardens and orchard. One of the neighbouring farms she subdivided and enclosed with hedges, planting shelter-belts and clumps of trees. The remaining fields were drained

4.3 Dowager Countess of Loudoun *(Private Collection)*

to improve the quality of the ground. Alongside the river and streams she planted other trees and created walks through the woods. It was noted that she supervised the works herself, and many of the trees she actually planted and pruned herself. Prior to starting this work, Lady Loudoun had been in poor health, but the fresh air and purpose that she had set herself resulted in her health becoming better, so much so that she lived for many more years.

The planting and draining improvements made by Lady Loudoun were noted by her neighbours, and as a result Mr Steel, Robert Farquhar of Gilmilnscroft, Mr Dunlop of Garnkirk, and others copied them, adding to the beauty of the parish.

The famous diarist, James Boswell of Auchinleck, visited Sorn Castle on Thursday 20 March 1777, walking through the grounds and around the battlements of the castle. He noted that, 'The place looked to me like enchantment. The old Castle on the margin, or rather rocky bank, of the water of Ayr, the gardens curiously formed, and the old Lady of the Castle – ninety-seven [an error on Boswell's part]. She received me with amazing ease and cheerful vivacity, though by a fall she was now lame, could not walk, and was wheeled about in a chair. She was neat in her dress... The gardens were like those of Babylon. The lady was like a Peruvian princess. I mean, all was like romance.' Boswell also visited Lady Loudoun at Loudoun Castle on 2 November 1778, finding her still quite fresh. Dr Samuel Johnson, Boswell's great friend, also visited Lady Loudoun, accompanying Boswell on a visit in 1773.

In 1778 and 1784 Andrew Wight compiled two volumes on the *Present State of Husbandry in Scotland,* extracted from reports made to the Commissioners of the Annexed Estates. In it he gives a good report on Lady Loudoun's work at Sorn:

At Sorn Castle, the very venerable and highly respected Countess of Loudon resides, now in the 98th or 99th year of her age, as I am informed, and yet as entire in memory and judgement as in the prime of life. Her Ladyship has graced this country in many respects; but I am confined to her husbandry improvements. Fifty years ago, when this lady took up her residence at Sorn Castle, not a tree was to be seen, a scrubby wood excepted; and now the finest oaks and other barren trees are striving, as it were, which shall rise the highest. The plantations are extensive, and all trained in the best order, every thing directed by the Countess herself. The soil of her farm is far from being kindly; yet, by skill and perseverance, she has brought it into high order; not greater verdure can be seen any where. In a word, her farm graces the county of Ayr, and might grace the richest counties of Britain.

I had the honour, which will not readily go out of mind, to be introduced to this noble personage. She entered familiarly into a conversation with me, and surprised me with her knowledge in husbandry; discoursed on the qualities of various grasses; inquired into the method of raising potatoes from the apple; and expressed uncommon zeal for husbandry improvements. There perhaps does not exist in the world such another woman.

The wages of labourers are high in this county, from 12d to 14d per day, occasioned by the great drain of men for the army. This bears hard upon agriculture; but the public must be served; and, in the mean time, children are growing up to fill the vacancy.

In my former survey of this county, I had occasion to mention some ministers, exemplary not only for good living, but for good husbandry. I am glad to add to the list Mr Connal [sic], minister of Sorn, who adheres to the following rotation. Lime is at hand, fivepence per boll. He lays 100 bolls per acre on the sward, to be opened up for oats, pease, oats. Grass-seeds are sown with the last crop, barley sometimes instead of oats; and six years pasture finishes the rotation. This method cannot fail to produce good crops; and, where lime is to be had, it may suit even the humblest tenant. I only doubt a little whether lime be not here too often repeated. Judicious farmers are in theory, if not in practice, that, in the culture of a field, change of seed is more necessary than a change of manure.

Following the death of the Dowager Countess of Loudoun, Sorn Castle returned to John Campbell, 4th Earl of Loudoun. He was born on 5 May 1705 and served in parliament as a representative peer from 1734 until his death in 1782. He was also active in the army, and fought against the Jacobite army of 'Bonnie' Prince Charles Edward Stewart at the Battle of Prestonpans in 1745. He appears to have retreated into the highlands, missing the Battle of Culloden, but spent the following weeks tracking down Jacobites on the island of Skye. He served on the continent and was appointed Governor of Edinburgh Castle in 1770. He died at Loudoun Castle on 27 April 1782 at the age of 76. Having no children, he was succeeded by his cousin, James Mure Campbell of Lawers.

The 4th Earl of Loudoun had been in financial difficulties at the time of his mother's death, and placed the estate in trust for his creditors. To assist in paying off his debts, Sorn castle and estate were sold in 1782 following his death. They were purchased by William Tennent of Poole. He only resided in Sorn Castle occasionally, and sold it again around 1785.

The next owner was Alexander Graham of Limekilns House, which was located in the parish of East Kilbride. His coat of arms comprises – Or, a buckle Azure, between three roses Gules, on a chief engrailed Sable as many escallops of the field. The crest was an arm from the shoulder holding a tilting spear Proper. The motto was *Pro rege*. Again he must only have owned the castle for a few years, for it was acquired by John Stevenson of Dalgain. It was perhaps he who was responsible for repairing the old tower, and for adding a considerable extension to it in 1793. It was at this time the drawing room and new staircase were added, creating a more spacious and comfortable house. The cost may have been too much for him, for the castle was placed on the market once more.

In the summer of 1797 the estate was purchased by James Somervell of Hamilton Farm, which stood by the side of the River Clyde in the parish of Rutherglen. He was a partner in the successful Glasgow colonial business of Somervell, Gordon & Co. His widow, Mrs Agnes Somervell, planted considerable shelterbelts around the castle policies in the early nineteenth century. James Somervell died soon after acquiring the estate, and it passed to his son, William Somervell (d. 1818). On William's death he left it to his sisters, Christina Somervell (who married Nicol Brown of Lanfine House, near Darvel) and Agnes Somervell. Christina Brown died in 1823.

Agnes Somervell became the next lady laird. She was born on 9 October 1771 and appears to have been a successful steward of the estate, extending it considerably. Although never married, she appears to have been given the Scottish courtesy title of 'Mrs.' She added the estate of Dalgain to Sorn estate in 1831 and around 1833 purchased the lands of Hole, or Holl, bringing around two fifths of the parish under her ownership. On 21 May 1817 she had the remains of her ancestors disinterred from the old burial ground of St David's Church in Glasgow and re-interred at the Sorn Castle Burial Ground, located by the side of the River Ayr, south west of the castle. This was carried out as there were plans to construct a railway through the churchyard at the time. When she died on 18 June 1856 she was herself interred alongside them, and a simple headstone erected.

On the death of Mrs Agnes Somervell the estate passed to a relative, Graham Russell, who changed his surname to Somervell. Graham Russell was born on 13 January 1819. He was married to Henrietta Jane Stirling. She was born on 4 July 1824, the daughter of Charles Stirling of Muiravonside. Buried in Sorn kirkyard is her niece, Mary Olive Stirling (11 October 1878-27 December 1963), fifth daughter of General Sir William Stirling KCB RA (1835-1906) and his second wife, Anna Christian Stirling.

Graham and Henrietta Somervell had issue, James Somervell (who succeeded), Agnes Mary Russell Somervell (born 22 August 1852, dying at the age of one year, and being buried in Sorn Castle Burial Ground), and Louis Somervell, a Lieutenant in the 74th Highland Light Infantry, who was born on 1 June 1858 and who fell at Tel-el-Kebir on 13 September 1882 and was buried there. Elizabeth Somervell, Graham and Henrietta's only surviving daughter, was to marry John Archibald Middleton on 17 January 1872. Graham Russell Somervell was a Justice of the Peace, Deputy Lieutenant, and convenor of the county. In 1879 he owned an estate of 6,245 acres around the castle, valued at £3,787 per annum. He also owned 218 acres in Lanarkshire (around Hamiltons Farm), valued at £799 per annum.

In 1861 Graham Somervell donated a stained glass window to Glasgow Cathedral, the building undergoing a major renovation. The window, which was designed by Professor E Siebertz, depicts Christ and people kneeling at his feet, with the verse, 'Ask and it shall be given unto you.' At the bottom of the window is a stained glass depiction of Somervell's arms.

In 1863-5 Graham Russell Somervell engaged the famous Scots architect, David Bryce, to restore and enlarge the castle. Bryce is famous for his Scots Baronial castles, but at Sorn he was not given a free reign in the plans, and his work is more restrained, and thus perhaps less fanciful, than many of his pseudo-castles. In fact, a pepper-pot turret that would have appeared at the southern end of the entrance front is shown on the original drawings, but this was omitted, as were some gables on the roofline. The distinctive gatehouse, with the entrance pend through the building, was built at this time, also designed by David Bryce. Graham Somervell's initials and the date 1865 (GS 1865) appear on a rainwater head on the river side of the castle.

Earlier proposals to rebuild the castle came to nought. William A. Railton, of Kilmarnock, drew up plans dated 17 January 1862 for alterations and extensions, but these were not followed through. He did, however, produce plans for the new water supply, the drawing dated 4 March 1862, and for a new cistern on Sorn Hill, the plans dated 15 April 1869. Other works carried out at the castle around this time include the water tank, designed by William Railton, in 1869.

Graham Russell Somervell died on 11 November 1881. Henrietta Somervell died on 24 February 1912 and was buried alongside her husband in Sorn churchyard. James Somervell (19 September 1845-10 February 1924) succeeded. He was educated at Harrow, and called to the Bar at the Inner Temple in 1870. He became a Justice of the Peace and Deputy Lieutenant for Ayrshire, and a Justice of the Peace for Lanarkshire. He was married on 21 January 1892 to Kathleen Emilie Maclaine (1870-1947), eldest daughter of Captain Murdoch Gillean Maclaine of Lochbuie, but they were divorced in 1919. Somervell was a keen farmer, and made considerable improvements to the dairy stock at Sorn. He established Sorn Dairy Supply Company in Glasgow, creating an outlet for his produce. James Somervell unsuccessfully contested the Tradeston seat in Glasgow in 1885. In 1890 he was successful in standing as a Conservative Member of Parliament for Ayr Burghs, and held the seat for two years. Somervell was a Major and Honorary Lieutenant-Colonel in the Ayrshire Yeomanry. He had a son, James Somervell, born 20 May 1893 but who died on 1 August 1894. His second son, James Graham Henry Somervell, was born on 13 August 1894. He also had two daughters, Agnes Marion and Elizabeth Julia.

4.4 Sorn Castle – c.1900 *(Baird Institute)*

In the early years of the twentieth century James Somervell fell into financial difficulties. He let out Sorn Castle for the season, and a variety of tenants came and went at that time. Among these were Mr P. M. Inglis (1907), Professor Sir James Dewar (1908), a co-inventor of Cordite, and Rt Hon Charles Scott Dickson KC (1907-8). Somervell was actually taken to Ayr Bankruptcy Court in the first few years of the 1900s.

James Somervell was unable to keep the estate on a sound financial footing and he was forced into breaking the entail. The estate was placed on the market and was purchased by Thomas Walker McIntyre on 18 October 1908 at a cost of £75,200. Previously McIntyre lived at Kirkmichael House, Ayrshire. It was noted at the time that the gross rent of Sorn estate for the year ending 15 May 1908 was £3,256 8s 4d and rates and taxes paid were £396 8s 6d. At the time the estate extended to 5,462 acres.

Thomas Walker McIntyre was born on 30 November 1860, the son of James McIntyre, of the old Glasgow firm of Napier and McIntyre, iron merchants. James McIntyre was the son of John McIntyre, who was a partner with Robert Napier in the manufacture of steamships for Cunard in the nineteenth century. James McIntyre became a ship-owner, one of his vessels, the *Neptune*, being famous at the time for being reputedly the fastest vessel of its time. It was used during the American Civil Wars to gun-run for the Confederates.

4.5 Thomas Walker McIntyre of Sorn
(Dane Love)

Thomas Walker McIntyre was educated at Glasgow Academy and Merchiston Castle School. In 1885 he began in business as a partner in the shipping firm of Maclay and McIntyre, which was based in Glasgow. His partner was Joseph Maclay, later Sir Joseph Maclay, 1st Lord Maclay (1857-1951), and they operated as shipowners and ship-brokers. He married Jeanie Paterson Galloway (21 December 1861- 22 December 1947), the third daughter of James Galloway of Trinity, Leith, on 23 July 1889. They had four children, James Gordon McIntyre who succeeded; Jean McIntyre (15 October 1890-13 November 1953), who was married on 15 May 1917 to Sir James Hunter Blair, 7th Baronet, of Blairquhan (1889-1985); Marjorie McIntyre (30 November 1891-7 December 1963), who married, firstly, Guy Fitzpatrick Roger Vernon (died from injuries sustained in a motor accident, 11 June 1914) and secondly, on 16 August 1922, to Archibald Seton Montgomerie, 16th Earl of Eglinton and Winton (1880-1945); and Alison McIntyre (1900-1984), who was married on 25 January 1923 to Captain Henry James Johnstone RN of Alva (1895-1947).

For a time T. W. McIntyre was chairman of Glasgow Committee of Lloyd's Register, he was a director in the Laird Line, director of Clyde Steamship Owners'

Association, president in 1906 of Glasgow Shipowners and Shipbrokers Benevolent Association, he was on the board of directors of Glasgow and South Western Railway Company, and a member of the Trades House, Glasgow.

Thomas McIntyre was a keen Conservative and Unionist and stood for parliament unsuccessfully three times – he contested Kilmarnock Burghs in 1906 and South Ayrshire (twice) in 1910. He was chairman of Glasgow Conservative Association for many years. He was Provincial Grand Master of the Masonic Lodge from 1912-17 and a keen supporter of the local Lodge St John, Number 497. Locally he was a keen supporter of Sorn Church, a member of Sorn Parish Council, Sorn School Board, and president of Sorn Parish Agricultural Association. He served in the First World War with the Ayrshire Yeomanry and suffered wounds. He died on 20 September 1920. His wife, Jeanie McIntyre was a noted worker for the British Red Cross Society and a member of the South Ayrshire Women's Unionist Association. It was she who instituted the long-running 'Daffodil Sunday' at Sorn Castle, which attracted considerable visitors to the grounds, raising money for charity.

4.6 Arms of the McIntyres of Sorn Castle
(Dane Love)

T. W. McIntyre retired from most of his business interests when he purchased Sorn estate and became a landowner and laird thereafter. He established a nursery and orchard on Sorn Hill, and around 1915 rebuilt Hillhead farm, with premises for the manufacture of dairy produce.

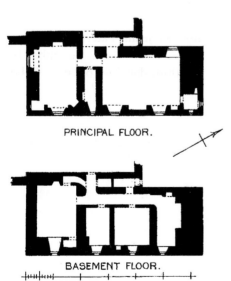

PRINCIPAL FLOOR.

BASEMENT FLOOR.

4.7 Sorn Castle – plans from McGibbon & Ross's *Castellated and Domestic Architecture of Scotland (Author's Collection)*

The most recent additions at Sorn Castle were added from 1907-14, to the plans of Henry Edward Clifford & Thomas M. Lunan of Glasgow. They added the viewing platform on the riverside front of the castle, the lower part of which is an arched colonnade, the upper part a balcony. The porte-cochere was added to the front of the castle, and the ground in front of the castle was raised at this time. At the north-east side of the castle they added the new billiard room. Clifford & Lunan were also responsible for designing the gateway to the gardens of the castle, erected in 1913, and the rebuilding (with upper floor) of Cleugh Cottage in 1917.

Captain James Gordon McIntyre succeeded to Sorn Castle in 1920. He was born on 21 July 1896 and received his education at Winchester, Balliol College, Oxford, where he graduated with a Bachelor of Arts degree in 1921, and Glasgow University, where he earned his Bachelor of Laws degree in 1923. He was appointed as captain in the Ayrshire Yeomanry in 1917, and served with distinction in the First World War, being awarded the Military Cross in 1918 for 'conspicuous gallantry and devotion to duty at the Battle of Sheria, Palestine, 6th November 1917.' Later in the same year he was awarded a Bar to the Military Cross and the Croix de Guerre (France) in 1919. A story claims that John Cameron Fergusson helped to save McIntyre's life during the war, and as a result he was granted the tenancy of West Auchenlongford farm on his return, McIntyre having purchased the farm from Glenbuck estate around that time.

McIntyre was a noted solicitor, being called to the Scottish Bar in 1922. He was appointed as a Justice of the Peace in 1930. In 1936 he became a member of the King's Counsel. He was Dean of the Faculty of Advocates from 1939-44. During the Second World War he joined the Ayrshire Yeomanry, serving in Gallipoli, Palestine and France. He was wounded shortly before the armistice. After leaving hospital he studied at Oxford, graduating B.A. with honours in jurisprudence. He then became a Bachelor of Laws, graduating at Glasgow University. One of his more notable successes was when he was involved in the case of Home Guard members below the rank of Sergeant. He campaigned right to the House of Lords that these men should be classed as a 'common soldier', meaning that should he die whilst in Home Guard duties, his family would not be subject to death

4.8 Lord Sorn *(Dane Love)*

duties. In 1944 he was appointed Senator of the College of Justice, a position that allowed him to adopt a title. McIntyre took the name Lord Sorn, the first Scottish judge to assume a territorial title since Lord Alness was raised to the bench in 1922. He retired from the court in 1963. Lord Sorn was married on 17 July 1923 to Madeline Scott Moncrieff (9 February 1898 – 22 October 1954), the younger daughter of Robert Scott Moncrieff of Downhill WS, Perthshire, on 17 July 1923.

They had two children, Robert, who succeeded, and Olivia McIntyre, born 8 February 1929. Lord Sorn died on 1 July 1983 and was succeeded by his son, Robert Gordon McIntyre.

During the Second World War the castle was requisitioned for use as a military hospital. Within the castle a number of army officers spent some time convalescing.

Robert Gordon McIntyre was born on 30 July 1931. He was educated at Eton, followed by Trinity College, Cambridge. Shortly after succeeding to Sorn he matriculated his coat of arms with the Lord Lyon on 6 June 1984. These comprise a shield divided into four quarters, the first and fourth quarters being gold in colour, with a red eagle displayed, having a black tongue and claws, with a roundel on the breast. The second quarter has a silver background, with a black-coloured galley, whose sails are furled but the oars are in action, with red flags. The third quarter contains a red hand holding a blue cross crosslet on a silver background. The crest comprises a hand grasping a dagger, and the motto chosen was *Per Ardua*, which means 'through difficulties'.

Robert, or Bobby McIntyre, as he was better known, was married on 10 May 1969 to Rachel Anne Watherston (b. 17 August 1948), younger daughter of Jack G. Watherston of Jedburgh, Roxburghshire. They had six sons, James, or Jamie (b. 18 May 1970), Gordon Thomas (b. 8 March 1972), Ewan Jack (b. 7 February 1974), Fergus Robert (b. 25 October 1977), Gavin Malcolm (b. 5 March 1979) and Rory (b. 23 December 1983).

Bobby McIntyre was a director of Dalblair Motors Ltd. in Ayr, which he purchased in 1970. The business sold and serviced Ford cars. He had a deep interest in cars and other vehicles, and built up a collection of old or strange examples at Sorn, including a tank. The collecting of vehicles ran in the family, for Thomas McIntyre had gathered sixteen cars before the First World War, and his father, Gordon, had owned Arrol Johnstones, an Itala and a 1914 Rover 12. Bobbie McIntyre's collection at various times included the ex-Mike Hawthorn Ferrari 212, an ex-Scarletti 1960 Ferrari 250Gt and a Ferrari 330Gt, formerly owned by Jimmy Stewart. He had plans to establish a museum of old cars at Sorn Castle, but he died on 22 March 1988 prior to setting this up.

The collection was sold at an auction held in the grounds of the castle on Saturday 2 July 1988 by auctioneers, Sotheby's. Amongst the sale of 181 lots (not all of which were owned by McIntyre), were a Sherman Tank, De Tomaso Ford Pantera 1973 (estimated sale value of £10-20,000), Aston Martin DB6 Volante Vantage (£18-25,000), 1939 Delage D6.75 (£18-22,000), and a Lanchester 30 hp Straigh Eight of 1929 (£25-35,000).

Mrs McIntyre remarried in 2007 to Charles May, and moved to live with her new husband at Eachwick Hall in Northumberland.

The castle was inherited by Jamie McIntyre, who was educated at Millfield and who was married in May 2008 to Jemma Folley, younger daughter of Mr and Mrs

Brian Folley, of Marlow in Buckinghamshire. Jamie McIntyre is a keen racing driver, competing in historic sportscar racing championships.

The castle has appeared in a number of television programmes, such as *Changing Step*, a film set in Spring 1917 in which the castle acted as a military hospital. The film was written by Anthony Sher and directed by Richard Wilson, and was filmed at Sorn in 1989. In recent years the castle has opened its doors to the public during the summer.

GILMILNSCROFT HOUSE

Gilmilnscroft estate was owned by the Farquhar family for many years, perhaps the earliest reference to them being in the late fourteenth century. The first known owner appears to have been Robert Farquhar, who married Agnes Wallace, probably a daughter of the Riccarton Wallaces, according to George Robertson's *Genealogical Account of the Prinicpal Families in Ayrshire*. They lived in the last years of the 1300s and Agnes seems to have survived him. In 1407 Agnes Wallace, or Farquhar, granted an infeftment to her son, Alexander Farquhar, in which she is styled the 'Gudewife of Gilmillscroft', a 'gudewife' being a tenant's wife.

Nothing appears to be known about Alexander Farquhar, and the next member of the family we are aware of is Thomas Farquhar, who claimed to have received a charter from King James I, who reigned from 1406-37. However, there is no record of this charter in the official records. And yet the charter appears to have been seen by George Robertson, for he states that 'the date of this charter is somewhat obliterated', and that Thomas was styled as son of Alexander Farquhar.

Thomas was succeeded by his son, John Farquhar, who obtained a charter to the lands of 'Castle Cavil' from the Commendator of Melrose Abbey in 1445. Castle Cavil is an older spelling of Castle Kyle, or Kyle Castle, the ruins of which lie five miles east of Cumnock at Dalblair in the Glenmuir valley. John Farquhar married Margaret, a daughter of the laird of Barquharrie, which lies in Ochiltree parish.

The next Farquhar of Gilmilnscroft that appears in the records was Alexander Farquhar, who was married to Janet Campbell. Alexander obtained a charter to the lands of Camys (probably Kames, near Muirkirk) and Glenshamrock (near Auchinleck) from

4.9 Arms of the Farquhars of Gilmilnscroft
(Author's Collection)

the Abbot of Melrose in 1535. This charter makes note of his obligations to the abbey:

> Be it kend til all men, me, Alexander Farker, to be bonden and oblisset to ane reverend fadder in God, ye Abbot of Melrose and Convent, notwithstanding that have laitten to me in feu heritage and myn airs, the lands of Ower and Nether Camys and Glenshamroch, I nevertheless bin and obliss me and myn airs to the said reverend fadder and convent that I sall never molest nor trubul, nor mak requisition to, the persouns which are at this present tyme namit and wrytten in the rental of the said abbey, under payn of forfaultin my feu.
> [Signed] Alex. Farchar, with my hand.

On 7 June 1541 Alexander Farquhar received a Crown Charter to the lands of Gilmilnscroft. In this charter he is described as being 'of Gilmilnscroft', as opposed to 'in Gilmilnscroft', which hints that the Farquhars had merely been tenants of their lands previously, no doubt from the Abbots of Melrose, whereas Alexander

4.10 Gilmilnscroft House *(Baird Institute)*

was now the owner of these lands. This all took place in the years prior to the Reformation, when the great landholdings of the abbeys were broken up. A daughter of the family, Catherine Farquhar, was around 1546 married to John Hamilton of Camskeith.

Alexander was succeeded by his son, Andrew (d. 1556), who in turn was succeeded by his son, Alexander (d. 1625). Alexander was at that time still a youth, and the estate was looked after by older relatives. Alexander was married in 1586 to a daughter of Charles Campbell of Glaisnock, a descendant of the Campbells of

Loudoun. On 11 May 1583 he received a Crown Charter of the Mill of Dalsangan, which was located near to Crosshands in Mauchline parish. A daughter of Gilmilnscroft, perhaps of this Alexander, was married on 18 July 1618 to Charles Campbell of Glaisnock. However, the daughter may have died fairly young, for Campbell was remarried to Helen Lockhart. Alexander died in 1625, whereupon he was succeeded by his son.

Robert Farquhar of Gilmilnscroft (d. 1646) obtained a Crown charter on 15 March 1634 of the 'holdings of Gilmillscroft united', in the name of himself and his son, also known as Robert. He also received ratification from parliament of the lordship of Kylesmuir and Barmuir, along with George Reid of Daldilling in 1641. On 15 August 1643 he was appointed by parliament as one of the Commissioners of Ayrshire.

This Robert Farquhar (d. 1670) succeeded. Prior to his father's death, he was, on 11 February 1646, appointed as one of the Committee of War for Ayrshire, for furthering the service of the kingdom. At that time the estate was a considerable size, extending to £37 13s 8d lands of old extent. He was married on 22 September 1651 to Elizabeth, daughter of James Ross of Balneill in Wigtownshire. Her tocher was worth 8,000 merks. The witnesses to this marriage were James Dalrymple of Stair, John MacDowall, brother of Sir James MacDowall of Garthland, and Alexander Baillie. This marriage produced no heirs, and when Robert Farquhar died in 1670 he was succeeded by his cousin, Robert Farquhar, grandson of Alexander.

This Robert Farquhar (d. 1698) was previously the proprietor of the lands of Lightshaw, near Muirkirk. He was the son of Mungo Farquhar of Lightshaw, a younger son of John Farquhar and Sarah Campbell, daughter of William Campbell

4.11 Gilmilnscroft House, c. 1910 *(Baird Institute)*

of Glaisnock. Robert was a supporter of the Covenant, but he managed to avoid any real conflict and escaped the troubles unscathed. According to Robertson, 'he conducted himself with so much prudence as to avoid the resentment of the Court, whilst he preserved the confidence of his own party.' His colours were, literally, with the Covenanting side, for the Dalgain parish Covenanting banner was long preserved by the Farquhars at Gilmilnscroft. Originally it was hidden there, but after the Glorious Revolution of 1688 the flag had the gold crown with the initials *W R* added, representing King William of Orange, and the date 1689. The flag long after hung in Gilmilnscroft House, but around 1930 was transferred to Sorn Castle.

It is claimed that Gilmilnscroft is haunted by the ghost of one of two brothers. It is said that the laird and his brother supported opposing sides during the time of the Covenanters, and that they often debated the merits of both causes. One evening, fired by alcohol, the argument became so heated that one of the brothers (it is not known which) started a fight resulting in the other being thrown from a window to his death. The surviving brother was thereafter so overcome by guilt that his spirit haunts the house to this day. A number of modern sightings of him have taken place.

Robert Farquhar was married to Julian, a daughter of Nisbet of Greenholm, another well-known Covenanting family. They had three sons and three daughters. The eldest son, James, succeeded. The second son, Hugh Farquhar, served as a colonel in the army. The third son was named George Farquhar. Sarah Farquhar was married to John Reid of Ballochmyle. Margaret Farquhar married Robert Craufurd of 'ye parochine of Cumnock', and Barbara Farquhar was married to Rev William Steel of Lochmaben. The witnesses to this last marriage were James Farquhar of Gilmilnscroft and Patrick Nisbet of Greenholm.

During the time of Robert Farquhar's ownership, Gilmilnscroft was largely rebuilt. A fireplace of 1682, bearing initials *RF IN 1682* (for Robert Farquhar and Julian Nisbet), exists in the master double bedroom on the second floor, having been brought back into the main house from an out-house. It is thought that it may have been located in the first-floor great hall of the original tower house. According to the Hearth Tax records of 1691, Gilmilnscroft had eight hearths at that time.

The Irish dramatist, George Farquhar (1677-1707) is said to have been a descendant of the Farquhars of Gilmilnscroft, though the connection has not been proven. He was born in Derry, the son of a clergyman, William Farquhar, and died in London. He was noted as a playwright, famous for his restoration comedies, and is still known for works such as *A Discourse upon Comedy* (1702), *The Recruiting Officer* (1706) and *The Beaux' Stratagem* (1707).

James Farquhar succeeded in 1698, his retour being dated 2 May 1700. In 1700 he was married to Jean Porterfield, daughter of William Porterfield of that Ilk, and of Duchal Castle in Renfrewshire, and his wife, Annabella, daughter of Stuart of Blackhall. They had three sons and five daughters. Robert predeceased his father.

The other sons were Alexander, who succeeded, and William. The daughters were Annabell, who married Andrew Brown of Waterhead; Jean, who married John White of Neuk; Anna, who married John Wylie in Burnhead; Margaret, who married Duncan Campbell of Barbieston; and Mary, who married Duncan's brother, Charles Campbell.

Gilmilnscroft was rebuilt and extended again in 1708. At this time the new scale-and-platt staircase was introduced to replace the original spiral staircase. It is possible that original vaulting on the ground floor, which was typical of late castles or tower-houses, was removed at this time. Windows on the ground floor were enlarged and the dormer windows on the second floor were changed with the raising of the wallheads to their lintel height.

Alexander Farquhar (d. 1779) who succeeded was thrice married. His first marriage to Agnes Campbell, eldest daughter of John Campbell of Whitehaugh (1682-c.1757), produced no issue. He married again to Elizabeth, daughter of Joseph Wilson of Barmuir, who was the Provost of Ayr from 1720-22. This marriage produced one daughter, Jane Farquhar. His third marriage was to Jean Cuninghame, a daughter of Cuninghame of Polquhairn, in Ochiltree parish, and again there were no children. He died in 1779.

Jane Farquhar (d. 1809) succeeded her father. She was married in 1777 to John Gray (1751-1823), son of Rev James Gray of Strathblane in Stirlingshire. John Gray was a considerable landowner himself, having succeeded his uncle, Rev Andrew Gray of New Kilpatrick, to the lands of Kilmardinny, near Glasgow. On his marriage to Jane Farquhar, he assumed the surname Farquhar Gray. He died in 1823. Jane Farquhar and John Gray had six sons and one daughter. James Gray Farquhar succeeded (the surnames being reversed). Alexander was their second son – he had been in the army but on his retiral became a farmer. John Farquhar became a lieutenant in the 40th Regiment but was killed in action under the Duke of Wellington at the Battle of Salamanca on 22 July1812. William Farquhar became a merchant in Glasgow and died in 1833. Andrew Farquhar became the Comptroller of Customs in Irvine then Glasgow and was married in 1820 to Margaret, daughter of Benjamin Barton, Commissary Clerk of Glasgow, by whom he had one son, John, and a daughter, Jane. The sixth son, Robert Farquhar, died in 1807. The daughter, Eliza, was married to John Ashburner MD, who practised medicine in London. They had no family.

John Farquhar Gray of Gilmilnscroft was a friend of the poet, Robert Burns. On 25 July 1787, at a meeting of Lodge St James Tarbolton, held in Mauchline, at a time when Burns was the Depute Master, Farquhar Gray was made an honorary member. It is claimed by Joseph Train that Farquhar Gray was the Justice of the Peace who performed Burns's marriage with Jean Armour, which probably took place in 'the writing office' of Gavin Hamilton's house in Mauchline in 1788, although other locations have been suggested by different people at different times.

The next owner of Gilmilnscroft estate was Lieutenant Colonel James Gray Farquhar (1778-November 1828) who succeeded his mother in 1809. He was a military man, becoming Lieutenant-Colonel in the Ayrshire Militia. In 1801 he had succeeded to a considerable estate in Northumberland, following the death of Robert Farquhar of Rothbury, a Lieutenant Colonel in the 81st Regiment, and who was a descendent of Robert Farquhar of Gilmilnscroft (d. 1698). He was married in 1801 to Margaret Cochrane Baillie (1783-1849), daughter of Major James Baillie (who served with the 7th, or Royal Fusiliers, and was for a time fort-major at Fort George, near Inverness) and his wife Margaret Ross, eldest daughter of Lord Anchorville, a Senator of the College of Justice. They had two sons and two daughters – John Gray Farquhar (1804-1838), James Gray Farquhar (who died at the age of four years), Margaret Gray Farquhar (d. 12 June 1879), and Jane Gray Farquhar (d. 25 March 1884). James Gray Farquhar died in November 1828 at the age of 50 years. He was buried in the Farquhar plot at Mauchline kirkyard, which had been the family burial ground prior to the erection of Sorn parish. A large granite stone marks his grave. Margaret Baillie outlived her husband by 21 years, dying in November 1849 at the age of 66 years.

John Gray Farquhar (1804-1838) succeeded to Gilmilnscroft in 1828. It was probably he who added the large Georgian block to the house, considerably enlarging the mansion and hiding the original tower house to the rear. This new extension to the house was L-shaped in plan, fitting tightly around the existing L shape of the original house. It was of two main storeys, the entrance doorway reached by a flight of six steps. To either side of this were stone pillars supporting a simple canopy. The front of the house was four bays wide, and on the north-east side the extension was four bays wide. This new block was two storeys in height, surmounted by a simple slate roof.

John Gray Farquhar was not married and on his death in 1838 the estate passed to his sister, Margaret Gray Farquhar (1811-1879). When she died her estate was valued at £3,543 13s 11d. She in turn was succeeded by her sister, Jane Gray Farquhar (1816-1884).

Following the death of Margaret Gray Farquhar, and knowing that she was the last immediate member of the Farquhar family, Jane Gray Farquhar decided to investigate who her nearest heir was. After some research she was informed by the Lord Lyon that Sir Walter Rockcliff Farquhar, 3rd Baronet, was her nearest heir male. He did not want to inherit the estate, so she arranged in her will for Gilmilnscroft to be left to his son, Henry Thomas Farquhar (1838-1916). Henry was amazed to discover that he had a distant relative who was willing to leave a considerable estate with mineral rights and other wealth to him. When Jane Gray Farquhar died on 26 March 1884 Gilmilnscroft was passed over to him. At her death the value of her estate was £14,054 19s 7d. At this time the estate owned by the Farquhars extended to 2,836 acres.

These distant cousins had to trace back their ancestry for over two hundred years to find a common ancestor. Sir Robert Farquhar of Mounie, or Monzie (d. 1676), was a cadet of the Farquhars of Gilmilnscroft and he made his fortune in the middle of the seventeenth century, becoming one of the richest men in Scotland at the time. He was a merchant in Aberdeen, exporting grain, and also dealing in other produce. He is also known to have been a benefactor to the city. In 1646 he was the Deputy Receiver of Scotland and Provost of Aberdeen from 1644-5 and 1650-51. At the time of the Covenanters he supported them during the troubles in Aberdeen. He was knighted in 1651 and was one of the first graduates of Marischal College. On his death in 1676 his lands passed to his nephew (or grand-nephew) James Farquhar of Lenturk in Aberdeenshire. His grandson, Walter Farquhar (1738-1819), was created a Baronet, of Cadogan House, Middlesex, on 1 March 1796. He had been a physician to the Prince of Wales, afterwards King George IV, and had saved the king's life, hence the grant of the baronetcy. He was succeeded by Sir Thomas Harvie Farquhar, 2nd Baronet. Sir Thomas was the founded of Farquhar's Bank, which eventually became part of Barclays Bank. A second son, Sir Robert Townsend-Farquhar received his own baronetcy in 1821, but his line died out on the death of the 6th Baronet in 1923.

This 6th Baronet's younger brother, Sir Horace Brand Farquhar (1844-1923), was something of a major fraudster. He collected donations and subscriptions to both the Liberal and Conservative party funds, mainly from those individuals who were keen on obtaining knighthoods or peerages. He himself was able to obtain a baronetcy in 1892, a barony in 1898, a viscountcy in 1917 and an earldom in 1922. It was only after his death that the full extent of his fraudulent dealings became apparent, and it was reckoned that he was lucky to escape a prison sentence whilst alive. He was married to Emilie Scott, who brought him a fortune, but at his death his estate was valued at nil, and although he was able to amass a number of titles, these all died out as he had no heirs.

Sir Walter Rockcliffe Farquhar, 3rd Baronet, was married in 1857 to Lady Mary Octavia Somerset (1814-1906), eighth daughter of of the 6th Duke of Beaufort. They had five sons and five daughters, and Henry Thomas Farquhar succeeded as the 4th Baronet in 1900. He was given the estate of Gilmilnscroft in 1884, prior to his father's death.

Sir Henry Thomas Farquhar was born on 13 September 1838, the son of Sir Walter Farquhar, 3rd Baronet, of Cadogan House, and Lady Mary, daughter of the 6th Duke of Beaufort. Henry worked in banking, mainly in London, but spent some time living at Gilmilnscroft after inheriting it in 1884. His London home was in Gloucester Place, in the fashionable Portman Square. He was appointed a Deputy Lieutenant for Ayrshire. On 8 July 1862 he was married to the Hon Alice Brand (1840-1925), daughter of 1st Viscount Hampden, who was Speaker in the House of Commons from 1872-84. They had two sons and two daughters. There were

4.12 Sir Henry Farquhar of Gilmilnscroft, Bt. *(Antonia Reeve)*

considerable celebrations in August 1912 when they celebrated their golden wedding, being presented with a gold centrepiece and a gold timepiece from the tenantry and neighbouring tradesmen. It was noted in his obituary that 'the relations between him and his tenantry were characterised by the utmost harmony.'

Sir Henry's eldest son, Trevor Farquhar (b. 27 December 1865), was a lieutenant in the Seaforth Highlanders and died on active military service in the Black Mountain Expedition on 23 October 1888. His second son, Lieutenant Colonel Francis Douglas Farquhar DSO (17 September 1874-20 March 1915) was a major in the Coldstream Guards, and served on the staff in the Boer War (1899-1900). He was decorated with a Distinguished Service Order and five clasps, and was mentioned in despatches. He served with the South African Field Force, 1900-01, and in the first Chinese Regiment 1901-2. From 1903-4 he served in Somaliland, gaining a medal with clasp. When the Duke of Connaught became Governor General of Canada he was appointed military secretary. During the First World War he was commanding Princess Patricia's Canadian Light Infantry Regiment in France but was killed in action at Flanders. He was given the French Legion of Honour and various other awards. Francis Farquhar had married Lady Evelyn Hely-Hutchinson, daughter of the 5th Earl of Donoughmore, on 27 April 1905. The eldest daughter of Sir Henry Farquhar was Gertrude Farquhar (6 June 1863-14 June 1914), who was never married. The second daughter, Katherine Farquhar (7 January 1865-24 November 1933), was married on 30 July 1887 to Sir Almeric William Fitzroy, KCB, KCVO, DSO (1851-1935), great-grandson of the 3rd Duke of Grafton.

In 1888 Sir Henry Farquhar restyled Gilmilnscroft once more, adding turrets and other baronial devices to create a neo-Gothic castle. It was said that Sir Henry was his own architect at this time, adding to the house in a whimsical fashion. The Georgian block of around 1830 had a third storey added to it, comprising steep roofs with strange gothic dormer windows. Instead of the steps at the front door, a new carriage porch was added, having gothic arches on three sides and a crenellated

81

parapet. On the ground floor of the entrance front the windows were replaced with heavy gothic bay windows. Some further alterations were made around 1909 to the plans of Ayr architect, James Kennedy Hunter.

Sir Henry Thomas Farquhar died in London on Saturday 15 January 1916 and his body was brought back to Sorn for burial. He was succeeded in the baronetcy by his nephew, Sir Walter Farquhar (1878-1918), followed by his son, Sir Peter Farquhar, 6th Baronet (1904-86), and then *his* son, Sir Michael Farquhar, 7th Baronet (1938-), who is the Master of the Beaufort Hunt.

4.13 Arms of the Farquhars of Gilmilnscroft as on the house
(Dane Love)

However, the Gilmilnscroft estate was maintained by the trustees of Sir Henry Farquhar on behalf of his grand-daughter, Norah Farquhar, daughter of Lieutenant Colonel Francis Douglas Farquhar, who would inherit at the age of 25, in 1931. By that time she was married and living elsewhere, so the house was let to various tenants for a number of years. Nevertheless, a large party was held at Gilmilnscroft to mark the coming of age on Friday 21 May 1931. A celebratory dinner was held in a marquee on the lawn.

4.14 Gilmilnscroft House - from the west, 2008 *(Dane Love)*

Olive S. Muir was one of the tenants of Gilmilnscroft at this time, staying there in 1935. She was to write a small book of poems and sketches, published in 1935 by John Miller, Glasgow. *Emblem of Peace* was written by her from September 1934-1935.

The next occupier of Gilmilnscroft was David Ross, who made his fortune in whisky. He was born in 1891, the son of John M. Ross. David Ross was a director of various companies and served as a Justice of the Peace for the City of Glasgow. He lived at Gilmilnscroft on occasion from 1932 until

4.15 Arms of the Somervells of Gilmilnscroft *(Dane Love)*

1936, renting the house from the Farquhar Olivers. However, he was able to buy the mansion and surrounding policies in 1936. David Ross was master of the Eglinton Hunt for a time. The Ross family remained in ownership until 1961.

From 1961 until 1966 the house was used as a private boarding school for boys, of which more under the chapter on Education.

In 1968 the estate was purchased by David Ronald Somervell (1912-2001), who had restored Burnside Cottage (known locally as the 'Round House') around 1960. Burnside was originally built around 1820 as part of Sorn estate. It was later occupied by Ian McGill RIBA FRIAS, architect. Previously Somervell had lived at Killochan Castle, near Girvan. He decided to restore Gilmilnscroft and remove

4.16 Gilmilnscroft House - from the north, 2008 *(Dane Love)*

most of the Victorian extensions that had made the house too large for modern living. Accordingly, much of the nineteenth century wings were removed, leaving only the ancient tower house with some later additions, which were reduced in size to make them smaller than the ancient block. It was at this time that the present porch was added, recreated in an eighteenth century style, and tying in with the old block where stonework indicated that one had been. A stone panel bearing the Somervell arms, with David Somervell and Jean Ogilvy's initials and the date 1968, as well as the motto 'Hold Fast to Faith' was added at this time.

David Ronald Somervell was a nephew of James Somervell of Sorn Castle, and had an affinity with the parish. He was born in 1912 and was married to Jean Helen Muriel Ogilvy (1914-2001). They had a number of children, their younger son, Louis John Charles Somervell (1 March 1949-17 December 1989), being buried with them in Sorn churchyard. He was killed on Arthur's Seat in Edinburgh whilst climbing.

David Somervell sold Gilmilnscroft in 1981 to the Countess of Lindsey and Abingdon, a daughter of Norah Farquhar Oliver, and moved to live in the former Sorn Manse. Some of the large stones that had formed part of the Victorian dormers were taken from Gilmilnscroft and used at the manse to buttress garden walls. David Somervell sold the Manse in 1993 and moved to Holly House, Montrose, where he died in 2001. At the time of the sale to Lady Lindsey, the estate comprised of 117 acres, of which 80 acres were grazing land, the rest were woodlands, formal gardens or lawns around the house.

Sir Henry Thomas Farquhar, 4th Baronet, had a son, Francis Douglas Farquhar (1874-1915), whose eldest daughter, Norah Frances Sapphire Farquhar (19 May 1906-19 September 1980) was married on 28 January 1925 to Mark Oliver OBE RSG (son of the writer and businessman, Frederick Scott Oliver of Edgerston, Jedburgh, Roxburghshire, and his wife, Katharine Augusta McLaren). Mark and Norah adopted the surname Farquhar-Oliver from 1931. They were divorced in 1948. Their second daughter, Norah Elizabeth Farquhar Oliver (b. 1932) married Richard Henry Rupert Bertie, 14th Earl of Lindsey and (9th Earl of) Abingdon (b. 1931) on 5 January 1957 and settled at Gilmilnscroft House, where they still reside.

The heir of the Earl of Lindsey and Abingdon is Henry Bertie, Lord Norreys of Rycote (b. 1958). He married Lucinda Sol

4.17 Arms of the Earl of Lindsey and Abingdon
(Dane Love)

Moorsom (b. 1960) in 1989, and they have two children – Willoughby (b. 1996) and James (b. 1997). Lucinda Norreys established the Norreys boot company in 2005, designing leather boots and shoes herself and having them made in Andalucia. These are imported to Britain and sold at upmarket shops and through an online shop.

DALGAIN

The estate of Dalgain was owned by the Mitchell family for many years. The original extent of the estate appears to have been considerable, for it was apparently broken up at times, and lesser branches of the same family established. The oldest record of a Mitchell of Dalgain dates from May 1600, when John Mitchell [I] is named in the marriage contract of his second son, Andrew, with Marion, daughter of Alexander Nisbet of Greenholm. He granted them the lands of Turnerhill in Mauchline parish, as well as those of Nether Heilar in Sorn. John Mitchell married a daughter of John Dunbar of Knockshinnoch, by who he had three known children, John who succeeded, Andrew, already mentioned, and Janet, who married James Campbell of Clewis. John Mitchell married for a second time to Janet Wilson, but there were no more children.

John Mitchell [II] succeeded. He married Mary Campbell, a daughter of the Campbells of Wellwood. John Mitchell died in 1643 and was succeeded by his son, also John [III].

John Mitchell [III] could be regarded as the father of Sorn, for it was he who granted the land on which the church, churchyard, manse and glebe were built in 1656. Little more is known about him, other than he had two sons, John [IV] and George, both of whom succeeded in turn.

John Mitchell [IV] is referred to in a Crown Charter of 1670 as 'Junior of Dalgain', indicating that his father was still alive at that time. However, he did not marry and on his death the estate passed to George Mitchell. He was married to Isabel Hamilton, by whom he had three sons and two daughters. Hugh, the eldest son, succeeded. The other sons were Gavin and James, and the daughters were Jean, who was married to William Hutchison in Dalgig, New Cumnock, and Sarah, who married Thomas Gemmel of Braehead.

Hugh Mitchell of Dalgain was married to Janet, daughter of John Campbell of Whitehaugh, in the parish of Muirkirk. They were to have many children, but some of these died in infancy. Of those who survived, were Jean (baptised 1 September 1697) who married John Campbell of Auchmannoch in 1719; Margaret (b. 1702), married in 1725 to Rev William Younger of Muirkirk; Agnes (baprised 12 July 1713), married in 1731 to Hugh Logan, Younger of that Ilk; Hugh (baptised 20 September 1719), who succeeded; and Andrew (1725-1811), who trained as a minister. Hugh Mitchell was appointed by the Scottish Parliament as a magistrate for Dalgain parish concerning the profanation of the Sabbath. He died around 1730.

Hugh Mitchell (b. 1719) inherited Dalgain estate at the age of eleven. The estate was run by his father's trustees for a time but they decided to sell it. Hugh Mitchell was trained for the law and when he qualified as a Writer to the Signet he spent most of his time practising in Edinburgh. His brother, Rev Dr Andrew Mitchell DD, acquired the estate of Avisyard, in Old Cumnock parish, which he left on his death to the Campbell of Auchmannoch family. He studied at Glasgow University and was minister of Muirkirk from 1751 until 1775, when he was translated to Monkton and Prestwick, perhaps influenced by his cousin, William Campbell of Fairfield and Whitehaugh, who held land in Muirkirk and Sorn parishes.

Dalgain was purchased from Hugh Mitchell's trustees by the Stevenson family. Dr Alexander Stevenson owned the estate in 1780, and it was he who established the village of Sorn as we know it today. Dr Stevenson was the son of a medical practitioner in Edinburgh but he removed to Glasgow, where he became a general practitioner. He was admitted as a member of the Faculty of Physicians and Surgeons in Glasgow in 1756, becoming its president from 1757-8. He was appointed Professor of the Practice of Medicine at Glasgow University in 1766, holding the chair until 1789, when he resigned. He was an active supporter in establishing Glasgow's Royal Infirmary, but he did not live to see it opened. Stevenson was described as a 'hodge podger', and was portrayed in an old rhyme that was current at the time:

> An obsequious Doctor appears next in view,
> Who smoothly glides in with a minuet bow,
> In manners how soft! In apparel how trig!
> With a vast deal of physic contain'd in his wig.

Stevenson lived in Glasgow's High Street before moving to a house on the eastern side of Virginia Street. He was married to Jean Picken, only child of John Picken of Ibrox and his wife, Jean Barns, sister to John Barns of Kirkhill. They had three children, John, who succeeded to Dalgain, James, and Jean, the latter dying unmarried. Dr Stevenson died in 1791. He was given a mock epitaph by John Dunlop, which was printed in Dr John Strang's *Glasgow and its Clubs, 1857*:

On Dr Alexander Stevenson

> Let hireling bards on splendid marbles tell,
> How kings and heroes lived, and how they fell;
> To private worth this humble stone we raise,
> Inscribed by Friendship with no venal praise.
> The man whose hallow'd dust lies here enshrined,
> Was bountiful, beneficent, and kind;

From honour's path he never did depart,
Mild were his manners, tender was his heart,
Joy and good humour fill'd his honest soul,
When mirth and fancy sparkled round the bowl;
And when dull care sat brooding on the brim,
The recreant fled his merriment and whim.
Friendship shall mourn and Medicine deplore
The heart that glows, the hand that heals no more;
While every reader joins the general tear,
For gentle, generous Stevenson lies here.

John Stevenson succeeded to Dalgain, which at that time extended to 1,378 acres. He was one of the local turnpike road trustees. He served as an advocate, never married and died sometime after 1812. By this time he was virtually bankrupt.

The estate passed to John Stevenson's brother, Lieutenant General Sir James Stevenson Barns of Kirkhill. James Stevenson was a colonel of the 20th Foot, serving with distinction in the Peninsular Wars. He joined the First Royals as an ensign on 11 July 1792 and served under General O'Hara at Toulon. In 1794 he served in the campaign in Holland, receiving wounds. He was on the expedition to Ferrol in 1800 and in Egypt in 1801. He served in Spain, Portugal and France from 1810 until the end of the war in 1814, receiving serious wounds at the Battle of Salamanca. He received the Gold Cross and Silver War Medal with three clasps for his 22 years service. He received the K.C.B. in 1831. When his grand-uncle, John Barns, died he inherited Kirkhill, adopting the surname Stevenson Barns thereafter. He died without issue on 5 October 1850. However, Stevenson had placed Dalgain on the market in 1827 and it was purchased by Lieutenant Colonel Joseph Burnett of Gadgirth (1753-1833), parish of Coylton.

Colonel Burnett retained the estate for only four years and in turn sold it in 1831 to Mrs Agnes Somervell of Sorn, since when Sorn and Dalgain estates have remained united.

In 1897 an old sundial was found at Dalgain and it was acquired by the Museum of Antiquities in Edinburgh. The dial, which is circular in shape and was made from greyish slaty sandstone, measures 6¾ inches in diameter. At the time the iron gnomon was broken. The dial bears the inscription *George Lamond 1686*. The provenance of the dial, and who Lamond was, is unknown.

BURNHEAD CASTLE AND GLENLOGAN HOUSE

Glenlogan estate was formerly part of Dalgain estate, Glenlogan House occupying the site of Burnhead Castle. This had been a typical old Scots tower house, which was partially still in existence in the middle part of the eighteenth century. It is thought that Burnhead Castle was given by the Mitchells of Dalgain to a second son in the early part of the sixteenth century.

Who the first Mitchells of Burnhead were is not known, and the earliest definite member of the family recorded was Robert Mitchell of Burnhead, who is mentioned in a Crown Charter of 1602 – 'Agnes, only daughter of the late Robert Mitchell of Burnhead'. The estate may have passed to a nephew or brother, Patrick Mitchell, of whom nothing is known. Patrick's son, John Mitchell of Burnhead seems to have succeeded in 1626 when he was granted a charter of confirmation by the superior of the lands, the 1st Lord Loudoun. This charter was witnessed by 'Dalgaine' and David Dunbar of Enterkine. On his death the estate passed to his son, also John.

In 1654 John Mitchell of Burnhead was forced to sell Burnhead estate due to the debts that he had accumulated. It was purchased by his distant cousin, John Mitchell of Dalgain. In 1680 all claims against Mitchell of Dalgain were discharged by a deed, which was witnessed by a number of notable local landowners, *videlicit*, John Reid of Ballochmyle, George Logan of that Ilk, Allan Logan his brother, and William Logan, writer of the deed. It was signed by Alexander Paterson, Jean Campbell (wife of Campbell of Whitehaugh) and others.

Shortly after the year 1700 Burnhead was sold to George Logan of that Ilk, whose family owned it for another hundred years. The Logans probably did not reside at Burnhead very often, for they owned Logan estate in Old Cumnock parish, as well as various other lands. However, the central block of the present Glenlogan

4.18 Glenlogan House – 2007 (Dane Love)

House may have been built soon after the Logan family took over, though it is doubtful if anything of the old Burnhead Castle was incorporated. A fairly plain Scots Georgian building, Glenlogan House comprises two and a half storeys, with smaller wings.

George Logan of that Ilk still owned the estate in 1710, at which time he purchased Nether Heilar from John Mitchell of Turnerhill and Daldilling. The disposition was witnessed by John Boswell, son of David Boswell of Auchinleck, and Captain H. Campbell, son of Sir Hugh Campbell of Cessnock.

George Logan was in all probability succeeded by William Logan of that Ilk, who was a writer to the signet in Edinburgh. He wrote a couple of pamphlets concerning Scots land ownership laws, one published in 1721. He died in 1727. He was succeeded by his brother, Allan Logan, who was trained as a minister and was ordained at Torryburn in Fife in 1695 and translated to Culross, also Fife, in 1717. He was married to a daughter of Lord Colville of Ochiltree. Allan Logan appears to have had the gift of prophecy, and in 1801 a chapbook was published in Glasgow which gave an account of 'the surprising Fore-knowledge and Predictions of the Rev. Allan Logan.' Rev Allan Logan of that Ilk died in 1733 and was succeeded by his son, Hugh Logan of that Ilk, who married Agnes Mitchell, daughter of Hugh Mitchell of Dalgain.

Hugh and Agnes Logan had four sons and four daughters. George Logan was baptised on 16 November 1732. William Logan was baptised on 15 January 1736 but must have died soon after, for a second William was born and was baptised on 24 December 1736. Hugh Logan was baptised on 22 July 1739. Janet Logan was baptised on 8 April 1734. She was married to James Goodlet Campbell of Auchline, a cadet of the Campbells, Earls of Breadalbane. Hugh Logan died around 1760. His eldest sons had predeceased him, so he was succeeded in the estates by Hugh Logan of that Ilk.

Hugh Logan was a contemporary of Robert Burns, and the bard wrote one of his mock epitaphs on Logan, which starts, "Here lies Squire Hugh", which cannot be repeated in polite company, but which can be found in *The Merry Muses of Caledonia* and some complete works. In a letter by the poet to James Dalrymple of Orangefield, dated February 1787, Burns makes mention of Hugh Logan: 'Let the Worshipful Hugh Logan, or Mass James McKindlay, go into their primitive nothing.'

According to James Paterson's *History of Ayrshire*, Logan's 'racy humour was wont to keep the festive table in a roar, and whose extreme hospitality is still spoken of with feelings of palliative respect.' His wit was collected into a book of anecdotes, entitled *The Laird of Logan*. Logan never married, but he is known to have had a number of illegitimate children. One was a woman who lived in Cumnock. Another was a son who became a stationer and music-seller in Paisley, dying between 1810 and 1820.

Hugh Logan lost much of his wealth due to his exuberant parties and entertaining, as well as his investment in the Ayr Bank. The firm of Douglas, Heron & Co. was formed in 1769, the major shareholders being the Ayrshire landed gentry. The company issued its own bank notes, but became quickly insolvent and ceased payment in 1772. Logan was one of 226 partners in the bank, who lost 4.4 times their investment, and to meet his debts he was forced to sell a large part of Logan estate.

Hugh Logan's commonplace book, in which are jottings by both him and Mr Walker, survived him, being in the possession of Mr Ranken, solicitor, Ayr, in 1900. He also had a few copies of his letters. In 1888 the Glasgow Exhibition included a chair that belonged to Logan.

Hugh Logan of that Ilk died on 12 March 1802 at Wellwood House, Muirkirk, and left Glenlogan estate to a relative, George Ranken of Whitehill, subject to Ranken paying his nephew, Hugh Goodlet Campbell of Auchline, a nominal price. Campbell disputed the will, and the case lasted many years before being settled by the House of Lords in Campbell's favour. However, Campbell died unmarried in 1814 and the estate was placed on the market soon after.

Burnhead was now able to be purchased by George Ranken of Whitehill, along with Nether Heilar, in 1819. It was at this time that the name of the estate was changed to Glenlogan, Ranken naming it in honour of his relative.

The Ranken family have their early roots at Sheil, now Shield, in the parish of Ochiltree, which they seem to have owned as early as 1508, when Peter Ranken is noted as having joined the Craufurds of Kerse in the clan feuds that they were then involved in. He was fined 40 shillings for his part in an incident whereby he and others prevented the court of the Bailliery of Carrick from sitting. He was succeeded by his son, William Ranken of Sheil, who was succeeded in turn by Lawrence Ranken, who heard Rev John Knox preach at Mauchline in 1544. He was succeeded by William Ranken of Sheil (d. 1623) but he lost out financially and he was forced to sell the bulk of their property. His son, also William, owned Mill o' Sheil in Ochiltree parish, and *his* son, William Ranken, took the title of Bankhead, the Sheil estate having been sold. His wife was the heiress of Robert Cathcart of Drumjoan. They had only one daughter, who married John Campbell of Skerrington. James Ranken,

4.19 Arms of the Rankens of Whitehill and Glenlogan
(*Dane Love*)

the third son of William Ranken (d. 1623), leased the lands of Fardenreoch and Caerniven in New Cumnock parish. His son, George, married Elizabeth, heiress of John Blackwood of Ardgrene, and inherited that property. Their eldest son, George, succeeded. A second son, William was the grandfather of John Ranken of Adamhill, who was a friend of Robert Burns. George Ranken, the eldest son, married Agnes Farquhar, daughter of William Farquhar of Lochingirroch (New Cumnock). He sold Ardgrene and died in 1740.

James Ranken (1720-1779) succeeded his father. He was married in 1750 to Jean Hutchison (d. 1790), daughter of William Hutchison of Dalgig and his wife, Jean, daughter of George Mitchell of Dalgain. James and Jean Ranken had three children, George who succeeded, Mary (b. 1750) and Agnes (1751-1791). Agnes Ranken was married to James Paterson (1738-1814) of Glentaggart, near Douglas, Lanarkshire, on 13 December 1776. They inherited the Paterson estate of Carmacoup, which lies between Muirkirk and Douglas. Their great grandson was Andrew Barton 'Banjo' Paterson (1864-1941), who is famed for composing the words to 'Waltzing Matilda' in 1895, as well as for being a poet, lawyer, journalist and writer of ballads in Australia, where he was born.

George Ranken succeeded and at New Cumnock on 19 January 1785 he married Janet, youngest daughter of James Logan of Knockshinnoch, by Margaret, daughter of John Begg of Dornal and his wife, Sarah Chalmers. George was born on 20 January 1759. Janet was born on 13 November 1763 and died 27 June 1853. George and Janet Ranken had fourteen children, four of whom were to die in infancy. They were, James Ranken, who succeeded; Thomas Ranken (26 June 1791-25 December 1831), writer to the signet in Ayr, who married Jane Campbell Logan (1791-1878), daughter of John Logan of Knockshinnoch; George Ranken (11 April 1793-17 October 1860), who married Janet Ranken Hutchison in 1821 and who emigrated to Saltram, New South Wales, Australia; William Ranken (4 July 1794-25 July 1867), doctor in Demerara for a time, and who assisted James Paterson with information for his *History of Ayrshire*; Hugh Logan Ranken (10 November 1797-20 October 1831), surgeon in Ayr, and Burgess and Freeman of Ayr by purchase, 30 May 1827, who died unmarried of a fever caught whilst working; Andrew Ranken (10 January 1799-25 October 1888), doctor in Demerara for a time; John Campbell Ranken (24 June 1802-16 November 1825), a lieutenant in the Honourable East India Company's Service (HEICS), and who volunteered to serve in the Burmese war with 40 of his company but was killed when storming a stockade at Prome, at the age of 23; Arthur Ranken (17 September 1805-14 June 1892), who married Annabella Johanna Cameron Campbell (1815-1904) in 1837, and emigrated to Lockyersleigh, New South Wales, Australia in 1826 – in 1844 he acquired land in Australia which he named Glenlogan; Jane Ranken (1795-1852), who died unmarried; and Agnes 1804-1825), also unmarried. George Ranken died on 1 December 1844 and was succeeded by his son, James. A brass plaque in memory of George and Janet Ranken and their eight sons was erected within Sorn church by their descendants in 1896. It bears the arms of Ranken and Logan on it.

James Ranken was born on 1 September 1788 at New Cumnock and served for over 30 years in the service of the HEICS, the bulk of which was spent as Postmaster-General of the North-Western Provinces. He was a doctor and staff surgeon in the HEICS. He died unmarried on 30 May 1848. He was succeeded by his nephew, George Ranken, the eldest son of Thomas Ranken (1791-1831).

George Ranken was born in Ayr on 1 August 1827 and was married in Ayr in 1859 to Frances (Fanny) Sarah Shaw (1839-1918). By this time most of the Ranken family had emigrated to New South Wales, where they established extensive farms, and the community of Glenlogan was named by them in honour of their homeland. George Ranken was a pioneer, surveyor, pastoralist, public servant and writer. He had been educated at Ayr Academy and trained as a surveyor. He emigrated to Victoria, Australia, in 1851 and served as a gold buyer in the Ovens district for the Bank of New South Wales. He also accompanied the explorer William Landsborough (1825-1886) through central Queensland in the early 1850s and they took up three runs in the Wide Bay and Burnett districts of Queensland in 1855. The partnership was dissolved in 1858 when George returned to Scotland. He went back to Australia with his wife in 1859, settling in Rockhampton. He was active in government in Australia, being appointed to two commissions to report on land laws there, on which subject he appears to have been an authority. He wrote *Bush Essays,* published in 1872, and a novel *Windabyne*, published posthumously in 1895. He also compiled *The Federal Geography of British Australasia*, published in 1891.

Glenlogan was leased for a number of years by the trustees of James Ranken, but at times various members of the family returned and stayed there. Amongst these were the daughters of William Ranken (1794-1867) - Mrs Schwarzmann, born Regina Ranken (1843-1930), and Mrs Jacobi, born Janet 'Jessie' Ranken (1845-1910) who resided in Strasburg for a period. The memorial in Sorn kirkyard to the Rankens of Glenlogan was designed in Australia and sculpted in Ayr.

Glenlogan House was let by the trustees to Henry Hamilton Houldsworth (later Sir Henry Houldsworth, 2nd Baronet (1867-1947)), ironmaster, who was part of the large iron and coal dynasty that owned many of the works in Ayrshire prior to the nationalisation of the industry. He leased Glenlogan around 1899, mainly for the shooting rights, as he also owned Carrick House in Ayr. From 1883 until 1909 the shootings and latterly the house (at that time referred to as Glenlogan Lodge) were rented by J. Douglas Baird, who tenanted the shootings of Glenlogan, Merkland and Limmerhaugh. He died on 21 February 1909. The house was occupied by Mr and Mrs F. D. Kiernander in 1912-13 and Mr and Mrs Thomas Fulton in 1914. In 1919 the house was leased by the Rt. Hon. Lord Moncreiff, 4th Baron (1872-1942). His wife, Lady Moncreiff, played an active part in parochial politics, but the Moncreiffs left the area in 1924.

Glenlogan estate was sold by the trustees of Thomas Ranken to James Hyslop Auld in July 1925. The Aulds had the estate for only a few years before it was sold once more.

In 1932 Glenlogan was bought by Mark Farquhar Oliver, who owned the estate for around seven or eight years. Mark Oliver rarely stayed at Glenlogan, owning property elsewhere, and the house was occupied by the factor, William Niven.

In 1940 Glenlogan estate was purchased by J. G. Stephen and on 7 September 1946 he added to the estate. John Graeme Stephen was born in 1894, the twin son (with James Howie Frederic Stephen (1894-1917)) of Frederic John Stephen (1863-1932) and his first wife, Agnes Renton Young. He was educated at Pembroke College until being called up to serve in the First World War, where his twin brother was killed. The Stephen family were the principal shareholders of the Linthouse shipyard in Glasgow, and J. G. Stephen remained a shareholder. He spent time in the drawing office before attending Glasgow University in 1919. A keen sailor, he took part in the International and Seawanhaka Cups, winning them both on a number of occasions. He established a ship model testing tank in a building at the adjacent Waterside farm in which he was able to test various designs of hulls for racing yachts. This was installed in the late 1950s when Stephen retired from Linthouse. The round tank was 39 inches in height, the side made from steel plates, and around 35 feet feet in diameter. At one side a flight of steps led down to a chamber below the tank, from where the underside could be viewed through a glass panel. The water was made to rotate around the tank and hulls could be trailed from a rope. Unfortunately, despite being noted as having historical interest, the sides of the tank were removed for scrap, leaving only the concrete base.

J. G. Stephen was married on 17 February 1932 to Maida Tennant Sloan (1902-1993) at Rhu Parish Church, Dunbartonshire, and they had two children, Mary Stephen and David Stephen. In his later life, J. G. Stephen was not too keen on shipbuilding, preferring agricultural and engineering matters. In the 1930s he had invented a machine that could bend steel for the manufacture of ship frames. This could be done cold, whereas previously the steel had to be heated, thus saving time and money. For the farmer, Stephen invented a machine that could cut and pick up silage at the same time, a machine still used today. This was developed around 1947-52, being based on one manufactured by Ferguson tractors. Massey was later to manufacture Stephen's chopper with considerable success.

Stephen worked hard on improving the agricultural condition of Glenlogan. When he first acquired the estate he only had four or five cows, but he increased the herd considerably. He also managed to increase the butter fat yield of the herd, and he was noted as being the first farmer in Ayrshire to dehorn his cattle. On one occasion he brought a lorry load of cockles and muscles which had been scraped off the hulls of ships at Linthouse. These were spread on the fields around Glenlogan to improve them. J. G. Stephen died at Torphins in Aberdeenshire in 1970.

Glenlogan House had been sold by J. G. Stephen in 1963 to Alexander Irvine Mackenzie, who was a chartered accountant. The Mackenzies broke up the remaining estate, selling Waterside farm to the Clarks in 1988. The house had been purchased by David and Susan Watts-Russell on 3 December 1986. They sold it and the remaining 87 acres of the estate on 31 October 2001. It was purchased by John Edward Lewis Sinclair and his wife, Mandy Sinclair. John Sinclair is an engineer and does independent contract work, mainly for defence industries. Previously living in Worcestershire, he has increased the size of the estate to around 100 acres.

AUCHMANNOCH HOUSE

Auchmannoch House is a typical Scots laird's house of the seventeenth century, perhaps dating from 1680, though it no doubt occupies the site of an earlier building. The main block stands two storeys in height, with an attic storey, and has corbie-stepped gables. Over the main entrance doorway, which is located on the north front, are the arms of the Campbell family, who owned the estate for many years.

It is believed that the Campbells of Auchmannoch, like many other local Campbell families, were a branch of the Campbells of Loudoun. According to James Paterson, writing in 1852, he thinks that 'all

4.20 Arms of the Campbells of Auchmannoch
(Dane Love)

the primary branches of that family were comprehended in the entail of the first Lord Loudoun, and therein set down in their respective degrees of propinquity, and that many families of that period subsequently sprang from *them*.'

The first recorded member of this family known today was Arthur Campbell of Auchmannoch (*c*.1540-*c*.1590). He was the son of John Campbell in Logan (*c*.1485-*c*.1553), who was mentioned in the protocol books of Gavin Ross. On 2 November 1524 he is listed as a voter in the election of a new parish clerk for Mauchline. John Campbell held a tack, or tenancy, of the lands of Logan from the Abbot of Melrose. He left three known sons – John Logan, who received the lands of Logan, Arthur of Auchmannoch, and a second John, probably by a second wife, who is mentioned in the Edinburgh Testament Registers of 17 June 1577. John of Logan's heirs inherited that estate, but his family seems to have died out fairly soon, and the lands became part of the Auchmannoch estate.

Arthur Campbell received a charter of Auchmannoch on 28 April 1554 from the Commendator of Melrose. This was written by John Nisbet, clerk of the Glasgow

Diocese, notary public, and refers to the forty-shilling lands of Auchmannoch in the lordship of Kylesmuir. It was given by David Boswell of Auchinleck to Arthur Campbell, son of John Campbell in Logan, and was witnessed by George Campbell of Cessnock, Richard Campbell, Hugh Farquhar and others. This instrument noted that Arthur Campbell had paid David Boswell 300 merks under contract, and that the lands of Auchmannoch were 'wadset' or mortgaged. Whether Boswell was unable to repay this, or else was happy to sell is unknown, but we know that ownership passed to Arthur Campbell.

Arthur Campbell resigned this and received a renewal of the charter from Michael, the Commendator, granted on 8 August 1565 to him and his second wife. Margaret Cunninghame, a daughter of the Cunninghames of Caprington Castle, Riccarton, was his second wife and she died in December 1580. Her will was registered in Edinburgh on 23 May 1582. Its contents make interesting reading:

> The testament dative and inventor of the goods, geir, sommes of money and debts of umql [umquhile or late] Margaret Cunnynghame, spouse to Arthur Campbell of Auchmannoch, quha deceast in the moneth of December 1580 years, faithfully made and given up by said Mr Arthur Campbell her spous as father and in name and behalf of Johne [who became a merchant in Mauchline], George, Arthur and William Campbells, their lawful bairnes and executor dative surrogate, May the 24th 1582 years at Edinburgh.
>
> Inventar
>
> The umql Margaret Cunnynghame had …. geir, sommes of mony and debts of the … pledged to her the tym of her decease forsaid, viz. twa …. And ane plough meire with ane file price thereof …. Price at forty shillings, item ane prize zow estimate at five pounds six shillings and eight pence, also some corn be the fallow the price put thereupon fifteen pounds eight shillings, item twa staei [oxen] price per heid five pounds therefore ten pounds, item ane milk cow price thirty pounds, item in ye barne and barnyard twenty three bolls of meall, price per boll six pounds, item eight bolls of beir [a type of barley] price ye boll five pounds, with fodder worth forty pounds, and the inplenishings of her house, together with the abulziements [clothes] of her body estimate at twenty pounds.
>
> Item there was owand by the said umql Margaret Cunnynghame to Andro Paterson for his hire four pounds, item to Agnes Reid for her hire three pounds, and to Agnes Cordiner for her hire three pounds, in 1580 years; and also for 1579 years, disbursements of the forsaid years having been made. (The missing parts shown …. are where a corner of the page has been torn off.)

Arthur Campbell was succeeded by his son, George Campbell (*c.*1560-*c.*1597) sometime between 1580 and 1591. He received a charter from King James VI, written at Dalkeith on 20 September 1590. A second son of Arthur was James Campbell, who acquired the lands of Montgarswood in 1603.

George Campbell was succeeded in turn by his son, Arthur Campbell of Auchmannoch (d. 1637). He was married on 10 November 1606 to Janet, daughter of John Campbell of Eshawburn, which is probably Ashawburn, east of Muirkirk. The retour is dated 1601. Arthur Campbell is mentioned in the testament of Robert Craufurd, younger of Smiddyshaw, who was married to Margaret Campbell, no doubt a relation. This testament is dated 1616 and George Campbell of Killoch and Arthur Campbell are noted as overseers under the deed. Arthur Campbell is mentioned in various other legal documents of the time.

George Campbell succeeded in 1637. He was a noted supporter of the Covenanters and fought with General Leslie in 1638-9. Soon after he wrote his will in which he appointed his relatives, John Campbell of Eshawburn, John Campbell of Killoch and his father as trustees of the estate in his absence. George was married in June 1632 to Jean Mure, daughter of John Mure of Stacklawhill, a scion of the Mures of Rowallan Castle. They had two sons, Arthur, who succeeded, and John Campbell of Netherton and Whitehaugh.

Arthur Campbell succeeded in 1668. He was listed by the Earl of Middleton in 1662 as 'Campbell, Younger of Auchmannoch' as having been fined £600 for his support of the Covenant. He appears to have been arrested and held prisoner in Avondale Castle at Strathaven, used at that time as a garrison for soldiers hunting down the Covenanters. He must have been released soon after, for on 28 September 1671 he was married to Margaret, daughter of John Shaw of Keirs Castle, which was located in Straiton parish, near to Patna. They had three sons, John, William and Allan, the last two never marrying. In 1701 Arthur Campbell is one of many Ayrshire gentry who aired their grievances. He died in 1703 and is buried in Mauchline kirkyard, where a flat tablestone bearing his coat of arms marks his grave.

John Campbell of Auchmannoch succeeded in 1703. He was married to Jean Mitchell, daughter of Hugh Mitchell of Dalgain and Janet Campbell of Whitehaugh. They had two sons, John and Arthur. John Campbell died in 1740 and was buried with his parents in Mauchline.

John Campbell (1725-1794) succeeded his father but he spent most of his life living elsewhere. For many years he worked as a merchant in Bristol. He never married and on his death in February 1794 at the age of 69 was succeeded by his younger brother. He was buried in the family plot in Mauchline.

Arthur Campbell of Auchmannoch succeeded to Auchmannoch. He was married in March 1779 to Burella Hunter (1758-1833), daughter of Robert Hunter of Pisgah (*c.*1728-79), who was the Professor of Greek at the University of

Edinburgh from 1741 until his death. They had four sons and one daughter – John, Robert, Andrew, Arthur and Elizabeth. Arthur Campbell died on 11 March 1828 at the age of 91 and was interred at Mauchline. His wife died in July 1833 at the age of 75. His eldest son, John Campbell, served with the Hon. East India Company but predeceased his father, dying in Calcutta, India, in 1803. The second son, Robert, succeeded.

The third son of Arthur and Burella Campbell, Major General Andrew Campbell (1783-1860), also served with the Hon. East India Company. He married Nicola Anna Maxwell, only daughter of Colonel Maxwell of Birdstown, Donegal, in the northern half of Ireland. Andrew Campbell was to succeed to the lands of Avisyard farm in the parish of Old Cumnock on the death of Rev Dr Andrew Mitchell DD, son of Hugh Mitchell of Dalgain. He died at Cheltenham on 25 December 1860 aged 77. His wife also died at Cheltenham on 5 April 1869 aged 70. Both were brought back to Scotland and interred at Mauchine.

The fourth son of Arthur and Burella Campbell, Arthur Campbell, purchased the estate of Nether Catrine from the heirs of Colonel Stewart in 1852. He was a Writer to the Signet and married Jane Barstow, daughter of Charles Barstow of Kelso, by whom he had one son and four daughters. The daughter of Arthur Campbell and Burella Hunter was Elizabeth Campbell, who married James Cuthbert of Dalleagles, in the parish of New Cumnock.

Robert Campbell of Auchmannoch succeeded in 1828. He was born on 26 January 1782. He served as a Justice of the Peace but was never married. He died on 19 August 1857 and was buried in Mauchline kirkyard, the burial ground of the family being acquired there prior to the creation of a separate parish of Sorn.

Captain Robert Campbell of Auchmannoch inherited Glaisnock House, in Old Cumnock parish sometime in the 1850s, and from then on spent more time there. In 1872 a survey of landowners in Scotland took place, and at this time his total properties extended to 3,928 acres, with a gross annual value of £2,156. He extended Glaisnock House soon after inheriting. The porch was built, incorporating his coat of arms, with mottoes *Sapiens qui Assiduus* and *I byde my tyme*.

Robert Campbell of Auchmannoch had registered his arms with the Lord Lyon in 1844. They comprise a Gironny of eight, gules and ermine, which represents the Campbell of Loudoun family, surcharged with the arms of Mure of Rowallan in a canton. In the chief position is a silver cup representing the Schaw of Hailly family, and a bugle horn on base for the Hunters of Pisgah. Above the shield is the crest, which comprises a double-headed eagle issuing from flames, and looking towards the sun. The motto is I byde my time. An earlier grant of arms, which has not been traced in the Lyon Office, appears to have been: Quarterly, 1st and 4th, a Gyronny of eight, gules and ermine, to represent Campbell of Loudoun; 2nd and 3rd – Argent, on a fess between three garbs Azure as many estoiles Or, to indicate Mure of Blacklaw. The crest was similar, a double-headed eagle issuing from flames, and looking to the sun, and the motto was the same. Robert was succeeded by his brother, Major General Andrew Campbell.

Andrew Campbell was married twice, firstly to Margaret, second daughter of Charles Hay, a descendant of the Hays of Hopes. She died in 1821. They had a son, but he died before his father. Andrew married again, on 28 June 1836, to Nicola Ann Maxwell, daughter of Colonel Richard Maxwell of Birdstown. Andrew Campbell died at Cheltenham on 25 December 1860, aged 76. His only surviving son succeeded, Captain Robert Mitchell Campbell, who was born on 16 September 1841.

4.21 Auchmannoch House *(Dane Love)*

Captain Robert Mitchell Campbell of Auchmannoch, Avisyard and Glaisnock (1841-1917) was married on 9 June 1870 to Marianne Letitia Georgiana Stevenson, daughter of George Stevenson of Tongswood, Hawkhurst, Kent. He was a Justice of the Peace and a Deputy Lieutenant. They had two children, Arthur Maxwell Mitchell Campbell, born 20 March 1874, and Montague Irving Mitchell Campbell, born 13 November 1879. Captain Campbell died at Cannes in France on 19 February 1917, aged 75 years. However, as he usually resided at Glaisnock House, outside Cumnock, Auchmannoch house and the shootings were let to James Robertson, wine merchant, of 48 West Nile Street, Glasgow, who was still in residence in 1905. In February 1902 a number of alterations were carried out at Auchmannoch House, the eastern wing being considerable rebuilt at that time. The architect was Allan Stevenson of Ayr.

If we return to George Campbell of Auchmannoch (*c.*1560-*c.*1597), his second son, John Campbell, became the progenitor of the Campbells of Whitehaugh, latterly of Fairfield House, which stood near to Prestwick Airport. John Campbell (c.1580-1655) married Helen Stevenson. He acquired the wadset of Nether Whitehaugh on 30 October 1641 and sasine dated 10 June 1648, of the 'forty-shilling lands of Nether Quhytehauch with the manor place and pertinants, formerly occupied by Hugh Campbell of Cessnock, now by them, in the lordship of Kylesmure, disponed to them by Sir Hugh Campbell of Cessnock by charter dated at the Castle of Tour, 30th October 1641.'

John and Helen Campbell's son, George Campbell (d. 1658), succeeded. He died without issue and was succeeded by his brother, John Campbell (c.1638-1694). He in turn was succeeded by his son, John Campbell (1682-c.1757). He is mentioned in the Ayrshire sasines of 27 August 1700. The 26 December 1726 sasine entry notes that he was the grandson of Helen Stevenson and heir tocher to Over Whitehaugh on 28 October 1712. The sasine of 21 September 1708 states that he had disposition of the twenty-shilling land of Limmerhaugh and Auchinlongford, and of Dalgain. John Campbell became a trader in Ayr, admitted a burgess on 27 June 1718, and was elected Provost of Ayr in 1743, serving until 1745. He was probably buried in Ayr old kirkyard.

John Campbell's son, William Campbell (1715-83), erected Fairfield House around 1760. This was a large classical country house located to the north-west of Monkton. Wiliam Campbell, 2nd of Fairfield (1749-1815), sold the two Whitehaugh farms around 1780. He also became provost of Ayr, from 1783-5. His will, dated 1788, notes that he held property in Monkton, Ayr, Edinburgh as well as Sorn, described as 'the 14 shilling and sixpence land of old extent of Bruntshield, commonly called Merkland, the sixteen shilling land of Middleheilar with ... fishings of salmond and other fishings in the water of Ayr,' and the half merk land of Auchenlongford in Bruntshield. At his death the Sorn estates also included the six shilling and fourpence land of Crossbog, 'alias Dalgain', 'superiority in the £25 15s 10d Scots land of Templehouse and the £50 Scots lands of Midtown'.

The last of the Whitehaugh or Merkland estate was sold in 1956, at that time comprising of Auchenlongford, Over Heilar and Low Merkland.

In 1918 Auchmannoch estate was sold by the Campbell family to the trustees of Major Sir Herbert Robert Cayzer of Lanfine, son of Sir Charles Cayzer, 1st Baronet, of Gartmore, the head of Cayzer, Irvine and Co., steamship owners. Auchmannoch House was occupied by William Duncan (1862-1952), a gamekeeper on Lanfine estate. Sir Herbert Cayzer (1881-1958) was created a baronet in 1924 and was raised to the peerage in 1939, taking the title Lord Rotherwick of Tylney. The house was later occupied by the Clark family, who left it in 1965 when the estate was sold.

The factor on Auchmannoch estate at the time of the sale was Allan Stevenson CE, who is noted as being an architect based in Ayr. His father had been the factor before him, and together they had served for 55 years to the Campbell family. Allan

Stevenson is noted for a number of major buildings in Ayrshire, such as the baronial building at the corner of Newmarket and High streets, Ayr (which incorporates the statue of Sir William Wallace), New Cumnock Town Hall, Burns Cottage Museum and Barr Parish Church.

In 1965 Auchmannoch was sold by Lord Rotherwick of Tylney to Captain J. G. McIntyre, Lord Sorn. The moor was added to Sorn Castle's sporting estate, and the house was let as a sporting lodge.

Auchmannoch House and immediate grounds of almost 8 acres were sold in 2001 to Rupert Hogg. Rupert Hogg is the managing director of James Finlay Limited, a multi-national company that specialises in the growing and production of tea. Finlay's is the current embodiment of the original James Finlay Limited that owned the cotton mills in Catrine.

CHAPTER FIVE

ECCLESIASTICAL

What is now Sorn parish originally formed part of a very large parish of Mauchline. In 1631 the Muirkirk of Kyle part was separated into a new parish of its own. In 1656 a further part of Mauchline parish was proposed to be removed, to create Sorn, or Dalgain, but the Covenanting and Commonwealth troubles intervened, and Sorn did not gain its ecclesiastical independence until 1692. Nevertheless, a new church to serve the proposed parish was erected in 1658, making it one of only two churches built during the Commonwealth in Ayrshire (the other being the Auld Kirk of St John in Ayr), at a time when the Episcopal form of worship was imposed on the country. A simple ecclesiastical building, it was constructed of locally-wrought sandstone. On the gable are crosses, and some have questioned why what appear to be Roman Catholic crosses should form part of the fabric of the building, but this is explained by the fact that the church was in fact Episcopal when first built.

Patronage of the church was under the control of the Earls of Loudoun to start with, but when Sorn Castle estate was sold, the patronage passed with it.

From the time of its erection until the creation of its own parish, Sorn did not have any minister serving it for any length of time. Rev John Campbell MA was admitted as minister of Sorn around the year 1658. He was a graduate of Glasgow University, qualifying in 1653. Being a supporter of the Covenant and refusing to swear allegiance to the king, he was deprived of his charge by Act of Parliament, 11 June 1662 and by Decreet of Privy Council, 1 October 1662. Rev Campbell was summoned to appear before a committee of the Diocesan Synod on 28 April 1664 for nonconformity.

With Rev Campbell thrown out of his church and manse at Sorn, the pulpit was filled by Rev Andrew Dalrymple. He had qualified as Master of Arts at Glasgow University in 1646 and had been admitted to Auchinleck church on 22 January 1651. However, like Rev Campbell of Sorn, Rev Dalrymple was thrown out of his church at Auchinleck in 1662. On 2 September 1669 he was appointed as an indulged minister at Sorn. Rev Dalrymple still held Covenanting sympathies, for on 8 July 1673 he was fined half of his stipend by the Privy Council for failing to pray for the king on 29 May that year, the anniversary of the Restoration. Rev Dalrymple was married to Elizabeth Ross and they had a daughter, Margaret, who married Adam Aird, Junior, of Catrine. Rev Dalrymple died in June 1676 aged around 50 years and is buried in Auchinleck, where a memorial with a Latin inscription commemorates him.

Around the same time that Rev Dalrymple was refusing to hold a service in honour of the king's restoration, Rev John Campbell was allowed to return to Sorn as an indulged minister, the act of the Privy Council allowing such having been written on 3 September 1672. Rev Campbell still remained a strong Covenanter, and is known to have preached at various conventicles, or field-meetings, in 1678. As a result he was accused of treason by the Privy Council on 19 December 1683 and tried before the Lords of Justiciary. Campbell admitted that he had broken his confinement, and that he had taken private services at various homes. He also admitted that he had not read the proclamation for the thanksgiving in the church at Sorn. As a consequence his indulgence at Sorn was revoked on 3 January 1684. He was imprisoned at that time for failing to find caution at 5,000 merks that he would no longer attend conventicles, baptise or marry anyone. Rev Campbell appealed, claiming that there was absolutely no way he could raise such a figure, so he was released after three weeks on the promise that he would refuse to undertake any such services. Following the Act of Toleration, 3 August 1687, Rev Campbell attended the first meeting of Ayr Presbytery after that date. In a minute he is styled as minister of Dalgain on 4 June 1690, but within a short time he appears to have left Sorn and become the minister of Craigie parish.

During the time of Episcopal rule, there appears to have been three ministers at Sorn. The first was Rev William Blair MA, a graduate of St Andrews University. He was presented to the charge prior to 1 July 1684 and got a testimonial for ordination on 5 August that year. He appears to have been admitted as minister within the next three weeks, and certainly before 31 August 1684. He did not remain at Sorn long, for in 1685 he was translated to Symington parish. He was 'outed' as a Covenanting minister in 1687 and deprived of his charge by Act of Parliament.

Rev Francis Fordyce is mentioned in 1686 as having a right to the stipend for the crop of Sorn glebe that year. If he was inducted at Sorn then it was for a very short time, for he was translated to Old Cumnock parish sometime before 3 November 1686. Rev Fordyce was the son of Andrew Fordyce, in Kirkton of Dyke (Moray) and was educated at Aberdeen's King's College, from where he graduated with a Master of Arts degree on 9 July 1672. He worked from 1673 until 1685 as a schoolmaster in Banff, during which time, on 3 April 1678, he was recommended for licence by the Presbytery of Fordyce. In Cumnock church Fordyce was noted for his strong Episcopal adherences and was detested by the parishioners. At the Revolution, in 1688, a band of 90 armed men forced him from the church into the kirkyard, forbade him to preach, and tore his ministerial gown. This indignity was used as an example of the persecutions the Episcopal Church suffered in a little leaflet entitled *The Case of the Afflicted Clergy of Scotland*, published around 1690.

The next Episcopal minister at Sorn was Rev William Anderson. He was also a native of Moray and was educated at King's College, Aberdeen, from where he graduated with a Master of Arts degree on 24 August 1680. He was admitted to Sorn around 1686 but at the Glorious Revolution of 1689 he was outed by the parishioners. Local tradition tells the tale of the villagers making their way to the manse to throw the minister out. Aware of them coming, the minister ran from the house alongside the River Ayr to the mouth of the Cleugh Burn. He was able to jump the foot of the burn, and then make his way along the narrow pass between the River Ayr and the cliffs towards the castle where he found safety. This narrow pass was known as the 'Curate's Steps' thereafter. Rev Anderson died in August 1690 aged around 30. He appears to have been in debt at the time, and the Faculty of Glasgow University, having intromitted with the stipend, granted 250 merks on 3 June 1691 to clear them.

With the Covenanting struggles over, the parish of Sorn was finally separated from Mauchline parish in 1692. A manse had been erected adjoining the churchyard, and a glebe and stipend was arranged. At this time Rev Mungo Lindsay was appointed minister of Sorn. He was born in 1666 and for a time in 1690 was a teacher at the Grammar School of Glasgow. He was licensed to preach by the Presbytery of Glasgow on 29 April 1691 and was called unanimously to Sorn and ordained on 30 November 1692. It was noted that he served the parishioners with 'exemplary diligence and fidelity.' He married Christian Begg, who lived at Corsebogue, or Crossbog, now a ruined house by the side of the River Ayr, about four miles upstream from Sorn. Rev Lindsay died in March 1738 and a mural memorial was affixed to the wall of the church by his widow. His epitaph reads:

> So long he lived in this Secure retreat
> Neather affecting to be Knoun nor great
> Humble and painful taught the great Concern
> Which yet he thought he never enough could learn.
> Skil'd in the sacred longues of heavenly truth
> the only language of JEHOVAH'S mouth,
> he led his flock throu the delicious fields
> (Heaven's gentle deuis & rain it yields)
> Shuning lau suits by deeds he us'd to write
> he sav'd their purse & clear'd their doutfull rights
> And with rare bounty Gratify'd the poor
> from the rich treasure of his blessed store,
> Which, by the laws of God & Man, descends
> to his long, dear, & Valouable friends.

Rev Mungo Lindsay and his wife had no family, and on his death he left £200 for the benefit of the poor of the parish.

The first minutes of the Kirk Session have been preserved, and show Rev Lindsay's desire to set the parish in order:

> Dec 18 1692 – Whilk day, after calling on the name of the Lord, the minister, Mr Mungo Lyndesay, inquired whether or no' there was any parish register belonging to the session or congregation; and it being answered and declared that there was none since the disjoining of the paroch from the paroch of Mauchline, the late prelacy being not long thereafter introduced into the national church, and during it the said paroch not being planted with any ordained minister, but men of prelatick stamp intruded thereupon, and in such tymes of confusion there was no register kept.
>
> The minister father inquired if any other elders used to sit as members of the session than those present; and it was declared that Robert Farquhar of Catarin, Andrew Wylie, portioner of Logan, John Peden of Blindburn, and Alexander McKerrow in Blackside, were yet living in the paroch, that had been established elders; that Robert Farquhar, though in the late times, through the power of temptation, and through the persecution, did swear that abominable oath called the test, yet, to the knowledge of many, he grievously repented that sin; of the others, two were also guilty of the same desertion.

The elders were all re-elected to the session.

During Mr Lindsay's ministry the jougs appear to have been used many times for the punishment of those who broke the Sabbath and other misdemeanours. The Kirk Session Minutes of 23 November 1698 make reference to them:

> Whilk day Jean MacLatchie was dilated by authority of two magistrates, James Farquhar of Gilmillscroft, and Adam Aird of Katarin, and was by them put in the jougges, from the ringing of the first to the ringing of the third bell, and then appeared to be rebuked before the congregation, for profanation of the Sabbath.

5.1 Jougs on the gable of
Sorn Parish Church (*Dane Love*)

Other entries from the early minute book of the kirk session make interesting reading on the goings on within the parish:

> May 11, 1700 – Hugh Mitchell of Dalgain was this day, according to the 31st Act of the present session of parliament, entitled 'Ane Act against Profaneness', named and chosen magistrate unanimously for this parish to carry said act into effect, Sir Geo. Campbell of Cessnock, Sher. Prin., having given him full powers.

> July 10, 1700 – Christian Beg in Corsebogue confess voluntarily that she inned some stuff on Saturday near the Sabbath, and on Sabbath night she caved some corn from the shaw, and gave it to the calfs. She was dismissed with a sessional rebuke, as she had not waited for a judicial summons, but told voluntarily; but the congregation is to be told that she was rebuked, and the magistrate has decerned her in a personal fine, which she is to pay.

Parishioners who were of an unblemished character and who moved elsewhere were often given certificates by the minister. The contents of an old one issued by Rev Mungo Lindsay is known:

5.2 Memorial to Rev Mungo Lindsay, Sorn Church (Dane Love)

The bearer, Matthew Hodge widow, (a member and elder of our session while among us) and Matthew Hodge his son, and Marie Blackwood spouses, were during yr abode here, and at yr removal from this place, viz. at Whitsunday last bypast, free of all public scandal knowen to this Session, and all shadow or appearance of it, qch is testified at Dalgain this twentieth and first of December jajivic [1700] and twentieone by Mo. Lindsay, minister.

In 1702 the church appears to have been altered, and new lofts erected to allow more people in to worship. The kirk session minutes detail what developments took place:

> At Dalgane Kirk, this 30th Oct 1702 – The Earl of Loudon and many other heritors present, met for the purpose of appropriating his room to every heritor for a seat, the aisle for the Earl was determined on, and for Dalgayne three pews south of the pulpit.

The minute details how the seating in the church was to be allocated, each heritor getting the number of seats equivalent to their contribution. It was also determined at this time to erect 'lofts' or galleries. The minute was agreed to by all the heritors of the parish, as well as the following additional people whose signatures appear in the minute: J. Beg of Heateth, Beg of Over Clewis, Patrick Boyle of Smiddyshaw, J. Brown of Hill of Auchmannoch, Gibson of North Limmerhaugh, Peden of Blindburn, J. Smith, portioner of Logan, and a Mr. Wyllie, portioner of Logan.

The next minister of Sorn parish was Rev William Steel, licensed by the Presbytery of Ayr on 27 April 1737. He was called to Sorn on 25 April 1739 and was ordained in the church on 29 August 1739. Soon after his appointment he commenced many improvements to both the manse and glebe. He created a garden of approximately half an acre in extent, which was beautifully laid out, and he planted the fields around the glebe with hedges. He was also able to build a new manse, mostly at his own expense, considering the heritors paid him a scantly wage. This manse, 'in point of strength, accommodation, and neatness, was then hardly equalled by any thing of the kind in this county.'

It was Rev Steel who was responsible for collecting subscriptions to pay for the erection of a bridge across the River Ayr opposite Sorn church. Rev Steel was held in high regard by his parishioners and, according to Rev George Gordon, writing in the old *Statistical Account* in 1796, he 'was not only distinguished by his abilities as a preacher, and a speaker in church courts, but also by his public spirit, his zeal, activity, and taste, in promoting every kind of rural improvement, at a time when such improvements were but little known in this part of the country.' In 1749 Steel had one of his speeches published, as *Speech in the General Assembly*, which appeared in a *Collection of Papers for augmenting the stipends of the Established Church*. As a result, Rev Steel was recommended in 1751 to the General Assembly of the Church of Scotland as one of the commissioners appointed for applying to the government for a general augmentation of ministers' stipends throughout Scotland. This appeal was defeated by the opposition of the landed gentry, who would have been responsible for paying such an increase. It was noted that Rev Steel and his fellow commissioners made an error in their application, for though they were unable to get an increase in the minister's stipend in cash, it was reckoned that the government was willing to allow an increase in their glebes, but this was not asked for, and thus was not offered.

Soon after his time as a commissioner, Rev William Steel demitted his charge at Sorn in October 1751 and took up an appointment as minister to the Protestant Dissenters at their church at Founders' or Salter's Hall in London. However, not long after being inducted Rev Steel contracted consumption, of which he died in April 1752. The parishioners of Sorn gathered a collection of £250 which was granted to his widow. He had married on 7 June 1744 Janet Brownlee, by whom he had three sons, John (who must have died young), Thomas (born 4 July 1746), and a second John.

In 1752 Rev James Connell was appointed minister of the parish. He was the son of James Connell, a merchant in Dumbarton, and he studied at Glasgow University, from where he graduated in 1740 with a Master of Arts degree. He was licensed by the Presbytery of Dunbarton on 12 August 1746 and was called to Sorn on 2 July 1752. He was ordained in the church on 26 August 1752. He was married to Anne Farquhar on 12 June 1755, the daughter of James Farquhar, merchant in Edinburgh. They had a number of children — Katherine (b. 25 March 1756); Agnes (30 June 1758-18 August 1786); Elizabeth (9 October 1760-3 January 1841); James (b. 27 February 1762); George (b. 8 August 1765), apprenticed to a Writer to the Signet in 1782; Jean (18 November 1767-5 August 1845); Alexander (9 November 1770-4 June 1841); and Arthur (24 December 1773-Dec 1819), who was a surgeon with the HEICS in Hyderabad. As a result of his large family, Rev Connell extended the manse on the west side, building a wing of a single storey with a slate roof. The value of the stipend in 1755 was £56 10s 0d. In 1757 a small augmentation was made to the minister's stipend, raising it to a quaint amount, namely 31 bolls 10½ pecks of meal, 16 bolls 4¼ pecks of bere (an old-fashioned type of barley), and £44 5s 7¼d Sterling, including £3 6s 8d for communion elements. A fair amount of the stipend was still paid by the parishes of Mauchline and Tarbolton.

Rev Connell was friendly with the great biographer, James Boswell of Auchinleck, and there are references in Boswell's journals to him coming from Sorn for tea with Boswell. One such visit took place on Monday 17 September 1781.

5.3 Memorial to Rev James Connell, Sorn Church *(Dane Love)*

During Rev Connell's ministry, around 1786-8, the interior of the church was repaired, with new seating and three new galleries, increasing its capacity. To save

107

5.4 Sorn Parish Church – Communion Token of 1756 *(Author's Collection)*

space internally, the galleries were reached by three separate stairways, built outwith the building. Rev Connell died on Tuesday 14 July 1789 aged 67 and in the 37th year of his ministry at Sorn. His wife moved to Edinburgh where she died on 7 December 1809. A mural memorial was affixed to the external wall of the church in Connell's memory, on which it is inscribed that he was 'Distinguished throughout the course of that Ministry by an Exemplary Discharge of the Pastoral Domestic and Social Duties.' The stone was erected by his son, James Connell of Conheath, a country house near Dumfries.

In 1756 circular communion tokens for the parish were struck. These have the name *SORN* on the obverse, surrounded by a circular border, and a monogram for the initial *JC* and *1756* on the verso, also encircled by a border.

Rev George Gordon was ordained as minister on 13 May 1790. Gordon was licensed by the Presbytery of Edinburgh on 28 July 1779. He was presented to the living at Sorn by William Tennent of Sorn Castle in November 1789. Not all of the parishioners agreed that Tennent should choose their minister, and on the day that he was ordained a small riot took place. A stone was thrown from the south side of the river, breaking a church window and striking one of the elders within. Other missiles struck the church bell. Those responsible for throwing the stones left the parish church after this and became what was known as 'dissenters', one of the first groups who disagreed with patronage. The dissenters then attended the secession church in Cumnock, but in later years a secession church was established within the parish at Catrine.

The heritors added a second wing to the manse soon after Rev Gordon's induction, on the east side of the original block, and 'these additions, joined to the beauty of its situation, and the interior repairs and improvements which it has lately received, chiefly at the expense of the incumbent, have rendered it both a commodious and a pleasant habitation.' In 1796 Rev Gordon contributed the account of the parish of Sorn to Sir John Sinclair's *Statistical Account of Scotland*. Rev Gordon was married twice, his first wife being Elizabeth Carruthers (d. 13 March 1799). He married again, on 14 February 1800, to Ann, daughter of Rev George Laurie DD, minister of Loudoun, a friend of Robert Burns. By her he had three children, George Lawrie Gordon (25 March 1801-30 December 1844), a captain with the HEICS who died at Manipur in eastern India; Louisa (b. 23 July

1802), who was married to Dr Charles Bryce on 6 October 1833; and Archibald Campbell Gordon (29 May 1804-30 November 1849), who became a MD with the HEICS and who died at Jallundur (now Jalandhar) in India. Rev Gordon continued his studies whilst minister at Sorn, and in November 1804 he achieved his divinity doctorate from Glasgow University. However, he died shortly after this, on 25 December 1805. His wife outlived him by many years, dying in Liverpool on 12 November 1834.

During Rev Gordon's ministry the glebe at Sorn was extended in order to improve the standard of living of the minister. The glebe had previously consisted of 5 acres 3 roods and 3¼ falls of ground, which included that on which the manse and outbuildings stood. Following a plea from Rev Gordon, the heritors and presbytery agreed to add 3 acres and 3 roods of ground to the glebe, so that it then extended to 9 acres 2 roods and 3¼ falls which, he noted, 'when duly improved, will equal, or perhaps even a little exceed, the necessary expence.'

Following the establishment of cotton mills at Catrine in 1787, and the new village built to house the workers, the church at Sorn became too small to accommodate all the parishioners. By 1791 Catrine had a population of 800, and it was a walk or ride of two miles from there to worship in Sorn. As a consequence, it was decided that a new church, or chapel-of-ease, was desirable in the new village, and on 30 March 1791 a petition was sent to the Presbytery of Ayr. This was signed by Claud Alexander of Ballochmyle, Rev George Gordon, and numerous heads of families in the district. They petitioned that 'owing to the great increase in the inhabitants of [Catrine], they the inhabitants intend building a chapel of ease and, in the meantime, request that the Presbytery would allow them to call a licentiate of this Church to preach to them.' The Presbytery discussed the proposal, but due to some difficulties decided to leave the decision until the next meeting. On 4 May 1791 the residents had written to state that Mr Alexander and a committee had agreed to contribute £40 as a salary for an assistant to Mr Gordon. This was agreed. On 9 February the following year, the inhabitants petitioned to be allowed to build a new chapel in Catrine. Claud Alexander also wrote to the Presbytery pointing out his support, and noting that if the Presbytery did not agree to the petition, then he expected that the residents would redirect their funds and goodwill to the Burgher Church, building an independent place of worship for themselves. The Presbytery agreed, and by July 1793 the church was open for worship. This eased the pressures at Sorn church, though the parish continued to be united for many years.

In 1796 there were a total of 27 heritors in the parish, responsible for the upkeep of the church amongst other things. They were also responsible for paying the minister's stipend, which in 1798 was £99 11s 7d.

Rev Lewis Balfour was appointed minister of Sorn in 1806, being presented by William Somervell of Hamiltons Farm and Sorn on 22 January and was ordained on 28 August that year. Rev Balfour was a notable man, being born at Pilrig House,

5.5 Memorial to Rev Lewis Balfour's children, Sorn Church *(Dane Love)*

in Edinburgh, on 30 August 1777, the third son of John Balfour of Pilrig and Jean, daughter of Robert Whyte, who was Professor of Medicine at Edinburgh University. Pilrig was a small estate between Leith and Edinburgh, later to be celebrated in Stevenson's *Catriona* as the place to which David Balfour went. Lewis Balfour was educated at Edinburgh High School, followed by Edinburgh University. He was licensed by the Presbytery of Edinburgh on 30 January 1805 and was ordained to Sorn.

Rev Lewis Balfour was married on 26 April 1808 to Henrietta Scott, the third daughter of Rev Dr George Smith DD of Galston (referred to as 'Cessnock Side' by Robert Burns). Whilst at Sorn he had two young sons die in infancy, and a memorial in the church wall commemorates them. They were George Smith Balfour (20 July 1813 – 3 May 1816) and William Somervell Balfour (27 May 1821 – 2 December 1821). In total they had thirteen children, namely, John Balfour, who became a surgeon with the Honourable East India Company (8 July 1809-13 December 1886); Marion Balfour (29 October 1811-14 December 1884) who married Colonel J. A. Wilson RA on 7 April 1835; Jane Whyte Balfour (6 November 1816-6 February 1907); Lewis Balfour (14 September 1817-13 February 1870), who was a merchant; James Balfour (30 July 1819-20 June 1824); Dr George William Balfour MD LLD (2 June 1823-9 August 1903), a heart-specialist in Edinburgh; Mackintosh Balfour (9 March 1825-7 June 1884), who was the manager of the Agra Bank in India; a son who was born and died in 1826; Henrietta Louisa Balfour (14 January 1828-25 November 1855), who was married on 14 December 1847 to Ramsay H. Traquair; Margaret Isabella Balfour (11 February 1829-14 May 1897); and James Melville Balfour CE (8 June 1831-18 December 1869).

During Balfour's ministry, in 1811, new communion plate was acquired for the church. Comprising four goblets and two

5.6 Sorn Parish Church pewter Communion vessels *(Dane Love)*

salvers, these were made from pewter and bear the date when they were presented to the church.

Margaret Isabella Balfour was to marry Thomas Stevenson CE (1818-1887) on 28 August 1848. He was a noted civil engineer, famous for his design and construction of lighthouses around Scotland, including Ailsa Craig, Turnberry and Muckle Flugga. They had a son born in 1850, who was named Robert Louis Stevenson. He was to become one of the world's best-known novelists. It is thought that RLS obtained his middle name from his grandfather's Christian name, though why the name was spelled differently is not known. Around 1889 the mother and aunt of Robert Louis Stevenson paid a visit to Sorn to see the place of their youth, spending a fortnight in the manse. Other members of the Balfour family, including RLS's uncle, Dr W. G. Balfour, a well-known heart specialist in Edinburgh, often attended family picnics to Sorn at the time. It is claimed by some that the manse of 'Essendean', which features in the first chapter of Stevenson's novel, *Kidnapped*, was based on the manse of Sorn.

Rev Lewis Balfour was translated to Colinton Parish in Edinburgh and admitted on 28 August 1823. He was to write a *Sermon on the Death of the Rev Daniel Wilkie*, which was published in Edinburgh in 1838. He also contributed an account of the parish of Colinton to the *New Statistical Account* of Scotland. Despite his large family, he continued to study and received his Doctor of Divinity from Glasgow University in 1853. He died on 24 April 1860.

In 1813 the Sorn Association for Religious Purposes was founded, meeting regularly to discuss religious matters for the next 21 years.

The next minister at Sorn was Rev John Stewart MA, presented by Agnes Somervell of Hamiltons Farm and Sorn on 22 September 1823 and admitted on 11 March 1824. Stewart was born in Greenock on 26 June 1793, the sixth son of Roger Stewart, a shipowner, and Jean Stewart. He was educated at Glasgow University, graduating with a Master of Arts degree in 1818. On 21 August 1821 he received his licence to preach from the Presbytery of Kintyre and was ordained by the Presbytery of Glasgow on 11 April 1823. He served as minister of Oldham Street Church in Liverpool from 1823 until he moved to Sorn, being translated here in 1824. Shortly after his arrival at Sorn, Rev Stewart was married on 1 July 1824 to Mary Gammell (d. 23 March 1872), daughter of General Andrew Gammell, who was the ADC to Frederick, Duke of York. They had three children, James Stewart MD (16 April 1825-18 April 1853); Harcourt Stewart (21 May 1827-1 September 1854), who was a master mariner but who was drowned in the China seas; Mary Gammell Stewart (b. 18 April 1830), who married Rev George Smytton Davidson, minister of Kinfauns Parish Church in Perthshire. Rev Stewart was translated to Liberton Parish Church in Edinburgh on 28 September 1843. In 1846 he wrote *A Letter on the Abolition of Tests in the Universities of Scotland*, which was published in Glasgow. When he died on 27 December 1879 he was the Father of the Church of Scotland, meaning that he was the oldest serving minister.

During Rev Stewart's ministry the church underwent considerable repair in 1826, when the pews were rearranged, the number of seats being increased to 611. For many years after this, the seating in the church was allocated to the parishioners. The three galleries were for the Sorn, Gilmilnscroft and Dalgain estates. When Dalgain estate was bought over as part of Sorn estate, this gallery was kept for residents of the former estate. In the main nave of the church the seats usually had the name of the seat-holder painted on them, such as 'Ballochmyle', or 'Auchmannoch', seating kept for residents from those estates. One seat had 'Schoolmaster' painted on it, and a number of others were inscribed 'Parish', meaning that anyone who had not otherwise been allocated seats could sit there. The roof was also raised at this time, making the church more airy. In 1852 there were 64 seats kept aside for the poor of the parish. As the church was being rebuilt a belfry was added and a bell was cast for it. It is inscribed *Caird & Co. Makers, Greenock, 1826*. The bell is around 20 inches in diameter.

In 1835 new communion tokens were produced for the church. These have the words *Sorn 1835* on the obverse, and *JS* on the verso, indicating Rev Stewart. The tokens are 13/16 inch in diameter.

During the ministries of Revs Balfour and Stewart there existed a Sorn Association for Religious Purposes. The minute book of this group was returned to Sorn in 1909 by Mrs Davidson, daughter of Rev John Stewart.

On 30 November 1843 Rev John Rankine was ordained as minister at Sorn, having been presented by Miss Somervell of Sorn. He was born on 28 December 1816, the son of John Rankine of Knockdon and Marion Sloan. He was educated at Maybole school, followed by Ayr Academy and the University of Edinburgh. He was licensed by the Presbytery of Ayr on 14 September 1842 and acted for a time as assistant minister at Lauder in Berwickshire. After being ordained at Sorn, he served for 42 years in the pulpit until his death on 30 April 1885. He had married Jane Simpson (1819-79) on 29 April 1845. She was the heiress of Charles Simson of Threepwood estate, which is located three and a half miles south west of Lauder, but is located over the border in Roxburghshire. One of Rev Rankine's speeches, *Address at Close of General Assembly* was published in 1883. In 1880 Rev John Rankine was awarded an honorary degree of Doctor of Divinity by the University of Edinburgh. From 1883-84 he was the Moderator of the General Assembly of the Church of Scotland.

Rev John Rankine's eldest son was Professor Sir John Rankine of Threepwood, KC, LLD, JP, (18 February 1846-8 August 1922). He was an advocate, being admitted to Faculty of Advocates in 1869, and appointed Advocate-Depute in 1885. He became Professor of Scots Law at Edinburgh University, holding that position from 1888 until his death. He was knighted in 1921. Rankine wrote a number of books in his field that were to become much admired at the time. The main ones

5.7 Sorn Parish Church – Communion Token of 1863 *(Dane Love)*

were *The Law of Landownership in Scotland,* and *Leases.* He also edited three editions of Erskine. The second son, Charles Simson Rankin, adopted the surname Simson of Threepwood and inherited his mother's estate. He was born on 15 October 1847 and became a writer to the signet. He died on 19 November 1911. Other children were Margaret Romanes (b. 25 May 1849), married to Rev John Brown D.D. of Galston then Bellahouston churches; Adam George (b. 17 April 1852), who became a merchant in Liverpool; Marion (Minnie) Elizabeth (b. 4 April 1854), married Rev Archibald Scott D.D (d. 1909), minister of St George's Church in Edinburgh and Moderator of the General Assembly in 1896; James (23 December 1855-10 April 1927), moved to Liverpool; Janet Simson (29 July 1858-16 December 1898), married Rev George Milligan, D.D., Professor of Divinity at Glasgow University; and two children who died in infancy, Graham Somervell (27 March 1861-30 March 1861); and Jane Tait (1 January 1863-18 September 1863).

In 1863 another new set of communion tokens were produced for the church. These were elliptical in shape, 1 1/8 inch long by 7/8 inch across. The obverse face has on them *Sorn Church 1863.* The date has rosettes before and after it, and a band of two beaded ovals surrounds it. On a border is the manufacturer of the tokens' name, *A. Kirkwood & Son, Edinr.,* written in tiny type. The verso of the token is inscribed, *This do in remembrance of me.*

Around 1860 the jougs from the kirk wall appear to have disappeared and who took them seems to have been forgotten. Writing in 1898, Helen Steven noted that they had been absent for around 40 years. The jougs, however, were recovered in 1912 and restored to the wall. According to the *Sorn Parish Magazine* of June 1912:

> It will be a matter of interest to the parishioner to learn that the 'Jougs' which hung on the Church and were abstracted fifty years ago or more, have been recovered, and will shortly again be placed upon the Church. The recovery of them has been effected by the Rev James Hill BD, of Auchinleck, in whose parish they have been in 'keeping' for

half a century. The jougs are in a good state of preservation, and we have to congratulate ourselves on their recovery, as comparatively few Churches in the country possess these ancient relics of ecclesiastical discipline and punishment.

In the late 1880s two stained glass memorial windows were added to the church in memory of locals. One of these was the gift of Mrs Henrietta Somervell of Sorn Castle. It was placed in memory of her husband, Graham Somervell, who died in 1881. It also commemorates her son, Lieutenant Louis Somervell, who was killed at Tel-el-Kebir in 1882. The second window was the gift of the officers of the 78th Seaforth Highlanders in memory of Lieutenant Trevor Farquhar of Gilmilnscroft, who died of fever whilst on an expedition in the Black Mountain in 1888.

The church at Sorn has its own Women's Guild, founded in 1883. This organisation was responsible for supplying the church with two lamps which stood in front of the pulpit by 1898. A harmonium for use by the Sunday School was also paid for by the Guild.

It was Rev Dr John Rankine who established monthly church services at Auchencloigh, at the northern end of the parish. As Auchencloigh was on the borders of Mauchline and Galston parishes, the ministry here was shared between the Galston, Sorn and Mauchline's Walker Memorial U.F. Church ministers.

During Rev Dr John Rankine's final years as minister five assistant ministers were appointed to help. In 1882 the assistant was Rev Matthew Charteris Thorburn (d. 1912), who became minister of Lumphanan, Aberdeenshire. The second assistant was Rev R. Spencer Ritchie. The third was Rev Dr George Milligan, who became minister of Caputh, and was to become Regius Professor of Divinity and Biblical Criticism at the University of Glasgow, and Moderator of the General Assembly of the Church of Scotland in 1923. Rankine's fourth assistant, for a period of ten months from May 1884, was Rev Robert Menzies Fergusson M.A. (1859-1921). The fifth minister was Rev Henry Begg.

Born a son of the manse on 12 April 1859, at Fortingal, Perthshire, R. Menzies Fergusson was licensed in 1884. He was to become minister of Logie Parish Church, Bridge of Allan. He was married to Isabella Haggart, and they had three children. Fergusson was a prolific writer, amongst his many works being *Rambles in the Far North* (1883), *Quiet Folk* (1889), *The Viking Bride and other poems* (1896), *Logie: A Parish History* (1905), and *The Ochil Fairy Tales* (1912). He wrote a total of 20 books, and some of these works are still in print. R. Menzies Fergusson mentioned Sorn in some of his books, basing some of the worthies in *Quiet Folk* on Sorn characters, and he regularly returned to attend functions in the village. He died on 25 July 1921.

Rev Richard Spencer Ritchie (1860-1917) was ordained to the church at Sorn on 21 July 1885. He had previously served in Sorn as assistant to Rev Dr Rankine. He only stayed in Sorn for just over three years, before being translated to Mains and Strathmartine, near Dundee in Angus on 21 November 1888. He died in Dundee on 19 April 1917, aged 57.

Rev Henry Cunningham Begg DD was ordained as minister to Sorn on 21 February 1889. He was a son of the manse, being born on 1 December 1856, son of Rev William Begg DD, minister of Falkirk. His uncle was the well-known Dr James Begg (1808-83) of Disruption fame. He received his education at Falkirk Grammar School, followed by the University of Glasgow. He was licensed by the Presbytery of Linlithgow in May 1884 and served for a time as an assistant minister at Maxwell Parish Church in Glasgow. On moving to Sorn he served for 30 years. A portable communion set, comprising a salver, cup and bottle, was 'Presented by Rev Henry

5.8 Sorn Parish Church *(Dane Love)*

Cunningham Begg to Sorn Kirk Session on the occasion of his Semi Jubilee, December 1913.' He was never married and died in the manse on 11 February 1919 and is buried in the kirkyard.

In 1892, to celebrate the bicentenary of the creation of the parish of Sorn, the congregation donated four silver communion cups and two patens to the church. These were made in the style of the early seventeenth century, around 1616-18, when Gilbert Kirkwood was a notable designer and manufacturer of such items. The stems are based on the cups from Fyvie church in Aberdeenshire, the bowl on that from Blantyre in Lanarkshire. A large function was held to celebrate the event, officiated by Rev John Keith BD, of Largs.

In 1900 the minister received a stipend of £205. Prior to May 1897 the stipend amounted to 175 bolls of victual plus £37 in cash. With rising inflation, this was insufficient for the minister, and James Somervell of Sorn Castle was instrumental in establishing an endowment of £1000, paid for from donations from the parishioners plus a donation from the Baird Trust. This fund produced £30 annually towards the stipend.

Prior to the installation of the organ, no music was played during services at Sorn. A precentor would sing a line, and the rest of the congregation would either join in or repeat the psalm line by line. At Sorn two of the precentors held office for many years – Helen Steven notes that the precentor in 1898 had been so for 47 years, and that his predecessor had held the office for 42 years. In 1901 a petition was presented to the kirk session requesting that music should be introduced to the ordinary church service, and this was agreed. Around 1910 the church building was restored, the supervising architect being Henry Edward Clifford of Glasgow, who was at the same time employed by the McIntyres in adding to Sorn Castle. During the restoration a new pipe and pedal organ was presented to the church by T. W. McIntyre of Sorn Castle. The organ had previously been used in Glasgow Cathedral during repairs to the permanent organ there. It was made in Germany by Messrs. Walcher. With the new organ being installed in the church, it was decided that a new Austrian fumed oak pulpit and platform be erected, all designed by H. E. Clifford. At the same time Professor John Rankine presented a communion table and chairs in memory of his father, Very Rev John Rankine DD.

Rev David Fyfe MacMath was appointed as the next minister of the parish. He was born in Forfar, Angus, on 24 October 1889, the son of Robert MacMath and Jessie Fyfe. He received his education at Forfar Academy followed by the University of St Andrews, from where he graduated with a Master of Arts degree in 1911. He continued to study and achieved a Bachelor of Divinity in 1914. He received his licence to preach from the Presbytery of Forfar in 1914, but was called up to serve in the First World War almost immediately. He served as a Captain in the Royal Field Artillery from 1914 until 1919. For his bravery he was awarded the Military Cross in 1917. On the resumption of peace, Rev MacMath was assistant minister at Galston before being ordained at Sorn on 18 June 1919. He was married on 6 August 1915 to Christina J. Cargill, daughter of Alexander Cargill, by whom he had two children, Ian Forbes MacMath (b. 3 July 1917) and Ronald Alexander Cargill MacMath (b. 27 September 1919). Rev MacMath was translated to St David's Church at Kirkintilloch on 15 October 1924. He retired from this charge on 31 December 1960 and died on 4 September 1962.

Rev William Lowyn Davies was admitted as minister of Sorn on 12 March 1925. He remained for three years, being translated to Auchendoir Parish Church in Aberdeenshire on 16 May 1928. During his ministry, in 1927, the former Dalgain Mill, located across the road from the church, was gifted to the congregation by Captain J. G. McIntyre of Sorn Castle. The members converted it into a church hall at a cost of £600 and it was opened on Wednesday 21 December 1927 by Mrs McIntyre and dedicated by Rt Rev Dr MacLean, Moderator of the General Assembly. Mrs William Niven presented Mrs McIntyre with a silver key, with which the door was opened. A new baptismal font was dedicated at the same time, the money for which was donated anonymously by a friend of Rev. Dr. Begg.

Rev James Gegg was appointed the new minister in 1928. He was born in 1896 at Motherwell in Lanarkshire, son of James Gegg and Jane Moffat. He was educated at Dollar Academy in Clackmannanshire followed by Glasgow University. He was licensed by the Presbytery of Hamilton in May 1926. His first appointment was as Assistant Minister at South Dalziel Parish Church in Motherwell, serving from 1925-27. He was ordained at Menmuir Parish Church, near Brechin in Angus, on 12 May 1927. However he did not remain there long, being translated to Sorn and admitted on 19 September 1928. Rev Gegg was a keen gardener and he also bred and exhibited game bantams and fancy pigeons, winning at numerous major bird shows through Scotland and England. He was also a keen Scoutmaster, and helped run the 39th Ayrshire (Sorn) Scout and Boy Scout troops. Rev Gegg was translated to Kirkhope Parish Church, Ettrick Bridge, Selkirkshire on 1 March 1951. He remained there until his death on 21 May 1961.

In 1951, when the *Third Statistical Account* was compiled, it was noted that the church had 212 members on its roll, of which 110 were men, the only parish in the county at that time with a larger proportion of men than women. It was noted that although around 150 attended the two annual communion services, normal Sunday attendance was usually around 60.

The manse underwent a number of modifications to bring it up to standard in 1951, awaiting the arrival of the new minister, Rev John Heron. Rev Heron was born in Kilmarnock on 6 January 1915, the son of William and Margaret Heron. He was educated at Prestwick High School followed by Kilmarnock Academy. On leaving school he found employment with Glasgow Rate and Salvage Association, working with them for eight years from 1932. During the Second World War he served with the RAF, between 1940-6. When he was demobbed, Heron studied at Glasgow University from 1947-51 to become a minister. He was married on 27 August 1946 to Elizabeth, daughter of Robert and Margaret Kennedy. He was a student assistant at Troon Old Church from 1949-51, and was licensed by the Presbytery of Ayr on 15 April 1951. Rev Heron's first charge as a minister was at Sorn, where he was ordained and inducted on 5 September 1951 at the age of 36. He remained in the pulpit here for six years, being translated to Strathaven Rankin Parish Church on 18 October 1957. He was then translated to Mochrum, in Wigtownshire, on 29 August 1968, and then to Ochiltree on 22 April 1971. He died in 2002.

Rev John Ernest Heathwood was admitted by the General Assembly and inducted as minister of Sorn on 20 April 1958. He was born on 30 September 1922 at Blackwood, Lanarkshire, the son of William Heathwood and Margaret Munro. Following an education at Glasgow Albert School from 1930-9, he served in the Merchant Navy for the duration of the Second World War. Heathwood then studied at Edinburgh Univeristy from 1948-52, graduating Master of Arts. He studied with the University of Indianapolis from 1953-6, gaining his Doctorate of Divinity. He was licensed by the Free Church Presbytery in Glasgow in April 1951 and was ordained at Prince Edward Island, Canada, in July 1953. He was translated to the Scots Presbyterian Church in New York in 1954 and was admitted by the General Assembly of the Church of Scotland in 1957. Heathwood was married on 21 March 1953 to Catherine Wilson (b. 1930) and they had two children, Elizabeth (b. 17 February 1957) and William James (b. 23 March 1959). Rev Heathwood stayed at Sorn for just over eight years, being translated to Glasgow Cowlairs-Somerville Church in Springburn on 18 August 1966. He was to be the minister there for only four years, for Rev Heathwood suffered a heart-attack and died on 18 November 1970.

On 17 May 1967 Rev David Reid MA HCF was inducted as minister of Sorn. He was born on 8 September 1905 in Ayr, the son of David Reid and Margaret Mackintosh Cowan. Following an education at Ayr Grammar School and Ayr Academy (from 1918-24) he attended Edinburgh University from 1924-7, graduating with a Master of Arts degree, followed by the New College from 1927-30. He was appointed as a student assistant at Leith Junction Road Church, serving from 1929-30, and was licensed by Edinburgh Presbytery in April 1930. Following a couple of years serving as an assistant at Buenos Aires St Andrew's Scots Church between 1930-2, he was ordained and inducted to Kirkcaldy Victoria Road Parish Church on 5 October 1932. From 1939-45 he served during the Second World War as a Chaplain to the Forces. On 12 May 1948 Rev Reid was translated and inducted to Dundee Clepington Parish Church. He was married on 2 November 1932 to Mary Gray Taylor Givan (26 November 1904-1 April 1993), better known as Maisie, daughter of James Givan of Airdrie. They had a son, Philip Reid, who was married to Marjorie Jean Robertson. In the autumn of 1968 the church organised a Christian Stewardship campaign, chaired by William Hale. Rev Reid died in Sorn Manse on 10 October 1977, having served the parish for ten years. He is buried in the new cemetery.

5.9 Rev Alexander Welsh
(Elizabeth Johnstone)

With the death of Rev Reid and the illness of Rev James Dickson of Catrine, it was decided by Ayr Presbytery that the two churches of Sorn and Catrine should be linked. The congregations were quite agreeable to this, as it would halve the costs of the minister's salary, as well as other expenses. At a service held at Sorn church on 3 September 1979 the two charges were officially linked. Rev Alexander Welsh was ordained to the linked charge of Catrine with Sorn on 27

February 1979. At first he lived in a council house at Fourfields, but in 1980 a cottage between Catrine and Sorn (Rowanlea) was purchased and used as a manse. It was at this time that Sorn Manse was sold, since when it has been a private house, owned variously by the Somervells, Paynes (from 1987) and MacMillans (from 1996).

Rev Alex Welsh was translated to Dennistoun in Glasgow in May 1986 and the Rev William Clement Robb (1940-2005) was inducted to Catrine and Sorn on 19 November the same year. Clem Robb was born at Elderslie, Renfrewshire, the son of Johnston Fraser Robb and Jean Stewart Clement. He was educated at Dumfries Academy from 1947-57 followed by Glasgow College of Science and Technology from 1957-8. He was trained at Glasgow University from 1963-8, graduating as a Licentiate in Theology (LTh). He served as a Merchant Navy Cadet from 1958-61. He was a student assistant minister at Greenock from 1961-8, and was licensed by the Presbytery of Greenock on 28 April 1968. His first charge was at Detting in Shetland, where he was ordained and inducted on 17 June 1968. Prior to arriving at Sorn, Rev Clem Robb had previously been the minister of Kilberry linked with Tarbert, in Argyll. Rev Robb was translated to Balmaclellan and Kells, linked with St John's Town of Dalry in Kirkcudbrightshire in May 1993.

In November 1987 the first two lady elders were ordained at Sorn and on 14 March 1993 a special service of praise was held in the parish church to mark 300 years of worship in the parish.

Clem Robb was to bring scandal to the church after he had gone. In 1994 police officers arrived at his manse and arrested him on a charge of abusing young boys at his home in Pollokshields and at Tarbert between 1981 and 1984. He was jailed for seven years. He was freed in 1999 and lived in Sorn for a time once more, before moving elsewhere, dying in 2005.

The next minister at Sorn (and Catrine) was Rev George A. Chalmers MA, BD, MLitt, who was inducted on 7 September 1994. Rev Chalmers had previously served at Banchory Ternan West Church in Kincardineshire. At the time of his induction his stipend was £14,481 per annum, plus 20% to the pension fund, 10% for National Insurance, plus manse. In 1995 the church income was £11,295, and with increasing expenditure a planned giving campaign was arranged for 1996. Following a period of illness, Rev Chalmers retired in July 2002.

5.10 Rev George Chalmers (Elizabeth Johnstone)

When Rev Chalmers left the churches of Sorn and Catrine, the Presbytery of Ayr decided to break the link and create a new one. The parishioners of Catrine and Sorn fought against this, but were outvoted. Thus Catrine Parish Church was linked with Auchinleck and Sorn found a new link with Muirkirk Parish Church. The manse, which was located between Sorn and Catrine, was sold, and the minister of Muirkirk linked with Sorn lived at Muirkirk manse. The new linkage was established on 27 August 2003.

Rev Alexander Welsh was inducted as minister of Muirkirk linked with Sorn in 2003, the second time he had been at Sorn. He left in 2007 to take up the position of hospital chaplain at Crosshouse Hospital, Kilmarnock. At the time of writing, September 2008, the church at Sorn had still to find a new minister. The roll at the time was 161 members.

MINISTERS:

1658-1662	Rev John Campbell MA
1669-1673	Rev Andrew Dalrymple MA (*c.* 1626-76)
1672-1684	Rev John Campbell MA
1684-1684	Rev William Blair MA
1686-1686	Rev Francis Fordyce
1686-1689	Rev William Anderson MA (*c.* 1660-90)
1692-1738	Rev Mungo Lindsay (1666-1738)
1739-1752	Rev William Steel (d. 1752)
1752-1789	Rev James Connell (1722-89)
1790-1805	Rev George Gordon DD (d. 1805)
1806-1823	Rev Lewis Balfour (d. 1860)
1823-1843	Rev John Stewart MA (1793-1879)
1843-1885	Rev Dr John Rankine DD (1816-85)
1885-1888	Rev Richard Spenser Ritchie (1860-1917)
1889-1919	Rev Henry Cunningham Begg DD (1856-1919)
1919-1924	Rev David Fyfe MacMath MA, BD (1889-1962)
1925-1928	Rev William Lowyn Davies
1928-1951	Rev James Gegg (1896-1961)
1951-1957	Rev John Heron (1915-2002)
1958-1966	Rev John Ernest Heathwood (1922-1970)
1967-1977	Rev David Reid MA HCF (1905-1977)
1979-1986	Rev Alexander Welsh
1986-1993	Rev W. Clement Robb (1940-2005)
1994-2002	Rev George A. Chalmers MA BD MLitt
2003-2007	Rev Alexander Welsh

5.11 Sorn Church – interior 2008 *(Dane Love)*

CHAPTER SIX

EDUCATION

The earliest parish school was probably erected near to the church in 1696. This came about as a result of an Act of Parliament for the Settling of Schools in every parish. The Kirk Session was responsible for running the school and the heritors were duty bound to pay the schoolmaster's salary and for the maintenance of the schoolhouse. On 24 February 1698 Rev Mungo Lindsay organised a meeting of the heritors in the parish with the intention of getting them to pay the schoolmaster's salary. A number of heritors attended this meeting, but 'not being the major part of the heritors of this paroch, found and declared themselves not to be in a capacity to stent the paroch in a salary for schoolmaster.' However, on 2 November 1698 he still had no schoolmaster in the parish and instigated proceedings whereby he notified the Presbytery of Ayr 'q[uhi]ch was taken against the heretors of the paroch because they would not stent th[e]mselves.'

On October 1712 Rev Mungo Lindsay notified Presbytery that he had obtained the services of Thomas Abercrombie as a suitable schoolmaster for the parish. Abercrombie was tested by the Presbytery, Samuel Lockhart and John MacDermeit being appointed to try him instantly. The two men reported back that they found Abercrombie qualified to teach Latin, and thus was appointed to Sorn. The report then notes that 'after which the said Thomas Abercrombie signed the Confession of Faith.' Thomas Abercrombie does not appear to have been particularly settled at Sorn and moved on, for a letter from Rev James Lawrie, minister of Kirkmichael, to Andrew Ross, Professor of Humanity at the University of Glasgow, dated 26 January 1714, makes reference to him:

> At lenth I got nottice of Mr. Thomas Abercrombie, who owes his birth and education to yᵉ City of Glasgow School and University there; before I engadged him I saw his credentiall letters from some Minᵗˢ of Glasgow, and Mr. Law his regent, ample eneugh; and he was tried by two of the Minˢ of our Presbytry, qᵒ pretend to be very much masters of humanity, and passed his trials wʰ with very great applause; moreover, he taught a school in the neighbourhood, in the parish of

Sorn, q^r Mr. Mongo Lindsay, once Doctor of the Grammar School in Glasgow (q^o is paucis secundus, not to say nemini, in his skill that way), q^o give him a verry ample testimony; after all (wch deserves scarce to be mentioned) I made a kind of tryall of him myself, and found he had a competent stock, yet might be improved upon, all wch I ventur'd to do my outmost to get him settled, and endeavoured to get him schollars from severall places, got him provided in some of the best classicks, w^h notes, and the most approved translations, and so the work begun in Decr last. He had not been six weeks in the place, tho' behaving himself w^h all the prudent management imaginable, untill the country people begun to pick quarrels; but this was not likely to prevail; but we have a school in the principall toun of the jurisdiction at Mayboll. The schoolmaster there is related to verry many of the gentlemen about the place. They begun to think this new erection if it prosper'd, might eclipse y^r friend's school, and break his reputation; so to prevent this, they have not been wanting to fall upon projects for that effect; but that wch has done him most prejudice is y^t your late schollar Mr. ffergussone has wrote home to me (y^t was indeed readily to be conceal'd), but also to his ffather the Laird of Auchinblane (q^o is the schoolmaster in Maybole's friend, and seeing wonderfully prejudged at our new school), that you told him that this new schoolmaster Mr. Thomas Abercrombie was most insufficient for the office he had undertaken, and that this you were willing to attest, under your hand if need were; this story Achinblane hands about, in gentlemen's comp^y who were inclinable to send y^r children to this place, effectually to prevent it. I confess the story surprises me much; its so contrary to what in fact I find now by experience of the young man, who I think by assiduos applecotion, together w^h good helpe (q^{ch} God willing he shall not want), may come to be a verry able teacher; and its so unlike, dear Sir, that character you have, of generosity, candour, and justice, that I'm uneasy about it, and can scarce give the story credit, and I must be bold in saying it wold be ungrate, upon me and Mr. Thomas both, q^o are at great pains to raise your reputation on all occasions, and had resolved to have kept up a strict correspondence w^h you, for your direction, in the whole of the management of his school; and hoped in a year or two to have been able to send you a swatch of topping schollars; but I cannot express how much this story has dashed us, and we are both verry uneasy till you send us a satisfying answer. I presume to give my humble respects to my old accquaintance, your lady, and so I subscribe myself (expecting your answer p. post of ye 30, or as soon as possible, and if

you please let Mr ffergusone know nothing of it till we obtain it), dear
Sir, your sincere and most humble serv^t,
James Lawrie,
Manse of Kirkmichael.

On 27 January 1725 the heritors of the parish of Sorn (still noted as Dalgain at the
time) along with Rev Mungo Lindsay of Sorn, and Revs Andrew Rodger and
William Maitland, plus John Beg of Dornal (Dornhall in the notes), ruling elder at
Sorn, met at a special meeting at Dalgain kirk for the purpose of settling schools in
each parish according to law, and for the appointment of a schoolmaster.

The parish of Sorn seems to have had difficulty in persuading the local
landowners to pay their share of the schoolmaster's salary, for the minister often
had to report them to the Commissioners of Supply of Ayrshire. On 17 August 1726
it was noted that there was no schoolmaster at that time.

On 31 May 1727 Rev William Marshall, who was chaplain to the laird of
Gilmilnscroft (at the time James Farquhar), was compeired to attend a meeting of
the Presbytery of Ayr where he signed the Confession of Faith.

In 1734-6 the school still seemed to be unable to get a schoolmaster due to
there being little chance of getting a salary for him from the heritors. The ministers
at a meeting of the Presbytery of Ayr took the necessary steps to formally present
their case to the Commissioners of Supply of Ayrshire at their next meeting. Even
by 7 September 1736 it was noted by the presbytery that little had been done
regarding the difficulty. It appointed Messrs Reid Senior and Campbell Junior to
attend a meeting with the Earl of Loudoun concerning a school at Dalgain, 'it being
informed that his Lop has done something as to the settling a school at Muirkirk
with others concerned.'

By the end of the eighteenth century the schoolmaster received an annual
salary of £20, which was much less than the Ayrshire average of £30. The old
Statistical Account gives a rather scathing description of the school in 1796:

> The parish schoolmaster has no garden but he has a school and
> dwelling-house, both among the most wretched that are to be found
> in any cultivated country. The late Mr James Boswell of Auchinleck,
> the last time he was in this country, declared his determination to do
> every thing in his power, in order to redress this parochial grievance
> as soon as possible, but his death, which unfortunately happened soon
> after, prevented his doing any thing in the business, and has not been
> taken up by any other person. The schoolmaster's salary is £8 6s 8d,
> and the school fees are, for reading 1s 8d, reading and writing 2s 6d,
> writing and arithmetic, 3s, per quarter. Latin is not taught here. The
> average number of scholars is from 25 to 30, and the schoolmaster's

whole annual income, including his emoluments as session-clerk, amounts to about £20. The school is by no means in a flourishing state, and there is but little probability of its ever being so, till better provision is made for the master.

There is a good description of the school in the late 1820s in A. B. Todd's autobiography:

> The schoolhouse was, as it were, indented into the churchyard, with windows looking into it from the back and at the end, with the graves of many generations risen much above the floor of the little school of only one apartment. The schoolmaster's house, of two stories, but thatched, stood at the eastern end of the school, with its face, not to the road, but looking into a large and well-kept garden. The schoolmaster then was good old Adam Smith, a little man of stern aspect, very lame, one leg being drawn up and much bent at the knew. He could, however, walk at quite a speedy rate, especially when, unfolding his terrible tawse to their full length, he hurried down the school from his desk to punish some delinquent, which he generally did very severely if not very frequently, for he was a most rigid and stern disciplinarian, and kept the best order in his school of any master I have ever known.

Adam Smith was born on 18 August 1776 and served as schoolmaster in Sorn for 40 years. He died on 30 June 1847 and soon after a large memorial was erected over his grave in the kirkyard 'by a few old pupils and other friends'.

6.1 Main Street, Sorn – pre 1909 (*Baird Institute*)

On occasions when the dominie's son, Robert Smith, came down to Sorn from his home in Glasgow, the children would be given an impromptu day off! Robert Smith worked in a bank, and became involved in a scandal when he took money without permission and loaned it to a friend. It was not paid back, and he was found guilty of theft. He was banished to the penal colony in Australia's Botany Bay, and it is thought that he was never able to return to Scotland.

Proposals for a new school had rumbled on for some time after Rev Gordon's remarks in the *Statistical Account*, but it wasn't until 1849 that work on a new purpose-built building building commenced.

The new parish school was erected in 1849-50 with accommodation for 216 pupils. The building was described at the time as being 'in a style of elegance which is rarely seen in a rural parsonage.' In 1864, when the first log book starts, there were two teachers and three pupil teachers employed in the school. These were Thomas MacWilliam, schoolmaster, Mrs MacWilliam, Sewing Mistress, John Kelly, pupil teacher, Thomas Reid, pupil teacher, and James Aird, pupil teacher. At that time there were 162 pupils on the register. The average attendance in 1900 was around 100 and £100 worth of grants were available. It is said that the main passage through the school was paved with old gravestones that were lifted from the kirkyard and were laid face down. Thomas MacWilliam's son, Rev Thomas MacWilliam M.A. became a minister, serving in New Byth, Aberdeenshire, and Foveran, Aberdeenshire.

In 1872 the Education (Scotland) Act was passed, which resulted in the creation of school boards in every parish, the members of which were elected by the ratepayers. Sorn School Board was quick to act on the fact that the school was too small for the number of pupils in the parish. On 24 November 1873 it decided that the school should be extended to hold a further 40-50 pupils. The cost of this extension was £665 3s 6d, the mason work being carried out by George Reid of Catrine, the joiner work by Matthew Morton of Catrine, the plaster work by Shand & Taylor and the slating and plumbing by Miller & Sons. The architect of the new extension was William Railton of Kilmarnock. In 1888 Sorn Parish School Board reported that the schools were in good order, and that the board had earned an average grant of 18s 1d per head on the average attendance at Sorn Parish School, and 19s 5½d per head at Auchencloigh Public School, which had been erected to serve the northern end of the parish. In that year Sorn school had 143 pupils on its roll, with an average attendance of 114.

In 1900 the school was extended. By this time the roll was 99. A visit from the inspectors resulted in a report on what was happening in the school:

> The present organization of the school, whereby the Infants and the Senior Division are taught by the Head Master, is open to objection, and it is, from every point of view, desirable that the Mistress should

have charge of the whole of the lower part of the School. Her Classroom would be much improved for teaching purposes if a gallery, a separate exit to the playground and more suitable and convenient desks were provided.

The Infants show satisfactory attainment. The junior division is well taught. In several classes a rounder and firmer style of writing is required. In summing creditable accuracy is secured but greater speed in working should be aimed at and the children should be accustomed to solve simple problems involving the application of the Elementary rules.

In the Senior department the work is somewhat unequal. Reading is fluent but monotonous. Care should be taken to see that the pupils understand what they read, and they should be encouraged to express in simple words of their own the more difficult language of the reading book. Arithmetic is weak throughout. In no class does the summary mark reach 40 per cent and in the Fourth Standard it is only 25. Spelling required increased attention, especially in the Fourth Standard, a class which is not strong at any point. The Sixth, and about half of the Fifth Standard pupils have a good appearance in Composition. In the oral examinations in the class subjects intelligent answering is confined to a very small proportion of each class. Singing and Drill receive due attention. There are sundry cases of what appears to be illegal employment and it is to be hoped that the Board may see their way to take up a firmer attitude in regard to the working of the Compulsory clauses.

6.2 Sorn Primary School – 2007 *(Dane Love)*

Children from Burnside Row, and a few other locations on the southern edge of the parish, had been in the habit of attending school at Darnconner, which was funded by Auchinleck Parish School Board. This caused some argument over a period, and in 1904 the Auchinleck board contacted Sorn board with the suggestion of erecting a joint school in the area to educate the miners' children. This was turned down by the Sorn board. The Auchinleck board went ahead and built a new school at Darnconner, opened in 1906. The headmaster of the new school was instructed that no pupils from Sorn parish should be admitted to the new school, even although they had attended the older Darnconner School. When the children were sent home it brought things to a head, and Sorn Parish School Board quickly agreed to assist in the running costs of the school, paying a fee for each pupil from its parish educated there.

From 1911-12 Sorn school was altered and extended to the plans of Robert Ingram. The roll in 1910 was 132 children, but this increased considerably in 1911 to 171, possibly the highest roll it reached. At that time Edward Robertson, headmaster, was assisted by four teachers – Miss B. J. MacFadzean, Miss Elizabeth B. Weir, Mr John Thomson and Miss Sarah P. Shearer. In 1914 the roll was added to with the arrival of three Belgian refugees.

In 1918 operation of schools in the county was transferred from the local school boards to Ayrshire Education Authority, and thus Sorn School came under the control of the Ayr-based authority. In 1929 the running of schools was taken over by the Ayr County Council Education Authority.

Drawing was first introduced into the curriculum in 1910 following a visit of the Instructor in Drawing from the county council, G. Bonar Lyon. In 1930 the school clock was repaired and later in the same year drinking fountains were installed in the playground.

In 1939 the school roll was increased considerably with the outbreak of war. A total of 25 children evacuated from Glasgow were enrolled at Sorn in the 1939-1940 session, and it was noted that it was some time before the classes settled with the new incomers. The rivalry between the locals and the Glasgow evacuees was regarded as being good for the school, for the city children had more confidence whereas the locals were diffident. A couple of teachers came to the school from Glasgow to help.

The headmasters, latterly head teachers, were Thomas MacWilliam (served up to 1880), who also acted as Registrar of Births, Marriages and Deaths for the whole of Sorn parish. He retired due to ill health in 1880, and was presented with a dining-room clock and a purse containing over 50 sovereigns by Rev Matthew C. Thorburn. Edward Robertson was the headmaster from 1880-1910. He was followed by John Thomson (1910-22), who moved to Sorn from Kilmarnock on his marriage in 1910. He later moved to become headmaster at Catrine School.

James Robb M.A. was appointed headmaster in 1922. He remained at Sorn for

22 years, dying suddenly of a stroke in October 1944, aged 58 years. The school log book noted that he 'served the school and parish faithfully and well. Of a quiet, unassuming nature, Mr Robb never sought the limelight, but was content to find reward in the pleasure that accompanies service to others.'

William B. Bryson was appointed as headmaster on 8 January 1945 and soon after, in June that year, the playground was tar-macadamised for the first time. After the Second World War, free milk was issued to pupils from 1946, 45 bottles of $1/3$ pint being required. Mr Bryson moved to become head teacher at Saltcoats at the end of 1950.

In January 1951 David W. Parker was appointed as the next headmaster. He was a native of Kilmaurs, and had previously taught at Mauchline. He remained at Sorn for almost seven years, until 1957.

James Barclay was the headmaster from 1957 until 1967. The next headmaster was William Hale. He was appointed in 1967 and retired in 1975. He died on 22 October 1987 and is buried in the new cemetery.

The next head of the school was a woman, Miss Annie Cameron, appointed in 1975. She became Mrs Annie Clark, and she remained headmistress for 21 years until 1996.

Thomas Ferguson was the headmaster from 1996 until 2001 when he retired. In September 2001 a special exhibition was held in the village hall to mark the 150th anniversary of Sorn Primary School.

The next head teacher was Elizabeth (Liz) Cole, appointed in January 2002. She left the post in 2005. The next head teacher was Margaret (Mags) Houston, appointed in 2005. She moved to become head teacher at Darvel Primary School in 2008.

Originally many of the head teachers lived in the schoolhouse which adjoins the school, but it was sold in recent years and is now a private house no longer associated with the school.

In November 2007 proposals to close Sorn Primary School were made by East Ayrshire Council as part of their survey of schools within the area. If the school was to be closed, the pupils would be transferred to either Catrine or Mauchline primary schools. However, after a concerted campaign to save the school, East Ayrshire Council relented and agreed to keep the school open.

OTHER SCHOOLS

A small public school was established at Auchencloigh, where the schoolmaster in 1867 was James Watson. Miss Bella Cromar was appointed teacher on 10 October 1884. The average number of scholars at the school in 1887 was 26.7, receiving a government grant of 15s 8d per scholar, plus £40 3s 2d from the rates – equivalent to £1 10s ¾d per scholar. The following year the roll had risen to 43, with an average attendance of 38. This earned a grant of £36 3s. Jessie Stewart taught in 1899-1900,

Miss Marion MacF. Forrester taught in 1901 and William Forrester (1843-1903) died at the Schoolhouse there. In 1906 the school had ten boys and 13 girls in attendance, taught by Miss Forrester. Miss Mary Ann Allan was the teacher in 1919, Mary J. Cow (1919), and Miss Moir (1921). In the 1930s and 1940s the teacher at the school was Mrs Janet C. Gardner. Around 1958 the teacher was Mrs Crawford. The school room had accommodation for 55 pupils, and an average attendance of 25 at that time. A grant of around £40 was available for pupils. Auchencloigh School educated pupils up to the age of ten, primaries one to five together in a single room, after which pupils had to move on to larger schools in the area. There was usually only ever one teacher there at a time. A census of the local population identified a falling roll, resulting in the school being closed in 1971, and the building demolished within a few years. However, it is claimed that within a year or so of the survey the school roll would have been significantly larger once more.

Auchencloigh schoolhouse was located across the road from the school building. It was for a time around 1897 also used as the local post office, under Kilmarnock.

There have also been a number of 'Adventure' schools in the district, run by men who were often crippled and who earned their living teaching what they knew to their scholars. One of these existed at Montgarswood Bridgend, for A. B. Todd attended it around 1832, when it was run by a former stonemason, James Begg. Two other schools existed in 1837; one of these was operated by John MacClymont and the other by a Mr Sloan.

A private boarding school for boys was established at Gilmilnscroft in 1961, known variously as Gilmilnscroft House School or Gilmilnscroft College. The house was purchased by Mr A. S. Robertson, a businessman in Glasgow, and it was converted to a school, opening for its first term in September 1961. Mr Robertson's son, Keith, had been a pupil at Clyde College Boarding School, which was located at Routenburn, Largs, but that school closed in 1961. When the new classrooms were ready at Gilmilnscroft, Keith Robertson and 33 fellow pupils from Clyde College moved to Gilmilnscroft to continue their education. The pupils came from all over Scotland, and also further afield – there were boys from the Bahamas, Hong Kong, Durban, India, Burma and Nigeria.

The first headmaster at Gilmilnscroft was Mr T. L. Jehu BSc (Edin.) BEd. He was a native of St Andrews and trained as a teacher at Moray House in Edinburgh. Prior to moving to Gilmilnscroft he had been the head of chemistry at Fettes School in Edinburgh. He stated that 'The aim is to provide a full senior secondary course leading up to university entrance and professional examinations.' By the end of the first session the school had 44 boys attending. Four new classrooms had been erected on the site of the old greenhouses, and the old coach house was converted into a science laboratory. In addition to Mr Jehu there were two other teachers at the school – Mr H Coltman BA (Cambs) and Mr A. D. Sterrey BA (Lond.). The school motto, *Mente Manuque* (by mind and by hand) was the same as the former Farquhar owners of Gilmilnscroft. The uniform worn was a black blazer, with scarlet and green trimmings, and a thistle badge, devised by Mr Robertson.

In addition to classroom lessons, the boys were encouraged to take part in sport and hobbies. These included a photographic club, aero-modelling club, model railway club, stamp-collecting society, wild-life society, playing golf at Ballochmyle, fishing on the River Ayr, rugby, tennis, cricket and swimming at Cumnock. Former students recollect that the school was operated on a tight discipline regime, but that they were free to visit Cumnock on a Saturday afternoon, where they met up with local girls, smoked cigarettes and drank coffee – all against the school rules! The rugby team was quite successful in its day, and used to play on a field loaned by a farmer. The boys had to repay the farmer by lifting potatoes from his field near to Sorn Bridge. On Sunday mornings the boys were marched in their school uniform down to attend the service at Sorn Church. They were allowed to sit in the Gilmilnscroft loft.

Gilmilnscroft School only operated for about four or five years before it was closed. Mr Robertson's son caused some sensation in the district when it was discovered that he had shot his girlfriend between Galston and Moscow, before turning the gun on himself.

6.3 Sorn village *(Jamie McIntyre)*

CHAPTER SEVEN

INDUSTRY AND COMMERCE

COAL-MINING

One of the main industries in Sorn parish was the mining of coal. According to the old charter books of Gilmilnscroft estate, coal has been wrought in the Burrow Lands of Sorn since the year 1497. The charter books also describe that ever since the year 1613 the standard Gilmilnscroft coal creel measured 14 inches wide, 16 inches deep and 30 inches long. A creel of these dimension filled with coal was priced at 2d Sterling. Apparently approximately the same size of creel was still in use in 1796, and this was classed as half a load, sold at 3d. Around 7 of these loads was equivalent to 20 hundredweight.

Seams of coal of various thicknesses have been noted throughout the parish, but not all have been worked extensively. The old *Statistical Account* makes reference to a seam five feet thick located on a high moor in the north-east part of the parish, below Blacksidend. This had been wrought in a very small scale in the seventeenth century, being only four or five feet below the surface of the moor. However, it was much neglected in the eighteenth century and its existence was more or less forgotten until rediscovered in 1796. Similarly, coal was noted to be plentiful around Brocklar, but as there was no pump suitable for drawing water from the pit, this had not been worked.

One area that had been mined with considerable success was in the immediate vicinity of Sorn Castle. Owned by the estate, there were two seams of coal, each of which was around one foot thick, separated by a band of hard till, around two feet thick. These seams were located around 8 or 9 fathoms below the surface of the ground, but as they did not suffer from water they were easily worked. In 1796 there were nine colliers employed in this mine, producing around 150 loads per week. The price obtained for this coal had only recently been raised from sixpence to eightpence per load. In 1790 the price got was only fourpence per load. The proprietors of Sorn estate were also at that time prospecting for new seams of coal.

A long-established colliery was located on Gilmilnscroft estate, owned by the Farquhar family. According to John Farquhar Gray, writing for the old *Statistical Account* in 1796:

When I came to this place, there were only about 6 men employed at the colliery; their wages were 14d per day, and their output 10 loads per man, sold at 3½ d per load. Without including those employed in drawing to the bank, the number now employed at our colliery, and the adjacent one of Burnhead, will average about 20; their out-puts from 12 to 15 loads per day, per man, sold at 6d. Their wages are from 2s to 2s 6d. The main seam is about 8 feet thick, with 6 inches of fire clay in the middle. Immediately above this seam, there is a stratum of the same kind of clay, 18 inches thick; above this 18 inches of coal; then 20 inches of hard black slate; and over that near 3 feet of coarse coal. The former practice had been to work only the lower seam, leaving about 6 inches of it for a roof; but I have lately gone back, and brought away both that roof and the next 18 inches of coal. The field is irregular below, having many steps, throwing the coal up and down, a circumstance which increases the expense of working it. Had we a sale for iron-stone the case would be very different, as these steps are composed chiefly of that mineral. My present going pit [1796] is 30 fathom deep, driven by a horse-gin.

On Gilmilnscroft estate a number of larger mines were sunk by Gilmour, Wood and Anderson, an Auchinleck mining company. Gilmilnscroft Colliery No. 1 Pit was sunk to the south of South Logan farm, near to the former South Logan Check Bar (NS 553240). This pit mined the Lugar Main coal 216 feet below the surface of the ground. A mineral railway linked the pit with the Muirkirk Branch of the railway near to Auchinleck. The pit head buildings were located east of the mineral line, which branched into five sidings at one point. It was still operating in 1918, by which time it was leased by William Baird and Company. The pit was operated in conjunction with Gilmilnscroft No. 4, the manager being Robert Bowie, the under –manager being George Weir. The two pits had 35 miners working below ground at that time, eleven working on the surface. As with the Gilmilnscroft pits numbered 1 to 6, the mine was closed on 31 March 1925.

Gilmilnscroft Colliery No. 2 Pit was sunk to the south east of this, to the north of the road past Glenshamrock road-end (NS 557237). A shaft 276 feet deep led down to the Lugar Main coal seam. This pit, which was much smaller than Pit No.1, was connected to a branch of the same mineral line. Apart from the railway passing through the works, there was only one other siding here.

East of No. 2 Pit by a few hundred yards was Gilmilnscroft Colliery No. 3 Pit (NS 561236). The mineral line passed Gilmilnscroft No. 2 and continued to Gilmilnscroft No. 3, the pit head being located between two bings on the north and south side of it. The mineral line continued for a few hundred yards past the pit-head buildings. The rail branched into four sidings here. On 23 May 1883 James

Muir, of Mill Street, Catrine, was accidentally killed in the pit. On 19 February 1900 William MacConnell was also killed in this mine. At the time the Gilmilnscroft pits were leased by the Gauchalland Coal Company, of Troon.

Gilmilnscroft Colliery No. 4 Pit was located in the gusset of the roads at Glenshamrock (NS 553239), and lay more or less on the opposite side of the road from No. 1 Pit, to which it was linked. A branch line from the main mineral line made its way into the pit complex, branching into six lies, which had a large shed over it from where the wagons were filled. At this pit, by the side of the road, was a smithy.

Gilmilnscroft Colliery No. 5 Pit was located to the east of the Auchinleck road, between it and Glenshamrock farm (NS 552233). Not shown on the 1856 Ordnance Survey map, it appears operational on the 1911 edition. At that time there were three pit-head buildings and a small bing to their southern side. No mineral railway is associated with this pit.

Gilmilnscroft Colliery No. 6 Pit was located to the east of Glenshamrock farm and was sunk in 1909. It was the last pit sunk by Gilmour, Wood and Anderson. Originally it had no mineral line for the removal of coal, but sometime after 1911 a track was laid to the south of the pit, linking it with the lines that served Berryhill and Barglachan pits. On 24 January 1913 William MacGarrey was killed in an accident in this pit. John MacLelland was also killed here on 2 July 1924 at the age of 65. The manager at Gilmilnscroft was William Hastie for many years, and in 1894 there were 343 miners working down the pit, and a further 65 on the surface. The firm was later bought out by the Gauchalland Coal Company (of Troon) and at a later date by William Baird and Company Ltd. In 1907 the manager was Robert Bowie, and it employed 282 miners below ground and a further 49 on the surface. In 1918 Bowie was still the manager of the Gilmilnscroft pits numbered 1, 4 and 6. Pit No. 6 had 161 miners working in it in 1918 and 24 surface workers.

The Burnhead Colliery was owned by Hugh Logan of that Ilk at the time of the old *Statistical Account*. It was located on Burnhead farm, or what became Glenlogan. Four 'Old Coal Pits' are shown on the Ordnance Survey map of 1860. One of them was in the wood immediately south of Glenlogan Bridge (NS 563260). A second was located on Barrsbrae Bank, halfway between Glenlogan Bridge and Glenlogan House (NS 565260). The two remaining pits were located in the wood immediately west of Barrhill cottage (NS 563259 and NS 564259).

Another old coal pit on Glenlogan estate was located on the moss south of Mid Heilar farm, almost due west of Templandshaw Loch (NS 586246). This mine was abandoned by 1860. In 1866 a borehole (known as Heilar No. 6) was sunk just to the south-east of this pit. The bore was 507 feet in depth, and it found a seam of coal 24 inches in thickness 23 feet below the surface, a further seam (Lugar Main) 45 inches thick 31 feet down, and a 24 inch seam of Lugar Blackband ironstone 504 feet down.

The Eglinton Coal Company operated the Glenlogan Pits in 1865. On Saturday 1 April 1865 a rock fall in Glenlogan No. 10 pit killed three young men. The victims, John Brown, William Wallace and Edward Pillin, who were all aged between sixteen and eighteen years, were engaged in a process named 'brushing' when a fall of debris landed on them. They were killed instantly. Two other miners, Patrick Marley and John Wallace, made a lucky escape at the time.

Glenlogan No. 11 was located at the southern side of Shaw Hill, on the farm of Shiel (NS 570247). This pit mined ell coal 36 feet below the surface. Glenlogan No. 12 pit was located a little to the south-west of No. 11 Pit (NS 568245). This pit mined ell coal 96 feet below the surface of the ground. All of these pits had been abandoned by 1911.

On Roundshaw farm a number of pits were sunk that were known as the Ballochmyle pits, from the estate of which Roundshaw was part. Ballochmyle Pit was sunk in 1876 and was owned by William Walker of Auchinleck. The original manager was Adam Hunter. In the late nineteenth century there were 220 men employed below ground at Ballochmyle, and a further 42 above ground. The pit was closed by 1900. Ballochmyle Pits No. 5 and No. 6 were located on the road into Roundshaw (NS 566235). Lugar Black Band Ironstone was mined here 1032 feet below ground. These pits were linked to Ballochmyle Nos. 7 and 8 to the north-east (but in Auchinleck parish) by an old tramway which predated the arrival of the railway on this part of the moor. The tramway continued past Dykeneuk Cottage, which was located midway between Berryhill and Glenshamrock farms, to the Catrine-Auchinleck road. Coal was unloaded here and transferred to the road.

In the immediate vicinity of Roundshaw farm was Common No. 16 pit, a large colliery located on the east side of the Dippol Burn, along with Common Ironstone Pit No. 15. The pit head workings were located in Auchinleck parish, but the large bing was located in Sorn parish.

The Dalgain pits were located to the east of the village, by the side of the Dalgain Burn. A rather small-scale operation compared with other pits, the first mines sunk here appear to have been in the 1860s. They were owned by Graham Somervell, and in 1879 the pit brought an income of £12 per annum. Coal had to be transported to Mauchline by horse and cart, the railway never reaching this place. Two shafts were sunk by the Dalgain Coal Company in the early twentieth century and these produced coal until 1929, when the drift mine was closed.

A new mine was sunk at Brocklar around the year 1867. A report on an accident in the pit that took place on the Sunday night of 30 June 1867 describes the pit as being 'newly opened'. When the incident took place the pit was out of order, and one of the managers, named Mr Nimmo, went down the hutch to the bottom. He was the only person in the mine at the time, and how he was killed is not known. Some groans were heard, and calls were made to find out if he was alright. With no replies the engineman went down the pit. He found Mr Nimmo in 'a state of insensibility'. He was brought to the surface, taken home and attended to by Dr Ballantine. There were no outward signs of any injury, and it was thought that he had internal injuries caused by crushing. He died two days later.

Just within the boundary of the parish, but more readily associated with Auchinleck, was Berryhill No. 1 mine. This was located on the north side of the Dippol Burn, just to the south of the Gilmilnscroft No. 5 Pit. It operated sometime between 1856 (when it doesn't appear on maps) and 1911, when it is shown simply as 'Old Shaft'. The pit mined the Lugar Main seam 198 feet below the ground.

Two small shafts of a coal mine existed at Grange, located up the Burn o' Need. These were disused by 1898 and were probably sunk to supply coal to the nearby limekiln, located near to the confluence of the South Grange Burn with the Burn o' Need. Investigative borings in recent years found that the coal was just 30 feet or so under the surface of the ground, and that the coal seam was around 30 inches thick. The coal was discovered to have a high sulphur content, making it unsuitable for mining as burning this coal produces a high degree of pollution.

A new mine was sunk on the farm of South Logan around 1925. The pit was run by the Dalgain Coal Company, which was a partnership between the McIntyres of Sorn Castle and the Farquhar-Olivers of Gilmilnscroft. The mine head was located to the north-east of South Logan farm, near to the small burn. The mine suffered due to faults in the rock and the lack of finance and the company was wound up in July 1935.

The largest, and most recent coal mine in the parish, was the Sorn Mine, sunk at East Montgarswood by the National Coal Board in 1952 and producing its first coal in 1953. The mine had two sloping in gaun e'es, or open shafts, which had rail lines leading down into them. Number 1 mine was 2,150 feet in length, dropping into the ground at an angle of one in four, with a direct rope haulage system.

7.1 Sorn Mine *(Baird Institute)*

Number 2 mine was 2,135 feet in length. The Hurlford Main and MacNaught seams of coal were worked, the coal being transported by road to the screening and washing plant at Mauchline Pit. The spoil heap was located down an incline by the side of the Burn o' Need. The mine was envisaged to have a lifespan of 25 years, but it was to become one of the NCB's most successful surface mines, producing a high-quality household coal. There were 246 miners working down the mine at Sorn initially, and a further 18 above ground. The output of the mine at the start was 1983 tons. Over its lifespan, the mine had an average workforce of 233, rising to a peak in 1970 of 294. In 1979 a development plan was drawn up which would have resulted in £330,000 worth of extensions into virgin seams, but this was shelved. The National Coal Board announced the closure of Sorn mine in 1981, as part of an extensive money-saving scheme, with the loss of 230 jobs. At that time the pit was losing £1 million pounds despite producing 1,600 tons of coal each week. In 1982 the miners proposed buying it from the coal board if it was to close, as they reckoned that there was enough coal in the mine to keep it open for another 26 years. This failed to happen, and the mine was finally closed on 29 April 1983, the last 'pick-and-shovel' mine in Scotland. On that date sixty men were transferred to Killoch Colliery; the remainder spent the next two months salvaging equipment and machinery at the mine before it was totally closed.

Mining was a dangerous occupation and in addition to those already mentioned, a number of other men from Sorn were killed. In the kirkyard is a stone to James Dempster, killed in Common No. 10 pit (Auchinleck parish) on 31 January 1868 aged 20 years.

MINERS' ROWS

A number of miners' rows were built on the moors south of Sorn to house miners employed in the local pits. Burnside Row was located on Roundshaw farm, on the southern edge of the parish, next to the Dippol Burn. This row of 12 houses was owned by William Walker, a coalmaster from Auchinleck, and was known locally as 'The Poverty'. The row comprised of two blocks of six houses, located between the road and the burn. By 1900 they were the property of William Walker Hood, coalmaster of Ballochmyle Colliery. At that time they were occupied by Matthew MacCrorie (overseer), Francis Johnston (engineman), John Frew (collier), George Peden (mason – he had two houses knocked into one), Richard Brown (surfaceman), Robert Mitchell (collier), William Sweaton (collier), Thomas Sanders (roadsman), John Fleming (roadsman) and Andrew Armour (roadsman). One of the houses was empty at that time. Annual rent of these houses was £3 11s 6d. The houses were still in existence in 1934 but were demolished by 1939. Adjacent to Burnside Row was Roundshaw Cottage, which comprised of two semi-detached houses. In 1900 these were occupied by Robert Whiteside, manager, and James Drummond Begg, cashier at Ballochmyle Colliery.

Better quality houses were located at South Logan farm, by the side of the Catrine to Auchinleck road. These were officially known as Meadowside Cottages, but to the locals they were better known as the 'Dundie Raw'. This name is thought to derive from the dundie coal which lay under the ground here – a description of burnt coal. This could happen when molten rock touched the seam, allowing it to burn slowly under the ground. Another definition claims that the name came from 'dandie', descriptive of the better quality miners' houses which these were. The houses were built in the years 1873-4 by Messrs Gilmour, Wood and Anderson, mineral tenants of Gilmilnscroft Colliery at that time. The first two families to occupy the houses were the Logies and Dunlops. The row comprised of 20 houses, located on the south side of the road, overlooking the Bogend Burn. These were arranged in five blocks, the front door facing the main road. Gardens were located to the rear of the houses. There were a further five homes at the Hillend huts, adjacent, which were smaller.

7.2 Meadowside Cottages *(Peter Robertson)*

Meadowside Row was later to become the responsibility of the Gauchalland Coal Company, which was based in Troon, the proprietor of which was Adam Wood, who was also harbour manager at Troon. The residents were employed in the Gilmilnscroft Collieries. In 1900 the occupation of the principal occupiers of the houses were 12 colliers, 4 miners, 2 labourers, 1 pitheadman, 1 fireman, 1 roadman, 1 gatekeeper, 1 bottomer and 1 widow.

One of the Meadowside cottages (number 7), became empty around 1882 and thereafter was kept by the coal company and was used as a hall. A monthly church service was held here, shared by the ministers of Sorn and Catrine, as well as a weekly Sunday school, established in 1882. Amongst the Sunday School teachers were Gertrude and Kate Farquhar, daughters of Gilmilnscroft, the latter to become Lady Fitzroy. Previously services were held by Rev Matthew C. Thorburn, assistant minister to Rev Dr Rankine, in kitchens at Meadowside, much to the annoyance of the 'guid wives'. The harmonium was introduced at services in 1906, resulting in increased attendance. Here also the annual soiree of Meadowside was held, the first one taking place in 1908. The reading and recreation room was added in 1884, being opened by Rev R. Menzies Fergusson, and the books were the gift of Sir Walter and Lady Mary Farquhar of Gilmilnscroft. The Reading Room was given a wooden floor in 1909 and the hall was renovated in 1921.

Rent of the main Meadowside houses was £5 4s 0d per annum in 1900, the Hillend huts being £3 9s 4d. When the Gilmilnscroft Mines closed in 1925 the houses were proposed to be demolished, but they were still occupied until 1937 and were demolished before 1939, when only a strip of ground survived, owned by Mrs Norah Farquhar Oliver.

Glenlogan Miners' Houses were located on the farm of Shiel, on the Heilar Road, and were owned by the Rankens of Glenlogan but were leased to William Baird & Company, iron and coal masters, who sub let them to their workers. The rent in 1900 was £2 10s 0d per house, all charged the same. There were four rows of houses, the front row being located adjacent to the Heilar Road. This row had ten houses in it, with small gardens located to the rear. The house at the eastern end had an Ordnance Survey benchmark on it, indicating that the row stood 567 feet above sea level. Centrally placed in front of this row were two water closets that were shared by the residents. Parallel with this row, located to its rear, was the second row, again with ten houses, although the house at the western end had been extended to one side. The third row of houses was located behind the second row, but it did not run parallel with the front two rows. This row also had ten houses in it, the gardens located on the north side of the houses. A fourth row erected parallel with the third row was located further south again, but this row only had four houses in it.

In 1900 the front row at Glenlogan had six empty houses, the other four occupied by a widow, two miners and another man. The second row had six empty houses, the four occupied houses being home to miners. The third row had five empty houses, the other five occupied by miners, and all of the houses in the fourth row were occupied by miners. In February 1914 the council Sanitary Authority visited the rows at Glenlogan and condemned them as being unsuitable for habitation. However, the First World War commenced and the occupants had to remain for another four years. The houses at Glenlogan were gradually emptied before 1919, the last occupant of the houses being Mr Todd. The houses were demolished around 1921.

GLENLOGAN IRONSTONE WORKS

Ironstone has been worked at various places in Sorn parish. In the old *Statistical*

Account there is a reference to considerable quantities of ironstone being located on the north-eastern part of the parish, below Blacksidend. This has not been worked.

Ironstone was mined at an early date in the parish at Pennel Burn, which forms the boundary between Sorn and Muirkirk parishes on the east side of Auchenlongford Hill. The iron mine is shown on Armstrong's map of 1775. The workings are still partially visible on the ground, to the west of Nether Whitehaugh farm. The haematite was quarried and mined and then was taken on pack horses to Ayr. From the harbour it was shipped to Bonawe, by the side of Loch Etive, where the Lorn Furnace Company had established iron furnaces in 1753, using the plentiful supply of timber to smelt iron ore into ingots. The pig iron was then transported back by the same route to the iron forge at Terreoch, on the southern side of the River Ayr, within Auchinleck parish. There the pig iron was worked into malleable iron. The River Ayr was diverted through a lade and was used to power bellows and hammers. The forge at Terreoch used charred peat or wood as a fuel, but the wood became scarce and the peat could not be dried quickly enough, so the works were abandoned fairly soon. This forge, which was known as the Spadeworks in some accounts, was established by the 3rd Earl of Cathcart sometime around 1732, and is thought to have been the only charcoal-fired blast furnace in southern Scotland.

Pennel Burn Mine was reopened in the late nineteenth century (approximately 1850 to the late 1880s) and again in the early 1900s to work the haematite. The shafts were located in the same vicinity as the older mine, and large spoil heaps and settling ponds were created by the side of the burn. A series of tram routes were created across Meathhill Moss to bring the ore down to the public road at Crook Moss, these now re-used as forestry roads. Another tram route branched to drop down to North Limmerhaugh farm. A couple of buildings were erected at the pit, the ruins of which remain. That on the east, or Muirkirk, side of the burn appears to have been the main mine-head. This building measures 83 feet by 20, and to the west are what may have been cottages.

The principal areas where ironstone has been mined is on the south side of the parish, on the lands of Glenlogan. The ironstone was used in the ironworks that had been erected at Lugar in 1846 by John Wilson of Dundyvan and James and Colin Dunlop. By 1860 a mineral line was laid from the pits south over Airds Moss, past Darnconner and linking with the Auchinleck-Muirkirk line. Around half a mile to one mile of railway was laid in Sorn parish, various branches being laid into the pits that operated at different times.

The first ironstone pits to be worked at Glenlogan were probably those located nearest to the Glenlogan Miners' Houses. The first mine may have been sunk in 1845 when blackband ironstone was discovered on Glenlogan estate. A large number of miners came into the area to work the mine, but by the end of March 1852, with the depression in the iron trade, the mine was abandoned. Two former pit bings are shown on the 1860 Ordnance Survey map of the area to the south-west of the miners' houses, and these probably were associated with the first ironstone pits. Five further ironstone pits existed after this, and these are shown as 'Old Ironstone Pit' on the 1860 map, indicating that they were by then disused. Two of these were due south of Henryston farm. Two others were located south of Shiel farm, and the fifth was located to the south-east of the miners' houses. These old pits were not connected to the Darnconner branch of the railway, but by an older tram road that headed south over Airds Moss to the Peat Moss and thence westwards alongside the Dippol Burn to the road between Sorn and Auchinleck.

The eighth and ninth Ironstone pits were located on the north side of Shaw Hill, to the south of the miners' houses, and these were the first pits to be linked by railway past Darnconner. The easternmost of these two pits, located at the end of the road from the miners' houses, was also a coal pit.

Glenlogan No. 10 pit was located to the south-east of Shiel farm (NS 576249). This mined Lugar Blackband ironstone 216 feet below ground. Glenlogan Nos. 11 and 12 were coal mines. All of the Glenlogan pits were abandoned by 1911 and their pit-head buildings demolished.

In 2005 Glasgow University Archaeological Research Division carried out a survey of the former Gilmilnscroft Colliery and Glen Logan Ironstone Works site prior to tree planting.

MINES IN SORN PARISH

C = Coalmine   I = Ironstone Mine   + = After < = Before

Name		NGR	Dates Opened	Closed	Original Owner
Ballochmyle 5/6	C	566235	1876	<1900	William Walker
Berryhill 1	C	553229	+1856	<1911	
Brocklar a	C	564280	1867	<1897	
Brocklar b	C	565280	1867	<1897	
Brocklar c	C	565278	1867	<1897	
Brocklar d	C	559280		<1860	
Brocklar e	C	560280		<1860	
[Daldilling]	C	574261			
Dalgain a	C	561267	<1879	<1897	Graham Somervell
Dalgain b	C	562267			Graham Somervell
Dalgain c	C	565278		1929	Dalgain Coal Co.
Gilmilnscroft 1	C	553240	<1911	1925	Gilmour, Wood & Anderson
Gilmilnscroft 2	C	558236	<1911	1925	Gilmour, Wood & Anderson
Gilmilnscroft 3	C	560236	<1883	1925	Gilmour, Wood & Anderson
Gilmilnscroft 4	C	551239	<1911	1925	Gilmour, Wood & Anderson

Gilmilnscroft 5	C	553233	+1860	1925	Gilmour, Wood & Anderson
Gilmilnscroft 6	C	558234	1909	1925	Gilmour, Wood & Anderson
Gilmilnscroft a	C	557262		<1860	
Gilmilnscroft b	C	559261		<1860	
Gilmilnscroft c	C	559260		<1860	
Gilmilnscroft d	C	559260		<1860	
Gilmilnscroft e	C	559258		<1860	
Gilmilnscroft f	C	561258		<1860	
Gilmilnscroft g	C	561259		<1860	
Gilmilnscroft h	C	561260		<1860	
Gilmilnscroft i	C	562258		<1860	
Gilmilnscroft j	C	559259		<1860	
Gilmilnscroft k	C	560259		<1860	
Burnhead a	C	563260	<1796	<1860	
Burnhead b	C	564260	<1796	<1860	
Burnhead c	C	563259	<1796	<1860	
Burnhead d	C	564259	<1796	<1860	
Glenlogan e	I	569255	+1845	<1860	
Glenlogan f	I	568253	+1845	<1860	
Glenlogan g	I	564251	+1845	<1860	
Glenlogan h	I	565253	+1845	<1860	
Glenlogan i	I	567253	+1845	<1860	
Glenlogan j	I	569252	+1845	<1860	
Glenlogan k	CI	571253	<1860	+1860<1897	
Glenlogan l	I	570250	<1860	+1860<1897	
Glenlogan m	I	571255	+1845	<1860	
Glenlogan 10	C	575249	<1865	<1897	Eglinton Coal Company
Glenlogan 11	C	570247	+1860	<1897	
Glenlogan 12	C	568245	+1860	<1897	
[Nether Heilar]	C	583250	+1860	<1897	
[Heilar]	C	586246		<1860	
Grange a	C	571309		<1898	
Grange b	C	571309		<1898	
Sorn	C	529276	1952	1983	National Coal Board
South Logan	C	553246	1925	1935	Dalgain Coal Co.

LIMEWORKINGS

A number of limeworkings existed in the parish. One of the principal ones was located at Haggisbank, by the side of the River Ayr, at Holehouse. There still survive the remains of the stone wall of the limekilns, and a number of tracks behind where the limestone and coal were taken to the kiln head. A single limekiln is located at Haggis Bank itself, and two limekilns together can be seen east of Holhouse mill. Adjacent were old limeworkings, one of which has filled with water to create a lochan. These limeworkings were abandoned before 1909.

Another limeworks existed at Brocklar, on Sorn estate. These were originally two separate limestone quarries, on either side of the Cleuch Burn, it being the boundary at one time between Sorn and Dalgain estates. They were worked in the mid-eighteenth century, but when Sorn estate took over Dalgain the works were merged. It appears the Dalgain workings were the older. In 1796 12 men were employed at the works, quarrying limestone and smelting lime. The contractor had planned producing 12,000 bolls of lime (around 750 tons), but due to the wet weather that year and a shortage of men had failed to reach this target. These works were abandoned for a time. They were reopened in 1837.

A third limeworks was located on Gilmilnscroft estate which seems to have been worked from around 1715. A detailed account of it, written by James Farquhar Gray of Gilmilnscroft, is included in the original *Statistical Account*:

> The average quantity of lime raised at this work, during the 18 years that I have been concerned in it, is about 9,000 bolls of shells, each consisting of 5 Winchester bushels; but in some particular years we have sold 14,000 bolls. This was actually the quantity sold last season, and so great was the demand, that, could it have been prepared, we could have sold double that quantity. We have contracted with workmen for raising 20,000 tons next season. As the quantity brought to market varies, the number of hands must vary in proportion. A good workman will, in a year, raise 500 tons, equal to 2000 bolls; but as little can be done in winter, you may reckon a man for every 1,000 bolls, besides those employed in bearing and in carting the lime and coals to the draw-kiln. The bare, which, 18 years ago, was only 15 feet, is now 30. This circumstance has, of late, obliged us to have recourse to the expedient of mining the rock, which consists of about 7 feet thick, in so many beds; with a roof of hard till 18 inches thick. This stratum of till, with 10 feet of blaze over it, makes a good roof, and allows us to work the mine from 16 to 20 feet wide, leaving pillars about 18 feet square. When I entered upon this work, the wages of the workmen, both above and below, were from 9d to 14d per day: they are now from 14d to 2s. This limestone has been worked 80 years. It is carried to the neighbouring parishes of Auchinleck, Ochiltree, Mauchline, and Stair, to the distance of 10 or 12 miles.

A small limeworking existed on Glenlogan estate, located by the roadside east of Barrhill. Old maps show an 'old limestone pit' here, indicating that the limestone was worked underground, rather than by quarrying. Immediately east of the pit, in the field below Henryston, was a limekiln. It was disused by 1867 and today nothing on the ground survives to mark either.

Another old limekiln, abandoned by 1867, was located on the hillside above the Pottery Row

The lime workings at Auchmannoch were established by Arthur Campbell in 1796 when he erected a draw kiln. A number of limestone quarries were hewn from the ground, these existing between Meadowhead and Todhills (closed by 1860), with a limekiln located adjacent to the Mare Burn. A second old quarry and limekiln existed north-east of Crofthead, south of Cockreoch Hill, again disused by 1860. A small limestone quarry was located by the side of the Stra Burn, which becomes the Auchmannoch Burn, on the upstream side of the bridge into Auchmanoch House. Within the same immediate vicinity was a limekiln. Shown as being in operation on the 1860 Ordnance Survey map, these limeworkings appears to have closed soon after. Upstream from Auchmannoch, adjacent to Coplar, was another pair of limekilns, shown on the Ordnance Survey map of 1896. Limestone from an old quarry at Coplar was smelted here.

Auchencloigh Quarry, disused by 1897, was located at the side of the road passing Auchencloigh School towards Auchencloigh farm. It was used to quarry limestone which was smelted at the adjoining limekiln, remains of which survive.

At Carleith, on the boundary between Sorn and Galston parishes, were a number of quarries for limestone. Carleith Quarry was located to the east of Meikle Carleith, almost due south of Monk farm. This quarry was disused by 1897. The limekilns associated with this working were located adjacent to the quarry, and were two in number. A small quarry and limekiln also existed immediately east of Little Carleith, next to the Killoch Burn.

In 1836 production of lime in Sorn parish was noted as 9,000 bolls, according to the *New Statistical Account*.

QUARRYING

A number of quarries have existed in Sorn parish at various times, sometimes only opened up to allow stone for building to be obtained, at other times worked for a longer period to supply demand for stone. Near to Bridgend of Montgarswood was a flagstone quarry. It was disused by 1856.

In the vicinity of Sorn Castle, according to the *Statistical Account* of 1796, there was a quarry from which 'a beautiful kind of stone, of a blue-grey colour, and of a close texture, which takes a polish little inferior to that of marble, and is therefore admirably fitted for the purposes of hearth-stones, pavements, steps of stairs, etc.' Another place where a marble-like stone could be found was on the north-east corner of the parish, but this remained unworked.

In a deep glen on the east side of the parish spar has been worked, but only in small quantities. The spar quarry was located at Burntshield Burn, now known as the Wyndy Burn. It operated at the end of the eighteenth century, but not to any great extent.

Stone had been quarried in a small scale over the years as building projects demanded it. By the side of the River Ayr, at the west end of the Kilnknow Park, a sandstone quarry worked stone, perhaps used when Sorn Castle was extended in the nineteenth century. A steel crane at the head of the quarry was used to haul the stone up onto a roadway that led to the public road at Smiddyshaw. The quarry was disused by 1910.

Lead was found near to Holhousemill, but was never really worked on any commercial scale.

The original Tincornhill Quarry was established before the First World War and was leased for many years to Ayr County Council. The roads department used the whinstone in the construction of roads. It was closed sometime after the Second World War.

The large Tincornhill Quarry to the east of Sorn was established in 1993 by Barr Ltd. The whinstone quarried was used for various building projects all over southern Scotland, as well as in the manufacture of concrete at their Killoch plant in Ochiltree parish. For the previous three years the residents of the village had campaigned against the reopening of the quarry, claiming that it would destroy the locality. As part of a goodwill gesture towards the parishioners, who would have to endure numerous lorries hauling the stone through the village, and a legal requirement of the planning consent, the Tincornhill Quarry Fund was established. Barr Holdings Ltd. contributes £10,000 in cash and £5,000 in kind to a fund which can be used to assist projects that will benefit the parish of Sorn. The fund will operate for a period of 15 years and will be used for long-term sustainable environmental projects.

MILLS

The River Ayr has been dammed at a number of locations and the waters diverted to drive mills. At the west end of the village is the former Dalgain Mill, now the church hall. This mill was used for milling corn and was the barony mill, the place where the parishioners had to take their corn for milling. To pay for this work, a percentage, or multure, was kept by the miller. Thirlage to particular mills was still the custom in 1796 but it was removed in 1799 when the 'Thirlage Act' was passed, which allowed tenants to break free from having to use particular mills. The dam was located almost opposite the roadway into the manse, and Damside Cottage was named after it. From the dam a lade directed the water alongside the roadway for 800 yards to the mill. The wheel was a breast paddle type. The mill had three pairs of stones used for grinding oatmeal and other provender. The mill building was three storeys in height. Millers at Dalgain were Robert and Hugh Wilson (1837) and Hugh Wilson (1851). In 1868 David (1800-74) and Robert MacNay were recorded as being the millers and farmers here. In 1890 Thomas Clark was the tenant of the mill, but at the time William Gray was recorded as being the miller.

Gray held the full tenancy by 1900. Dalgain Mill was closed around 1913 and latterly was used as a collecting place for milk, or a creamery. The building was converted into a church hall in 1927, the large skylights being added at that time.

The New Mill was located at the east end of the village, the site now occupied by the new houses in Woolmill Place. This was a worsted mill and was probably erected between 1843 and 1855. The curved dam was located 1,200 yards upstream,

7.3 Woolmill, Sorn *(Elizabeth Johnstone)*

near to Dalgain farm, and the lade directed the waters to the mill wheel. As there is no reference to this mill in the *New Statistical Account*, which was written in July 1837, it is thought that the mill was erected sometime after. In 1855 there is reference to Thomas Hendry, a 'worset' spinner in the village. The mill remained the property of the Hendry family for around 50 years. In 1901 New Mill, by then the property of Thomas Hendry & Son, Worsted Spinners, of which the sole partner was William Hendry, was sequestrated. Around this time the mill machinery was removed, and the building was converted into a woodworking shop. Here 'fiddles', which were used for sowing seed, were manufactured. The building was partially demolished in 1930 and converted into a store, used at various times by James Alston, blacksmith, Robert Johnston, coal merchant, and by James Murdoch for slating materials. Part of the old mill was used as an old men's recreation hall and a room was used by Sorn Athletic Club. At this time the mill and lands were part of the Oliver of Gilmilnscroft estate. The former mill buildings were demolished in the mid 1990s prior to the present houses being erected.

Holhouse Mill stands in ruins on the opposite side of the River Ayr from Waterside farm, at Glenlogan. The earliest reference to it appears to be from 1646, when it was acquired by John Campbell of Crossflat (Muirkirk) on the death of his brother, along with Brocklerdyke, Holehouse and Sund. In 1851 James Struthers is noted as being the farmer here and Thomas Murdoch lived at the mill – the mill was probably abandoned by this time. By 1868 it is noted that John MacCrae farmed here. He was followed by his son, Andrew MacCrae. When Andrew died in 1915 the mill was probably abandoned as a house, for by 1919 it is described as being in ruins. The mill appears to have been an oatmeal mill at one time, but latterly became a small farm, the mill lade being filled in. The mill building, which still stands in ruins, was built of river boulders set in mortar, the exterior faces of which have been roughly dressed. All the walls are two feet thick, apart from that on which the mill-wheel was supported, which is two feet four inches thick. A low circular base of around 30 feet in diameter may have been either a threshing floor or horse-gin. It is thought that a separate building nearby housed a kiln for drying grain.

There are believed to have been two mills in existence on the south side of the River Ayr, one of these perhaps being Wheelhouse. The mill lade was at one time still traceable. Further downstream, between Damhead and Bridgend, stood Linthouse, which was a lint or flax mill. Both of these mills seem to have become disused at an early period, perhaps when the planned village was created on the north side of the river.

Around one mile downstream from Sorn, on the holm below Sorn Hill, was a waulk mill, but this was disused by 1856, when the first Ordnance Survey maps were surveyed. The mill was used for fulling cloth. John MacMurtrie died at Waukmill in 1857 aged 87. The house survived for a time, and was occupied in the early 1900s by Mrs Stewart, whose donkey carried milk on panniers into Catrine. The land around the former mill was later used as a nursery, being operated in the 1940s by Robert Dale & Sons of Hillhead Nurseries.

An old plan of East Montgarswood farm, dated 25 September 1823, notes that there was the 'site of old mill' on the Mill Holm, downstream from Bridgend of Montgarswood.

OTHER TRADES

A tileworks existed at Bridgend at one time. This was located on the southern side of the Mauchline road, east of the Burn o' Need. The buildings formed a large 'U' shape, and the clay pit used for making the tiles was located east of the works. The works were in existence by the time of the 1857 Six Inch Ordnance Survey map, and date from sometime after 1825, the year in which the Duke of Portland is reckoned to have introduced tile drainage as a method of improving land to Ayrshire. The works disappeared early in the twentieth century.

Within Sorn was a smithy that had existed for many years. In 1782 William Hunter was a smith in the village, living at that time at 'Sandbed Holm of Dalgain'. In the late 1820s and up to 1837 at least, it was operated by David Boyle. Boyle was noted for a number of innovations, and he made one of the first iron ploughs to be used in Ayrshire. In fact, the first such plough in Tarbolton parish was made by Boyle.

A grandson of David Boyle was another David Boyle (1842-1911), who became the Superintendent of the Provincial Museum of the Ontario Education Department in Toronto, Canada. He was born at Greenock on 1 May 1842 and emigrated to Canada at the age of fourteen. He was apprenticed as a blacksmith in Canada but his interest in archaeology grew, and he became a noted archaeologist in Ontario. In 1888 the Canadian Institute Museum appointed Boyle as Canada's

7.4 Sandbed, Sorn *(Baird Institute)*

first full-time professional archaeologist. From 1896 to 1911 he served as curator at the Ontario Provincial Museum, a forerunner of the Royal Ontario Museum. He collected many artefacts in the 1890s and early 1900s and contributed much to the anthropological collections at the museum. His work laid the groundwork for the development of Ontario archaeology as a systematic and scientific discipline. From 1887 to 1911 he published his *Annual Archaeological Reports* for Ontario, the first Canadian periodical devoted primarily to the study of the archaeological record. As well as his work in history, Boyle was the author of a book of nonsense poetry for children! He died at Toronto on 14 February 1911. His biography, *David Boyle, from Artisan to Archaeologist*, was written by Gerald Killan and published in Canada

7.5 Waulkmill, Sorn *(Baird Institute)*

in 1983. Today Boyle is remembered through The Boyle Memorial Lectureship in Archaeology, which finances lectures by archaeological visitors to the Department of Anthropology at Ontario University.

Sometime around 1880 James Alston and his family moved to Sorn from Muirkirk to take over the smiddy, shoeing horses and repairing agricultural implements. James Alston (1859-1922) succeeded as the blacksmith in 1894 and was noted for his part in organising Sorn's 'Wee Race'. The smiddy operated until the mid 1950s. The former premises were later converted into a garage, which now specialises in the sale and repair of motorcycles.

Another smithy in the parish appears to have existed at Wealth o' Waters, William Piper (1780-1852) being noted as smith there. His family later moved to Barrshouse, where they operated a smithy for a time. A descendant, James Reid Piper, was a clerk at Pennelburn mine but moved to Grange, Burntisland, where he operated The Grange Whisky Distillery. This was sold around 1925 when he moved into farming, and tried to breed 'the ideal stock' of cattle in farm buildings designed and erected by himself. On 12 February 1936 he sold a bull at Perth market for 2,200 guineas, which was a considerable price at the time. Piper was a considerable benefactor to the parish church for many years.

7.6 Barrshouse *(William Frew)*

The arrival of the motor car resulted in a couple of garages being established in the village. One of these was operated by W. & N. Anderson (by the 1930s), who also had two petrol pumps to supply the needs of the vehicles. Anderson hired out motor cars, as did Robert Lightbody Jr., who had the second garage in Sorn.

In 1837 a number of carpenters and joiners existed in Sorn, namely John Baird, John Caldow at the New Mill, Sorn, John Gemmell at Lintmill, Robert Granger at Holmhead, and Hugh MacCulloch. In 1900 Alexander Gibson had a joiner's shop in the Main Street.

Gas was produced on Sorn estate in the 1800s for use in the castle. The Gas Cottage was located within the estate policies, but by 1900 it was occupied by John Dougan, ploughman, and by 1940 by George Campbell, the estate carter.

A pottery seems to have operated at Sorn in the early 1800s. What was produced there is not known, but it was probably basic kitchenware. The Pottery Row Cottage survived long after the pottery closed, and in 1941 was owned by William Withers, a joiner.

Along the same side of the River Ayr from the Pottery Cottage is another old cottage, known as Stepend. Owned by Gilmilnscroft estate, it was run as a laundry, in 1941 being operated by Mrs Jessie Proctor.

At Westtown farm a well was sunk into the natural rock to extract mineral water from the ground. A partnership named Burns County Mineral Water Ltd. was incorporated on 27 December 1995 to bottle the water in a plant at Westtown farm and sell it to Water Direct, which supplied water coolers to offices and workplaces. The partners were G. & A. Henderson of Westtown and Mr & Mrs Whillock of Blythswood Enterprises Ltd. Burns County was closed down in 2001 when the Henderson family set up Sorn Spring Water Company Ltd. which continues with the bottling and supply of mineral water to customers.

SHOPS

In Sorn village a number of small shops have existed over the centuries. In the late 1820s Peggy Barbour ran a small sweetshop, located between the old mill and the smithy. There children lucky enough to have some money could buy 'blackman, peppermints, ballads, bakes, bawbee-scones and bools.' William Lapraik (1800-56) was a merchant in the village. In 1837 Robert Kirkland Dalgleish was a grocer, as well as a wholesale dealer in meal and cheese, and ran the post office. John Ferguson is also noted in 1837 as being a grocer and dealer in meal and cheese in the village. At the same time Hugh Baird and Robert Wilson in Damside operated shops or business premises.

There were four boot and shoemakers at work in Sorn in 1837 - James Lapraik, John Reid, Hugh Simpson and John Wilson. Andrew Scott was a tailor.

In 1837 J. Pigot and Company compiled a directory for Ayrshire in which Sorn was listed. At the time the village post office was run by Robert Kirkland Dalgleish, and there are details on the delivery and despatch of the mail – 'letters from Kilmarnock and north arrive every morning at seven, and are despatched every afternoon at half past two. Letters from England arrive from Douglas every afternoon at half past two and are despatched every morning at seven. Letters from Mauchline arrive (by foot post) every morning at half past nine, and from Cumnock every night at nine and are despatched every afternoon at half past two.'

Helen Steven noted that around 1850 the mail gig with letters and parcels from Ayr and Kilmarnock bound for London passed through the village every morning. Mail was collected at Sorn and letters were transferred to the Glasgow to London

7.7 Coalford *(Baird Institute)*

coach at Douglas Mill. Letters would reach London 44 hours after being lifted at Sorn. In 1898 a post-cart carried the mail from Sorn to Mauchline every day. The Post Office had Elizabeth Dalgleish as postmistress in 1867 and Robert Watson as postmaster in 1901, and he held this position for many years. Watson also acted as session clerk to the church and Registrar. The sub-postmistress in 1941 was Helen S. Anderson. The post office was originally located in a building in what was Dalgain Street, but it was relocated to its present position at the north-eastern end of Sorn New Bridge, within Coalford house. The Sorn office was closed on 25 September 2002 and for a few years the village was not serviced by the post office. However, in December 2004 Eileen Paterson re-opened the post office as well as Eileen's shop in the same building.

In 1867 Isaac Slater's *Directory* lists some businesses that existed in Sorn at that time. David Gibson ran a bakery, James Alston was a blacksmith, James Baird and Robert Watson were boot and shoe makers, John Headley had a joinery, Hugh Simpson was a flesher or butcher and also a grocer, Elizabeth Dalgleish had a small grocery, in addition to the post office, Mary Struthers was a linen and woollen draper, John Andrews was a tailor, and Helen Merry and Agnes Retson were dress-makers or milliners. John Cameron operated as a mason, Thomas Hendry as a worsted spinner, and William MacMillan was a miller.

In 1900 the village had five or six shops. James Murdoch had a grocery, as did William Hendry, who was a provision merchant and woolspinner. Another shop was operated by Mrs Jessie Bryce and a fourth by Mrs Elizabeth Jardine or Caldwell. Thomas Irvine Caldwell operated this shop in 1934, located in what was the old post office. Charles Nisbet had a bakery in Main Street. Other business premises in the village included Joseph Johnstone's tailor's workshop, Robert Watson's shoemaking workshop, and Alexander Gibson's joinery shop.

A branch of Catrine Co-operative Society Limited was opened in the village in 1926, at first located in the shop belonging to Jane Murdoch, Coalford. By 1928 a purpose-built shop was erected in Main Street. This was supplied by the larger shops and warehouses in Catrine and customers were able to collect their dividend for making purchases at Sorn. The Co-op had been established in Catrine on 23 March 1866, enrolled as a co-operative society on 17 April 1866. The drapery, boot and shoe department in Catrine was opened on 8th July 1873. During the Second World War the small Sorn shop was operated by Sarah Jane Harrison, and in later years it was operated by Mrs Brown. The shop premises were rather small, but it had a distinguished façade with two pillar-like buttresses topped by ball-finials. The co-op shop was closed in the 1960s and the commercial front was removed and the building refitted as the old-folks' cabin and meeting room.

CHAPTER EIGHT

AGRICULTURE

In the second half of the eighteenth century there were great strides forward in agriculture. It was at this time that the fields were first created, with the planting of hedges and the erection of stone dikes. In the 1780s many of the farm houses in the parish were rebuilt, and many of the smaller pendicles or crofts were merged with neighbouring farms to create larger units. In around twelve cases the old croft house was abandoned. Thus, in the eighteenth and early nineteenth centuries, the following farms became redundant, their houses either being left to fall into ruins or cleared away: Yardneuk, Roddinhead, Berryhill, Plucks, Tinkhorn, Brownknowe, High Blindburn, Greenfaulds, Blairkibbock, Scroggs, Burnside, Shillingland, Backside, Neuk, Bruntland, Todhills and a number of others.

Of those farms that were rebuilt, mention should be made of Auchencloigh farm, on the Galston road, which had a marriage lintel erected when the farm house was rebuilt. This bears the initials *17 JR ◊ IP 29*, which stands for James Richmond and Isabel Paterson (portioner of Carleith) who were married on 27 August 1724.

On the estates farms were let for either eighteen or nineteen years. In 1796 older leases tended to be for five shillings per acre, or thereabouts, but new leases made saw the rent increase to around 10 or 12 shillings per acre. Better quality ground near to the village, and the holms of the River Ayr, were leased at up to 20 or 30 shillings per acre, or in a few cases more.

There were some restrictions on what the tenant farmer could do, such as he could only plough one third of the land at one time, a cycle of oats for two years, the third year bear or grass, the fourth hay, and the next five years pasture. However, it was noted that this cycle was not adhered to, and the farmers often just grew oats for three or four years, followed by five years of pasture.

The old *Statistical Account* of 1796 gives a picture of agriculture in the parish at that time. It describes the parish as having around 13,460 acres (about 57% of the parish total) of arable soils, though not all was in a state of cultivation. There were about 200 acres of woodland, 3,000 acres of moss and 7,000 acres of hills, moors and other pastures. The soil could yield a good crop of oats. Few of the tenants had more than a ploughgate of land (that is, around 50 acres, though the figure appears to be indetermined, sometimes described as being the amount of land that can be successfully ploughed by an individual), and most had much less.

In 1796 there were around 5,000 black-face sheep in the parish, 240 horses and 1,470 black-cattle. Around two-thirds of the cattle were milch-cows, the rest being young cattle. It was noted that a number of farmers had moved to Sorn from Dunlop parish, and with them brought the method of making Dunlop cheese, which became the norm. Some of the cheese and butter produce was sold as far away as the Glasgow markets. A few farmers had introduced pigs. There were around 80 ploughs and 160 carts. Potatoes were a stable diet for the residents, almost everyone growing their own, and in some cases they were fed to the cattle and horses.

It was also noted in the *Statistical Account* that many of the small proprietors in the parish, who owned their own small farms or pendicles had been negligent of their lands, and were forced into mortgaging their property. With little to repay the debts, these properties, worth £50 to £100 per year, needed to be sold off. Others in the parish, 'though men of sober and inoffensive characters, yet discover no spirit of activity or enterprise... Their lands, accordingly, are, for the most part, worse cultivated than those of the tenants, who pay a reasonable rent; their habitations are in some instances more wretched, and their mode of living in every respect more uncomfortable.'

During the Victorian era many farmhouses were enlarged, and farms extended, taking in former crofts or smallholdings. East Montgarswood was built in 1831 by Henry Richmond, the old steading (which became Montgarswood Cottage) being occupied by the farm foreman. On Sorn estate, Graham Somervell engaged the Kilmarnock architect, William Railton, to design a new farm steading, the drawing dated 22 May 1857. His successor, T. W. McIntyre, engaged Ingram & Brown, of Kilmarnock, to design other alterations to various buildings on Sorn estate. Farmhouses that were rebuilt elsewhere include Auchencloigh, erected in 1890. Many old steadings were abandoned by 1897, when the Ordnance Survey compiled detailed maps of the parish, such as Dallyearnoch, Benniehill, Plucks, Tincornhill, Benthead, Burnhead, Lindsayhill and East Whiteflat.

Graham Russell Somervell of Sorn Castle was a keen supporter of his agricultural tenants, and encouraged them in the improvement of their farms. In September 1870 he brought Miss Harding to the parish in order to teach the wives and daughters of the farmers on his estate the principles of making Cheddar cheese. In the early 1880s he instituted a class in Sorn to teach the young farmers agricultural chemistry, employing Alexander Goldie of the Science and Art Department of Darvel Public School to carry this out. To encourage the tenants to improve their output, he also instituted an annual competition for dairy produce from tenants of Sorn and Dalgain estates.

James Somervell of Sorn Castle did much to improve the herd of cattle he had on the estate, and to maximise his return was to establish the Sorn Dairy Company. The main centre for this was Hillhead farm, which lies near to the castle, and the business was one of the first to bottle milk in Scotland. Somervell's improvements made Sorn something of 'a kind of 'Mecca' of improved dairying long before the formation of the Kilmarnock Dairy School,' according to Helen Steven, writing in 1898. In 1887 the Glasgow International Exhibition had a model working dairy and

8.1 Sorn from Woodhead *(William Frew)*

this was operated by Somervell's business. The milk was bottled in stoneware containers, made from clay, many of them having two shades of brown as their finished colour, though most were left the natural fired clay colour. The containers came in a variety of sizes and all bore the legend 'Sorn Dairy Supply'. A Cumnock Pottery pouring jug, probably used to fill containers from large milk churns, still survives.

The milk was taken from Sorn to Glasgow on a daily basis, where it was sold to the residents. One method of transportation used was by steam engine, hauling a cart in which the milk bottles were loaded. The steam engine bore a brass plaque with the legend 'James Somervell Esq. of Sorn'. Previously the milk would have been transported by horse and cart, for it is known that the Sorn Dairy Supply Company erected a stable and dormitory at 91 Sanda Street, off Queen Margaret Drive, in the North Kelvin area of Glasgow. This was erected at a cost of £1,000 and was erected in 1893 to plans by William Ingram, of W. & R. S. Ingram architects.

Most of the farms were still part of larger estates at the start of the twentieth century. Major landowners at that time were the Somervells of Sorn Castle,

Farquhars of Gilmilnscroft, Campbells of Glaisnock and Auchmannoch, and the Rankens of Glenlogan. Other groups of farms belonged to estates that were centred on mansions outwith the parish, such as the Alexanders of Ballochmyle, Campbells of Fairfield, Boswells of Auchinleck, Lord Howard de Walden, Marquis of Bute, Hamilton-Campbells of Netherplace, Howatson of Glenbuck, and Tufnell of Dallars.

Many of the estate owners began to sell off some of their property to the sitting tenants. In 1919 the Duke of Portland's estate sold Auchencloigh farm to the tenant, William Bone, for £4,300. In 1921 the Boswell's Auchinleck estate was partially broken up and Whiteflat farm was sold to the tenant, Mungo Bryson. In 1936, for example, James Frew made arrangements to purchase Barrshouse from Gilmilnscroft estate, the final payment being made to the owners of the estate in 1951.

In 1951, at the time of the *Third Statistical Account*, it was noted that there were around 70 farms and five small-holdings in the parish. Most farms were from 50 to 200 acres in size, averaging about 80 acres, usually with a dairy herd of around 25-30 cows, but on the higher hills the farms could be up to 3,000 acres in extent and used for sheep breeding.

In the twentieth century more small farms were abandoned and many were either cleared away or left to fall into ruins, their land being merged with neighbouring farms to create larger holdings. Farms disappearing at this time include West Heateth, Little Blackdyke, Mid Montgarswood and Springhill.

Middle, West and East Whiteflat farm were abandoned and later incorporated into Whiteflat farm. Middle Whiteflat had comprised of a house and adjoining byre, all of which was thatched. The building was burned to the ground in the early 1900s and never rebuilt. West, or Wee, Whiteflat was condemned around 1970. East Whiteflat disappeared before 1895.

The tower at Smiddyshaw farm was erected sometime in the late eighteenth century, probably as a wind-powered threshing mill, though the tower seems to have had multiple uses. The tower stands around 27 feet in height, and is octagonal in plan, around 16 feet across the flats. At present it rises through three storeys, each of which diminishes in height, the floor line marked externally by string courses. The first floor is around 15 feet above ground level and was originally used as a doocot. Around the walls are nesting boxes built from sandstone slabs, around two inches thick, on hand-made red bricks. The tower probably had a fourth floor, on which the windmill was located, but this has long-since gone. The tower, which was visible from Sorn Castle, was also ornamental in design to be a feature of the immediate policies.

In April 1994 David Shaw of Crofthead farm established Sorn Milk Ltd, in an attempt at maximising the return to farmers for their milk. The firm collects milk produced by a number of local farmers and sells it on to Lockerbie Creamery, where half is turned into cheese and half into butter. In 2008 the company was collecting milk from 86 farms across Ayrshire, Dumfriesshire and Lanarkshire, totalling 84 million litres per annum. Some of the milk is sent as far as Chester. In 2002 the firm also created the 'White and Wild' labled milk, which is sold to the customer as a quality milk produced by more environmentally friendly farms, where care is taken to protect and promote the natural wildlife. This milk, originally bottled by Graham's Dairies of Stirling and now by Wiseman Dairies, is sold at a premium to the customer.

8.2 Auchencloigh farm - c.1900 *(David Bone)*

Sorn Parish Agricultural Association was founded in 1872, though for a time used the name Catrine Agricultural Association. One of the first presidents was Charles Howatson of Glenbuck (who lived at Daldorch House) and T. Aitken was secretary. The association still organises an annual show, which for many years was held on the Burn Park at Catrine, by permission of the Alexanders of Ballochmyle, but which was moved to the Holm Field, near to Howford Bridge, where it is still held.

CHAPTER NINE

RECREATION

Sorn Constitutional Club was founded in 1832 and a Constitutional Hall was erected and presented to the club by James Somervell of Sorn Castle. This was located in Dalgain Street. In 1922 the hall was in danger of being closed, due to the difficulties in paying the rates. The *Sorn Parish Magazine* of February 1922 gives an indication of the uses made of the hall at that time – the Men's Club met in the building, and summer ice, billiards, draughts and dominoes were available to play. The hall was closed when the new Village Hall was opened. The hall, which was two stories in height, was later converted to become part of the Greyhound Inn, which was adjoining. As with the inn, the hall is now converted to housing.

The Village Hall was erected by public contribution. A fund-raising committee had raised money for a number of years, the chairman being J. G. Stephen of Glenlogan. The hall was officially opened in 1954 and has been used for many functions and groups ever since.

9.1 Drummer, Sorn Race Day
(William Frew)

At one time the Sorn Races were a highlight of the social year. The first race appears to have been held around 1750, in the month of March. When the races took place traders from neighbouring communities came to Sorn, resulting in a form of fair. It was also a time when many of the farmers and shepherds in the parish were able to meet and pass on gossip to each other. There were two main races – the 'big race' and the 'wee race', the latter taking place on the second day. The big race was for horses, but by 1898 Helen Steven noted that this had fallen in stature to something of a farce. The only horse taking part was one that had already been used to transport pigs in a cart from Kilmarnock. Once the pigs were offloaded, the horse was taken to the race field and being the only entrant was an obvious winner. The wee race had the local children as competitors. A collection raised money for prizes, and the children ran the length of the main street. At the race day the Drumclog drum and halberd were carried around the village, attracting the attention of the residents. The drum, which was said to have been used at the Battle of Drumclog in 1679, was for around 60 years beaten by Andrew 'Blackie' Reid, who was the last weaver in the village. The drum appears to have been repaired in 1751. When it was beat the children started running, and they had to make their way round the halberdier and back to the start. After the races the locals took part in a meal of veal and oatmeal and a dance in the hall.

William Aitken, the 'Railway Poet', wrote one of his verses on the Sorn Races:

And when the schule clock hauns drew near the magic 'our o' twa,
Oot cam the ancient halberdier, the committee and a';
'Wee Jamie' lookin' lairge as life, wi' swallow-tail and lum,
'Co' threshin' at it wi' the fife, and 'Blackey' wi' the drum...

The horses were a'body's talk – some five were entered in,
The first o' which could scarcely walk, the next yin couldna rin,
The third was no like yin wad fag, but then 'twas nearly blin',
The fourth yin was a sorry nag – a bag o' banes an' skin;
The fifth, though like a racin' beast, rode by a pigman chiel,
Wad no dae ought but jump and re'ist, and caper through the fiel';
A mair unlikely lookin' set could hardly shown their face,
Yet oot the five 'twas thocht we'd get a fairish kind o' race.

The children's race, which continued long after the horse race had stopped, seems to have died out shortly before the Second World War, if not before.

At Auchencloigh a hall was established in 1924 for the use of the rural community at the north end of the parish. The local Women's Rural Institute had been very successful and required a larger meeting place. In 1923 and 1924 funds were raised and on 14 February 1924 a public meeting was held in the community school. Alexander Watson of Barboigh was elected chairman of the new trustees. Miss Moir, president of the W.R.I. announced that the treasurer had placed £100 in the bank to start the hall fund. A collection made from families living within 3 miles of the hall had raised a substantial amount of money. It was agreed to commence work on a new hall, 50 feet by 24 feet

9.2 Halberdier, Sorn Race Day
(William Frew)

externally, designed by Hugh Hyslop of Mauchline, and it was to be built from materials carted free by local farmers. The feu for the hall was offered by William Bone of Auchencloigh, set at 2s 6d per annum. The foundations were dug by volunteers on 19 April 1924 and on 5 May 'practically every farmer in the district was carting building materials from Garroch Burn to Auchencloigh', building work starting that very afternoon. The hall, the cost of £233 paid for by subscription, was opened on Friday 27 June 1924 by J. Harling Turner CBE of Cessnock Castle, followed by a concert, tea and dance. A new kitchen was added in 1927, water was supplied to the hall in 1943 and electricity in 1951. The hall has been used by the Women's Rural, Auchencloigh Dramatic Club (founded in 1925 by Betty MacTaggart and disbanded in 1951), dancing club, and a carpet bowling club over the years. A new constitution was drawn up in 1998. The hall is still operated by Auchencloigh Hall Trustees, the chairmen of the trustees being Alexander Watson JP of Barboigh (1924-1942), James D. Anderson (1942-1958), John W. Jamieson (1958-1972), Matthew B. Jamieson (1972-1989) and Andrew Jamieson.

Sorn Curling Society was founded on 21 February 1795, the first meeting taking place at the Greenfoot Inn, Sorn. At the meeting those present decided that they would meet annually on the second Monday of January to elect office bearers. The first president elected was John Farquhar Gray of Gilmilnscroft and the other directors were Hugh Breakenridge, John Reid (treasurer), Hugh Caldar, George Rankin (secretary), John and William Goldie, William and James Kirkland and John Nimmo. There was an artificial curling pond created at Blindburn at one time. The small stream that flows on the south side of the farm was dammed at the roadside and a triangular pond was formed to the east of the public road, between it and the wood. It was known as the Lees Loch, and the curlers stored their stones at the nearby Lees cottage. A second large curling pond in the parish was located by the side of the Catrine branch railway, in the hollow between Clews Mount and Kenstey farm. This curling pond was an elongated rectangle in shape. A third curling pond was created on the level ground below the western front of Glenlogan House. An elongated rectangle in shape, dating to sometime after 1909, this pond can still be made out on the ground.

The curling team played against many local teams, being successful visitors on many occasions. It was common in the nineteenth century for teams to play each other with a prize of £5 or a load of meal for the poor to be supplied by the losers. An example was the match organised between Sorn (under Graham Somervell of Sorn Castle) and Thornhill (under Mr Villiers of Closeburn) on 30 December 1878. Ten rinks a side were played, Sorn winning by 60 shots. As a result Mr Villiers paid £5 for the poor of Sorn and Catrine. In 1879 Sorn and Auchinleck parishes joined to play Old and New Cumnock parishes at Lochside, New Cumnock. There were 160 players a side in the great bonspiel, Auchinleck and Sorn winning by 36 shots. The prize was one ton of meal for the poor of the parishes, but Charles Howatson of Daldorch gifted 4 bolls of meal to the losing parishes.

The celebrated Eglinton Jug trophy was won by the Sorn club on a number of occasions, including 1882 when they beat Mauchline by 3 shots.

Sorn Sheepdog Trials Association held annual dog trials in October each year, often at Blindburn farm. Sorn Farmers' Union existed in 1950.

Quoiting was a popular sport prior to the First World War, after which it struggled on for some years before virtually dying out. The last minute of Sorn Quoiting Club was written in 1936, when the club finally folded. Thomas Walker McIntyre of Sorn Castle donated a large silver cup for annual competition to Sorn Quoiting Club in August 1912. Notable quoiters from Sorn included Robert Lightbody, who was a taxi-driver in the early 1900s.

Football was played on a small scale in the parish, though no junior teams from

9.3 Sorn Quoiters *(Baird Institute)*

Sorn appear to have joined any of the local leagues. Sorn Juveniles played for a time in the field at the north-east corner of the crossroads at Smiddyshaw farm, before relocating to the recreation ground in the village. Spectators would stand on Sorn Bank to view the games. Catrine had a number of junior teams over the years, and many of the Sorn boys played with them. In the 1920s one of the Catrine teams played on a field at Meadowside, kindly loaned by Robert Graham in High Logan. Nevertheless, some sons of the parish did excel in the sport, among these being James Frew (1895-1985), who played for Cronberry Eglinton, Nithsdale Wanderers, Kilmarnock F.C., Stamford Bridge F.C., Chelsea (1922-7) and Carlisle. James Frew was captain of Carlisle for a time, but he retired from the sport in 1931.

A number of juvenile football clubs have operated in the village over the years, such as Sorn Thistle and Sorn Boys' Club.

A Golf Course was located on Sorn Hill, to the south west of Sorn Castle. The

9.4 Sorn Castle Golf Club *(Jamie McIntyre)*

land was owned by Sorn estate, and a Golf Club House was erected on Sorn Hill for the players. The course was established sometime around 1910. The clubhouse was used during the First World War for various functions, but the course was closed for the duration of the war. The golf club appears to have re-opened on 22 September 1922 and operated for a number of years thereafter. It was closed a year or two after Ballochmyle Golf Club was opened at Mauchline in 1937.

From 1991 onward the British Long-Bow Society in Scotland held a number

9.5 Sorn Castle Golf Clubhouse *(Jamie McIntyre)*

of competitions on local estates, in 1991 at Gilmilnscroft, in 1992 at Sorn Castle, and in 1993 at Glenlogan. However, the number of archers in attendance soon became too great for these venues, and the competition was moved to Culzean Castle.

For boys the 39th Ayrshire (Sorn) Scout Troop existed from 1928, being formed by Rev James Gegg, who acted as Scoutmaster initially. For girls the Sorn Girl Guides troop existed around the turn of the century, operating during the First World War.

An interest in politics was fostered amongst the residents, and various local branches of political parties were established. Sorn and Catrine Conservative Association was instituted on 15 January 1872, the main office bearers being local lairds, including Somervell of Sorn, Farquhar of Gilmilnscroft, Colonel John Robert Fairlie of Daldorch, and Charles Howatson of Glenbuck. Catrine and Sorn Liberal Association was instituted on 19 August 1884, mainly under the guiding hand of the Catrine ministers, Rev James M. Copland and Rev Aeneas C. Gordon.

A Sorn Men's Club was formed around 1948 and was gifted part of the old

9.6 Sorn Scouts at Wellwood *(William Frew)*

Wool Mill which they converted into a recreation room, opened in October 1949. The billiard table was gifted by David Ross of Gilmilnscroft. The club held regular meetings and lectures, on subjects as diverse as the 'History of Education' or 'Hiking in the Highlands'.

Many other organisations have existed in the village over the years (some linked with Catrine) — Sorn Dramatic Society (founded 1923), Sorn Players, a dramatic society which existed in the 1950s; Sorn and Catrine Horticultural Society, and Sorn and Catrine Nurse Scheme.

Sorn Bowling Club was founded in 1977 under the guidance of its first president, William Hale. The club created a new bowling green on land that had formerly been houses, to the east of the Sorn Inn. A timber club house was added, and the club has gone from strength to strength ever since.

The Catrine, Sorn and District Local History Group was founded on 24 April 1986, its first chairman being Edna McElroy of Mill Cottage, Sorn. Meeting regularly in Catrine since that time, the group have been active in preserving the history of the area, both by campaigning to save local heritage, and by publishing local histories. They produced *The Busy Wee Toon where the Drum aye gaed roon, At half-past five in the morning – A Collection of Verses from Catrine and Sorn*, in 1988, edited by Mary Bunting, and *200 Years of Catrine and Sorn Parish: A Cotton Tale*, in 1987, edited by Robert Dalziel and Terry Harrison.

CHAPTER TEN

SONS AND DAUGHTERS

WILLIAM AITKEN (1851-1931)

Buried in the kirkyard is William Aitken, who gained some fame as 'The Railway Poet'. His gravestone, which is located on the left side of the path approaching the church door from the gate, is inscribed:

> *William Aitken, Ex-Inspector G&SWRy. Born at Sorn 26th March 1851, died at Greenock 27th Oct 1931. Jean McClymont Richmond, wife of the above William Aitken, died at Greenock 30th April 1934 in her 83rd year.*

William Aitken was born in Sorn on 26 March 1851, which happened to be 'Wee Race Day', the son of a shoemaker. Whilst still a youth he moved with his family to Bridgend of Montgarswood. At the age of eight he started working in the fields and at the age of ten he was apprenticed as a shoemaker under James Baird at Bridgend. He had little formal education, only attending school when he could. On the first Monday in May 1871 he started work as a signalman at Kilmacolm for the Glasgow and South Western Railway Company. He was later employed as a district officer at Kilmarnock and Glasgow for the same company. At an early age William Aitken had begun writing poems, and he sent these to various local newspapers. His poems are shrewd observations on human life and character, and many of his more popular works were accounts of incidents and events in the life of the railway. As such he became known as the 'Railway Poet' or the

10.1 William Aitken's Gravestone, Sorn Parish Churchyard *(Dane Love)*

'Laureate of the Line'. His first book of poems was entitled *Rhymes and Readings*, published in 1880, with a preface by Rev Dr Rankine. *Lays of the Line* was published in 1882. In 1893 a third book of his poems was published, entitled *Echoes of the Iron Road*. In 1913 he published another work, entitled *Songs of the South-West*. Aitken became an Inspector on the Glasgow and South Western Railway. Aitken was a devout man, and for a time was active in the Railway Mission at Greenock, which he founded in 1885 under the name the Railwaymen's Christian Association. He was a member of the Congregational Church in Greenock, and was superintendent of the Sunday School. He composed an address entitled 'I'm jist a boy', which became a popular recitation piece at Band of Hope and Sunday School recitals.

Aitken died at Greenock on 27 October 1931 aged 80 years.

ADAM BROWN TODD (1822-1915)

Adam Brown Todd was born at Craighall on 6 February 1822, the fourteenth child of a small tenant farmer. Craighall stood on the northern side of Glover's Hill, between the farms of Barwheys and Boghead (of which it became part), in Mauchline parish. It no longer exists. Todd's father, Matthew, (1768-1850) had taken on the lease at Whitsunday 1795. He was a contemporary of Robert Burns, and knew him. His mother, Mary Gibb (1779-1861), was the daughter of James Gibb of Auchmillan. Young Todd moved to Barrshouse, south of Sorn, at Whitsunday 1826. It was from Barrshouse that Todd attended the village school in Sorn, which was located at the north end of the Auld Brig, adjacent to the kirkyard. In his *The Poetical Works with Autobiography*, he recalls the time when he was sitting at his desk in the school, looking out into the kirkyard. The level of the ground in the kirkyard was higher than the floor level in the schoolroom, and he gazed up at Saunders MacGowan as he dug a hole for a burial. The earth was being piled up against the school, and Todd was given a considerable fright when Saunders threw up an old skull, which rolled down the earth and landed at the window. So frightened was Todd that he ran out of the school and all the way home!

At Whitsunday 1831 the family moved to East Montgarswood farm, where his father was engaged as farm manager, or foreman, to Henry Richmond. In 1834 the Todd family moved to Castlehill farm, in the parish of Kilmarnock. When he was old enough, Adam Todd found work on various local farms, and at Galston tileworks, where he was paid 6s and 6d per week for a 14-hour day in 1838. In 1844 he moved to Wellhill Tileworks, in the parish of New Cumnock, of which he became tacksman in 1851, and remained there until 1861.

It was during his time working at New Cumnock that Todd had his first success as a poet, when 'The Storm' was published in the *Ayr Advertiser*. He was encouraged to write more, and in 1846 his first book of poems, *The Hermit of Westmorland, The Covenanter's Revenge, and other poems*, was published. From then on he contributed articles of various sorts to local newspapers, in particular the *Kilmarnock Journal*. Adam Todd took on a partnership in the Dalquharran Tileworks, which were located near Dailly in southern Ayrshire. He still lived in the Cumnock area, and travelled to and from the works on his mare, 'Brenda'. In 1862 he rented Taiglim farm in Old Cumnock parish but in 1863 moved to Afton Bridgend. In 1864 he settled in Cumnock. He built for himself a new stone bungalow in Glaisnock Street, known as 'Breezyhill', which still stands.

10.2 Adam Brown Todd *(Author's Collection)*

From that time on Todd wrote more extensively, for the *Ayrshire Post, Ayr Advertiser* and *The Cumnock Express*, of which he had been appointed editor in 1863. This newspaper, which was a local edition of the *Ayr Observer*, ceased publication in 1909. In 1863 he married the great grand niece of Dr Alexander Murray, Professor of Oriental Languages at Edinburgh University. A second volume of poems, *Poems, Lectures and Miscellanies*, appeared in 1876 and a third, *The Circling Year and other Poems*, in 1880.

A. B. Todd, as he styled himself when writing, had a keen interest in the Covenanters, instilled in him from birth, for his father was descended of the Fenwick Covenanters. He wrote two books on the stories of the Covenanters, *Homes, Haunts and Battlefields of the Covenanters*, published in 1886 and 1888, and *Covenanting Pilgrimages and Studies*, published in 1911. His interest in Covenanters resulted in him playing an active part in having new memorials erected, and he was secretary of the Cumnock Peden Monument Committee, which was to have the white granite monument to Rev Alexander Peden erected in the Barrhill cemetery in 1891. It was unveiled in 1892 before a crowd of 3,500. Other memorials that he had an active part in having erected were those at Lochgoin at Fenwick, to the poet James Hyslop at Sanquhar, and to the Battle of Bothwell Bridge.

Todd was also a noted Burnsian, and he presided at Cumnock Burns Club's annual dinner on a number of occasions. Adam Todd served on Cumnock Burgh Council for a time, and was noted for squabbling with James Keir Hardie, Todd being a Conservative in politics. Nevertheless, he was honoured with a public luncheon in Cumnock Town Hall on 3 October 1903 to celebrate his diamond jubilee as a journalist. At the event he was presented with an illuminated address and £168 15s. Todd died at his Cumnock home on Sunday 31 January 1915 aged 92. He was buried in Cumnock New Cemetery, where a tall sandstone headstone marks his grave.

A number of Todd's relatives emigrated to New Zealand, and Rev Garfield Todd went from there to became a missionary in Africa. He became involved in politics and eventually became Prime Minister of Northern Rhodesia (now Zambia). However, he was ousted by the regime of Ian Smith in 1964 and spent much of his life thereafter under house arrest.

JOSEPH TRAIN (1779-1852)

Joseph Train was born in the parish on 6 November 1779 of humble parents, his ancestors being land stewards on the estate of Gilmilnscroft. He received little schooling, but he was keen to educate himself. Around 1787 he moved with his family to Ayr and following a simple education enlisted in the Ayrshire Militia in 1799, serving until 1802. At this time he subscribed for a copy of Burns's works, published at a cost of one guinea and a half. His colonel, Sir David Hunter Blair, saw the copy lying in an Inverness bookshop and asked to buy it, only to be informed that it was ordered by one of his own men. He was so delighted by this that he gave the bookseller orders to have it bound in the best leather and given to Train free of charge.

Train then worked for James Finlay of Glasgow for a time, and in 1808 was appointed an officer of the excise. He served at first in Largs but in 1813 he was transferred to Newton Stewart. He worked for a time at Perth, where he was attempting to suppress the illicit distillation of whisky in the hills. His experience caused him to draw up a document suggesting how the excise could be improved and these were adopted in 1815.

In 1806 the first volume of poems written by Train was published, entitled *Poetical Reveries*. In 1814 *Strains of the Mountain Muse* was published, subtitled *Poems, with notes illustrative of traditions in Galloway and Ayrshire*, printed by Ballantyne in Edinburgh. The proofs were noted by Walter Scott and he immediately wrote to Train, asking to be on his list of subscribers, requesting one dozen copies. When the book was printed, Scott took it with him on his tour by ship around Scotland, and was so impressed by it that he asked that Train could help him to track down historical information and tradition from Ayrshire and Galloway, which he subsequently used in his novels. Train became friendly with Sir Walter Scott and sent the great author many stories and details thereafter. He also presented him with a number of antiquities, including Rob Roy MacGregor's purse and a drinking horn, reputedly gifted by Robert the Bruce to the leper hospital at Kingcase in Prestwick. He also passed on the jougs from Threave Castle, thumbscrews used to torture Covenanters, Grierson of Lag's sword, and a Roman battle axe. Sir Walter Scott noted that most of the knowledge he gained on the life of Robert Paterson, or 'Old Mortality', was supplied to him by Train, at that time 'supervisor of Excise at Dumfries, to whom I owe many obligations of a similar nature.' Other novels of Scott's that owe much to Train include *Redgauntlet, Guy Mannering, The Surgeon's Daughter, The Lord of the Isles* and *Peveril of the Peak*.

Train also supplied many historical details to George Chalmers, author of *Caledonia*, a historical account of Scotland. He was the first to trace Roman roads through Nithsdale to Ayr and compiled data on the Dei'l's Dyke, an elongated earthwork that snakes for 80 miles across Ayrshire and Galloway. Train moved to Cupar in Fife in 1820, followed by Kirkintilloch, Queensferry, Falkirk and finally Castle Douglas, all due to his position with the excise, from which he retired in 1836. He lived at Lochvale, St Andrew Street, Castle Douglas, with his wife, Mary Wilson, whom he had married in 1803. They had five children.

In 1845 Joseph Train wrote a *Historical and Statistical Account of the Isle of Man*, and in 1846 *The Buchanites from First to Last*. He wrote a number of articles that were published in *Chambers Journal* and the *Dumfries Magazine*. He died on 14 December 1852 and is buried at the old kirkyard of Kelton, near Castle Douglas. Plaques to his memory were erected in the MacMillan Hall, Newton Stewart, and in the Town Hall, Castle Douglas, both unveiled in 1909.

THOMAS WALKER (1750-1833)

Thomas Walker was a minor poet who lived at Poole, which was located near to Watston farm, Ochiltree. He was a tailor to trade, but spent much of his time writing verses. He became friendly with William Simson (1758-1815), schoolmaster in Ochiltree and Cumnock, better known to Burns aficionados as 'Winsome Willie'. Walker sent a number of his compositions to Robert Burns but the poet does not seem to have replied. This annoyed Walker, and he wrote scathingly to Burns, attacking his moral standing, in a poem starting 'What woefu' news is this, I hear?' in which he comments on Burns's affair with Jean Armour and his intention to leave Scotland. This goaded Burns into writing the poem 'Reply to a Trimming Epistle received from a Tailor' around August or September 1786:

> What ails ye now, ye lousie bitch
> To thresh my back at sic a pitch?
> Losh, man, ha'e mercy wi' your natch!
>   You bodkin's bauld:
> I didnae suffer half sae much
>   Frae Daddie Auld.

This poem, which extends to 12 verses, despite its remarks, was treasured by Walker, who believed it to be by the poet. However, no manuscript of the poem survives, and it has been claimed that the reply was composed by none other than Simson himself. This theory was noted by James Paterson in his *Contemporaries of Burns*, in which he relates how Simson told Burns that he had replied on his behalf, and that the poet replied, 'You did well. You thrashed the tailor much better than I would have done.'

Thomas Walker was to write a religious pamphlet, *A Picture of the World*, which was distributed widely and brought him some degree of fame. He later moved to Bridgend Cottage at Sorn, where he died in 1833 aged 82 years. His remains were interred in the kirkyard.

JOHN WRIGHT (1805-c.1844)

Wright was a minor poet born on 1 September 1805 at Auchencloigh farm, fourth child of five sons and two daughters of James Wright and Grizzle Taylor (she died in December 1842). He is said to have obtained his intellect from his mother, and moved around the age of seven to near Galston, where he assisted his father as a coal driver. At the age of thirteen he was apprenticed to George Brown in Galston and was trained at the loom as a weaver. He took an interest in his employer's weekly meetings for mutual improvement, and he borrowed books which he studied, learning to read. His poems reflect his love of the countryside, and his difficulties in love. Amongst his works were 'Mahomet, or the Hegira', which was 1,500 lines in length, followed by 'The Retrospect', published in Edinburgh in 1824.

10.3 John Wright, poet *(Author's Collection)*

He was to live in Ayr for a time, followed by Cambuslang, where he worked as a weaver. Wright was to leave his family behind and spent the rest of his life wandering the countryside, selling the second edition of 'The Retrospect'. According to John MacIntosh, writing in *The Poets of Ayrshire*, this 'led him into dissipated habits, ruined his health, and brought him to an early grave.' He died in Glasgow around 1844. About the same time *The Whole Poetical Works of John Wright* was published in 1843.

10.4 John Wright's Signature *(Author's Collection)*

FARMS AND SMALL LAIRDSHIPS

1900 – known dates
1899 – known dates, but not necessarily terminal
c.1750 – approximate dates

Auchencloigh
1663	John Richmond
1724	James Richmond
1774	John Richmond
1789	William Richmond
c.1810	Mr Falconer
1830-1873	Duke of Portland – William Bone (1800-1873)
1873-1905	Duke of Portland – David Bone JP (1830-1905)
1905-1919	Duke of Portland – William Bone (1874-1958)
1919-1958	William Bone (1874-1958)
1958-1979	William Bone (1915-2004)
1979-1990	William Bone (1915-2004) & W. David Bone (1949-)
1990-2003	W. David Bone (1949-)
2003-	David Herbert

Auchenlongford (East)
c.1750	Gilbert MacAdam
1779-	Fairfield Estate
1882-1907	Fairfield Estate – William Clark (1827-1907)
1919-1923	Fairfield Estate – Alexander & W Clark
1941-1956	Fairfield Estate – Robert Fitzsimmons Clark (1909-1991)
1956-	Robert Fitzsimmons Clark (1909-1991)
2007-	Gong Hill Ltd – Alexander W. Clark

Auchenlongford (West)
-1648	Alexander Pethein (d. 1648)

1648-	Alexander Pethein
1693-1723	James Peden (d. 1723)
1723-	James Peden
-1779	James Peden
1779-	Innes of Stowe
1882	George Park
1900	Glenbuck Estate – George Campbell (1818-1907) & William Campbell
1919	Glenbuck Estate – George Hogg
1923-1941	Sorn Estate – John Cameron Fergusson
-2001	Sorn Estate – Hugh Fergusson (1927-2001)
2001-*2008*	Sorn Estate – Hugh Fergusson

Auchmannoch

1900	Auchmannoch Estate – John Lambroughton
1941	Lanfine Estate – James and Hugh Lambroughton
1956	Lanfine Estate – Lindsay Clark
2008	A. R. MacIntyre

Auchmillanhill

1900	Netherplace Estate – Hugh Hodge
1919	Hugh Hodge
1941	Hugh Hodge – Alexander Hodge
2008	Hugh Hodge

Barboigh

1850-1882	- Hugh Watson
1900	Howard de Walden Estate – Alexander Watson
1919-28	Alexander Watson
1941	Alexander D. Watson (1907-87)
2008	Ian Watson

Barrshouse

1826-1831	Gilmilnscroft Estate – Matthew Todd
1857-	Gilmilnscroft Estate – John Piper
1882-1921	Gilmilnscroft Estate – John Piper (1832-1921)
1921-1936	Gilmilnscroft Estate – William Piper (1860-1937)
1936-1937	William Piper (1860-1937)
1937-1985	James Frew (1895-1985)
1985-	William Frew

Blackbriggs

1900-1905	Auchmannoch Estate – Robert Strathearn (1825-1905)
1918	Lanfine Estate – Robert Thomson
1941	Lanfine Estate – George R. Templeton
2007-	George R. Templeton

Blackdyke

1819	- Henry Richmond (1796-1871)
1882-1900	Sorn Estate – David Shaw (1814-1904) and Charles Shaw
1919	Sorn Estate – James and Robert Armstrong
1937-1941	Sorn Estate – Robert Armstrong

Blackdyke (Little)

1941	Mary Gordon Watson – Robert Shankland

Blackside

1692	- Alexander McKerrow
1782-1792	Dalgain Estate
1882-1894	Sorn Estate – Francis Dickie Weir (1842-1921)
1900	Sorn Estate – John Mackie
1919-1941	Sorn Estate – George M. Anderson
1947	Sorn Estate – Rae

Blacksidend

1882-1900	Gilmilnscroft Estate – Robert Steel
1919-1923	Gilmilnscroft Estate – James Wilson
1941	Norah Farquhar Oliver – John Wilson of Smiddyshaw
2007-2008	John Tannock of Longmore – Thomas Blacklock
2008-	Cessnock Estate

Blairkip (North)

c.1825	Sorn Estate – Baird
1882-1924	Sorn Estate – John Stewart Baird (d. 1924) & Charles Baird (d. 1924)
1927	Sorn Estate – David Baird and Hugh Baird
1941	Sorn Estate – Charles Baird Hastings
2008	James Hogarth

Blairkip (South)

1882	Sorn Estate – Thomas Baird
1900	Sorn Estate – John and Gilbert Baird

1919-1941	Sorn Estate – John Templeton
2008	Archie Baird

Blairmulloch

1882-1927	Sorn Estate – James Sloan (d. 1927)
1941	Sorn Estate – Hugh Reid Sloan (1898-1979)
2007-	Sorn Estate – Hugh Sloan

Blindburn

1692-1702	John Peden
1770	Hugh Mitchell
1782-1792	Dalgain Estate
1859	- James Welsh
1882-1900	Sorn Estate – James and John Baird
1919	Sorn Estate – David Hastings
1941	Sorn Estate – James Donald
2007-	Sorn Estate – Archibald P. Johnston & Sons

Bogend

1882-1900	Auchinleck Estate – George and John Peden
1919	Auchinleck Estate – George Peden
1941	Andrew and Alexander Peden
	George Peden
2008	P.R. Forrest

Bogend (of Carleith)

1900	Howard de Walden Estate – Matthew Jamieson
1919	Janet Jamieson
1941	John W. Jamieson

Brackenhill

1882	Auchinleck Estate – James Murray
1900-1919	Auchinleck Estate – James Alexander
1941-c.1970	James A. Tannock
c.1970-2008	Robert Crawford

Brocklar (High)

1782-1792	Dalgain Estate
1882	Sorn Estate – Matthew & John Young
1900	Sorn Estate – John Cameron & Hugh Fergusson (1859-1947)
1919	Sorn Estate – empty

1941	Sorn Estate - empty
2008	Sorn Estate - Peter Wren

Brocklar (Laigh)

1782-1792	Dalgain Estate
1882	Sorn Estate – Matthew Young (d. 1925) & John Young
1900-1945	Sorn Estate – John Cameron & Hugh Fergusson (1859-1947)
1941	Sorn Estate – James Fergusson
2008	Sorn Estate – Roy Jones

Burntshield

1779-	Innes of Stowe
1882-1900	Glenbuck Estate – John Wilson (1840-1921)
1915-1918	Glenbuck Estate – John Cameron (1862-1918)
1918-	Annie Cameron
1941	Annie Clark
2008	David Ogilvie

Carleith (Little)

1941	William Mair – Hugh Cunningham
2008	Andrew Jamieson

Carleith (Meikle)

1663	Andrew Richmond
1691	John Willock
1700	James Richmond
1704	John Richmond
1767-1792	John Richmond
	William Wallace (1805-1871)
1882-1900	Howard de Walden Estate – Robert Alexander Taylor
1900	John Mair
1919	Mary Mair (widow of William Mair)
1941	William Mair
2008	Jamieson

Catrine Holm

1900	Catrine House Estate – Adam & Simon Scott
1919	Catrine House Estate – John Hamilton

Catrine Mains

1882	Ballochmyle Estate – David MacKerrow

179

| 1900 | Ballochmyle Estate – William Park |
| 1919 | Ballochmyle Estate – David Shaw & Charles Shaw |

Catrineshaw

1792	John Gibson
1882	Catrine House Estate – James Campbell
1900	Catrine House Estate – Alexander Cochrane Duncan
1919	Catrine House Estate – William Marshall
1941	Catrine House Estate – William Maxwell
c.1965-2007	James S Hodge

Clews (High)

-1648	Robert Campbell
1648-	William Mitchell
1702	- Beg
1882	Thomas Letharday
1919	Auchinleck Estate – Robert Templeton

Clews (Low)

1512	James Campbell
1621	James Campbell
1643	John Campbell
1648	Robert Campbell
-1681	John Campbell
1681-	John Campbell
1747	James Campbell
c.1800	Auchinleck Estate
1895	Auchinleck Estate – James Campbell (1817-1895)
1941	William Hastie Bryson
2008	Mungo Bryson

Croftfoot

1882	Ballochmyle Estate – Mungo MacKerrow
1900-1919	Ballochmyle Estate – Margaret MacKerrow
1927-1956	Ballochmyle Estate – David MacKerrow
	William Bruce MacKerrow (1931-1981)
2000-	David MacKerrow

Crofthead

| 1823 | - Gardener |
| 1824 | - MacGaan |

1882	Sorn Estate – William Sloan
1900	Sorn Estate – George and John Templeton
1919-1941	Sorn Estate – Alexander Eccles
	Sorn Estate – Hugh Ross
	Hugh Ross
-1967	David & Mary Robb
1967-*c*.1990	Charles Shaw & David Shaw
c.1990-	David Shaw

Crofthead of Auchmannoch

1865-1916	Auchmannoch Estate – John Lambroughton (1836-1916)
1916-1918	Auchmannoch Estate – James & Hugh Lambroughton
1918-*1941*	Lanfine Estate – James & Hugh Lambroughton
2008	Nicholas Armour

Daldilling

1527-1544	George Reid
1596	George Reid
1641-1651	George Reid
1651-*1662*	John Reid
-1691	Rev William Reid
1691-*1698*	William Reid
1698-1740	John Mitchell of Turnerhill
1740-1792	Dalgain Estate
1836	James Struthers
1882	Sorn Estate – James MacKerrow
1900	Sorn Estate – Charles Sloan
1919	Sorn Estate – Thomas Wardrop
1927-1941	Sorn Estate – Robert & Andrew Clark
	Sorn Estate – Thomas Lindsay Clark Sr.
2007-8	Sorn Estate – Thomas Lindsay Clark Jr.

Daldorch

1794-1795	Hugh Breakenrig (Brackenridge)
1882-1900	Sorn Estate – John and Andrew Watson
1919	Daldorch Estate
1941	Daldorch Estate – James Kennedy Jr.
-2007	John Kennedy
2007-	Neil Kennedy

Dalgain

1691	Hugh Mitchell
1740-1796	Dalgain Estate
1882-1900	Sorn Estate – Robert Brown
1919	Sorn Estate – Hugh Gibson & John Gibson
1941	Sorn Estate – James Donald
2008	George Young

Darnhay

1882	- William Richmond
1900	Howard de Walden Estate – William Wallace
1919	William Smith Jr
1941	William Smith
	Alistair Watson
2008	William Cochrane

Dykeneuk

1882	Sorn Estate – John Morton
1900	Sorn Estate
1919-1942	Sorn Estate – Archibald Paterson Johnston
1947	Sloan
2008	Graham Hillary

Glenshamrock

1535	Gilmilnscroft Estate
1882-1919	Gilmilnscroft Estate – James Kennedy
1941	James Kennedy
	Douglas Kennedy
	Lees
	Messenger
	Wynn
2008	George Haye

Heateth (Hillend of)

1900	Dumfries House Estate – James Boswell
1919	James Boswell
1941	Hugh Gibson
-1981	Neil Raphael
1981-1990	J & R MacKinlay - John MacKinlay
1990-	Jackson
2008	Scot MacFarlane

Heateth (Little)
1882-1900	Dumfries House Estate – John Lymburner
1919	John Lymburner & Archibald Lymburner
1941-1963	Archibald Lymburner (1886-1963)
1963-1977	James Boswell Lymburner (1913-1977)
1983-	Robert Sloan of Darnlaw – James Robert Lawson
2008	Bryce Sloan of Darnlaw - James Robert Lawson

Heateth (Meikle)
1832	- John Hutton
1900-1919	Dumfries House Estate – John (1831-1912), Robert & William Boswell (1838-1912)
1941	Archibald Lymburner – John Lymburner (1908-1982)
-1981	Neil Raphael
1981-1990	J & R MacKinlay - Raynor MacKinlay
1990-1992	Derek Barrow
1992-	David Robinson

Heateth (Mid)
1845	- Archibald Lymburner (1819-1905)
1905	- John L. Stewart

Heilar (Mid) (known as Glendale since 1984)
1539	James Reid
1788	Fairfield Estate
1882-1900	Fairfield Estate – William & Gilbert Harvey (1834-1922)
1919-1946	Fairfield Estate – David Young
-1984	Major Kennedy of Doonholm -
1984-	Adam McIlheron

Heilar (Nether)
1600-	Andrew Mitchell
-1710	John Mitchell of Turnerhill
1710-1819	Glenlogan Estate – Logan of that Ilk
1900	Glenlogan Estate – Agnes Young
-1915	Glenlogan Estate – William Templeton (1838-1915)
1915-1926	Glenlogan Estate – James Templeton (d.1947)
1926-*1941*	William MacMurray
	Alastair Drummond
2007-	Alan Drummond

Heilar (Upper or Over)

1600-1608	- Durie
1682	William Duncan
1717-1722	Mungo Duncan
1762-1776	John Duncan (b. 1717)
c.1800	Mungo Duncan (b. 1762)
-c.1810	William Duncan (b. 1765)
c.1810-	Fairfield Estate -
1900-1923	Fairfield Estate – George F Milligan
1941	Fairfield Estate – George Milligan
-1956	Fairfield Estate

Henryston (Corbiehill)

1900	Gilmilnscroft Estate – George Rodger Templeton
1919	Gilmilnscroft Estate – Jane Templeton
1941	Margaret Templeton
	MacMurray
	George Young
-c.1997	Hugh Blythe
c.1997-	Allan Mackay

Hill of Auchmannoch

-1601	James Brown
1601-1649	William Brown
1702	J. Brown
1900	Auchmannoch Estate – Findlay Murchie (1827-1909)
1918-*1941*	Lanfine Estate – Charles Sloan
2008	David Martin

Hillhead of Sorn

1882	Sorn Estate – William & Thomas Retson
1900	Sorn Estate – John Wilson
1919	Sorn Estate – William Muir
1941	Sorn Estate – Thomas Templeton (1891-1971)
-1991	Sorn Estate – David Templeton
1991-	Sorn Estate – David Shaw

Hillhead of Gilmilnscroft

1882	- Andrew & John Tannock
1900	Gilmilnscroft Estate – Andrew Tannock
1919-1920	Gilmilnscroft Estate – John Sutherland (d. 1920)

1941	Gilmilnscroft Estate – David Ross
	MacClure
	Wiliam Gibson
	Wilson
2008	Prof. Ian Selman

Hole (Holehouse)

1654	William Aird
1687	William Aird
c.1750	James Aird
1716	Patrick Davidson
1782-1792	Dalgain Estate
c.1790-	Steele
c.1830	Robert Steele
1833	Sorn Estate
1882	Sorn Estate – Gavin Hamilton
1900	Sorn Estate – Thomas Clark

Holehouse-Hillhead (before 1897 – High Holhouse)

1782-1792	Dalgain Estate
1900-1919	Sorn Estate – John Williamson
1941	Sorn Estate – Barbara Cavan
2008	John Dunlop

Holhouse Mill (formerly Sands)

1882	John and Andrew MacCrae (1788-1871)
1900	Andrew MacCrae (d. 1915)
1919	Sorn Estate – ruins

Kenstey

1882	AuchinleckEstate – John C. Sharp
1900	Auchinleck Estate – Robert & James Sharp
1919	Auchinleck Estate – James Sharp & Margaret Sharp
1941	James C. Sharp
c.1980	James Hodge

Knowehead

1900	Sorn Estate – Robert Fitsimmons
1919	Sorn Estate – James Johnstone
1941	Sorn Estate – Thomas Ramage (1915-1997)
	Andrew Ballantyne Watson (1943-2004)

Limmerhaugh (North)

1702	- Gibson
1900-1919	Dallars (Tufnell) Estate – Alexander Park
1937-1941	Richard Lionel Tufnell – Ivie Park
2007	James Cowan

Limmerhaugh (South)

1900	Dallars (Tufnell) Estate – Thomas Kerr
1919	Dallars (Tufnell) Estate – James Smith
1941	Richard Lionel Tufnell – James Fallas

Lindsayhill

1882	John Boswell
1900	Auchinleck Estate – Adam & Simon Scott
1919	Auchinleck Estate – George Peden
1941	Andrew and Alexander Peden
	Derek Barrow
1995-	John Purdie of Birnieknowe

Logan (High)

1882	- William Wilson
1900	Auchmannoch Estate – David Graham
1919	Daldorch Estate – David Graham
1925-1928	Daldorch Estate – Robert Riddall Graham (1885-1928)
1941	Daldorch Estate – James Kennedy
2008	Roddy Middleton

Logan (Laigh)

1882-1908	Gilmilnscroft Estate – James Girvan (1823-1908)
1919	Gilmilnscroft Estate – William Girvan
1941	James Girvan
	Bryson
2008	Andrew Hannah

Logan (North)

1882-1912	Gilmilnscroft Estate – William Girvan (1867-1912)
	& William Girvan Jr
1919	Gilmilnscroft Estate – Annie Girvan
1941	Robert Kennedy
	John Weir
2008	Edward Hewitt

Logan (South)

1882-1919	Gilmilnscroft Estate – Thomas Campbell
1941	Thomas Campbell of Polquheys
-1977	Thomas Caldwell
1977-1996	- Mungo Howat
1996-*2008*	William Howat

Meadowhead of Sorn

1680	William Mitchell
1882	Sorn Estate – Robert Kennedy
1900	Sorn Estate
1919	Sorn Estate – Matthew MacTaggart
1929-1939	Sorn Estate – Robert Cunningham I
1939-1961	Sorn Estate – Robert Cunningham II
1961-	Sorn Estate – Robert Anderson
2007-	Sorn Estate – J. & W. Kay – Matthew Bell

Meadowhead of Auchmannoch

1882	Auchmannoch Estate – Hugh Lambroughton
1900-1901	Auchmannoch Estate – James Merrie Wilson
1918	Lanfine Estate – Alexander Mair
1941-1956	Lanfine Estate – William Cunningham

Merkland (Low)

-1654	John Reid
1654-1674	Mungo Reid (d. 1674)
1674-	Margaret Reid
1702-1715	John Reid
c.1750-c.1770	Gilbert MacAdam
c.1780	Fairfield Estate
	Fairfield Estate – Gilbert Clark (1759-1841)
1900	Fairfield Estate – Marion Clark & John Clark
1919-1956	Fairfield Estate – Alexander Stewart (1877-1959)
	Alexander S. Fergusson
2008	Gong Hill Ltd - Dennis Marshall

Montgarswood (East, or Little)

1603-	James Campbell
1695	William Campbell
1770	- Campbell
-1798	Henry Richmond

1798-	James Richmond
1852-1871	Henry Richmond (1796-1871)
1886-1900	Ballochmyle Estate – James Gall
1914-1919	Ballochmyle Estate – John Smith
1941	Ballochmyle Estate – David Shaw
2008	Robert Shaw

Muirhead of Auchmannoch

1900	Auchmannoch Estate – John & William Craig
1918-*1941*	Lanfine Estate – William Duncan

Nethershield (Nether Burntshield, or Benthead)

1882	Sorn Estate – Gavin Hamilton
1900-1925	Sorn Estate – Thomas Clark (d. 1925)
1925-*1927*	Sorn Estate – Alex Clark
1941	Sorn Estate – James Welsh
2007-	J. Morton Welsh

Newhouse

1900	Howard de Walden Estate – Agnes MacGavin
1918-	Lanfine Estate – Janet Jamieson
1941	Lanfine Estate – John W. Jamieson
2008	Scott Ashforth

Oxenshaw

1792	John Mitchell
1900-1918	Netherplace Estate – Alexander Paton (1843-1918)
1941	John Paterson
2008	J. & E. Paterson

Redgate

-1823	Ballochmyle Estate – Andrew Borland (d. 1823)
1882	Ballochmyle Estate – James and Cuthbert Nairn
1900	Ballochmyle Estate – John & William Harvey
1919	Ballochmyle Estate – James Nisbet Martin
1941	Robert Hillhouse

Roundshaw

1882	- James Weir
1900	Ballochmyle Estate – John Duncan
1919	Ballochmyle Estate – Robert Wardrop

1941	Robert Wardrop
c.1955	David Wardrop
c.1970-2008	Benjamin Welsh

Sawerston

1707-1727	John Paton
1759-1770	Robert Paton
1790-1810	Robert Paton
c.1810	Mr White
1837-1874	Thomas White (d. 1874)
1900-1927	Netherplace Estate – John MacKerrow
1941	John MacKerrow
2008	W. M. & J. D. Gibson

Shawwood

1882-1900	Catrine House Estate – Andrew Taylor
1919	Catrine House Estate – Matthew Nisbet
1941	Catrine House Estate – Thomas Houston
	James Hodge
2008	Thomas Neil

Shiel

1882-1922	Glenlogan Estate – John Harper (d. 1922)
1941	James Hyslop Auld
1976-	Trevor Hamilton
	Scottish Coal
	Rockwood Mining
2008	Adam MacIlheron - Colin Douglas

Smiddyshaw

1527	Hugh Craufurd
1612-1629	Robert Craufurd
1641-1646	William Craufurd
1662	- Craufurd
c.1665	Cessnock Estate
1702	Patrick Boyle
1770	- Somerville
1882	Adam Anderson
1900	Sorn Estate – Robert Strathern Jr.
1919-1941	Sorn Estate – Robert Strathern
	Sorn Estate – John Wilson

Sorn Estate – Sam Anderson (1921-1997)

2008   Sorn Estate – Alexander Anderson

Sorn Mains

*1882-*1901   Sorn Estate – Thomas Traill (d. 1901)

1919-1941   Sorn Estate – James Ramage

1980   Sorn Estate – Robert Ramage

2007   Sorn Estate – James Nisbet

Waterside of Glenlogan (Glenlogan Home Farm)

1900   Glenlogan Estate – James Baird

1919   Glenlogan Estate – Anthony Caven

1934   Glenlogan Estate – William Niven

1941   Glenlogan Estate – Robert Kelly

*c.1955-*1988   Glenlogan Estate – Thomas Lindsay Clark Sr.

1988-*2008*   Thomas Lindsay Clark Sr.

Waulkmiln

1900   Sorn Estate – Alexander Stewart

Weitshaw (High Burn o' Need to around 1900)

1900-1923   Sorn Estate – William Anderson

1941   Sorn Estate – George & James Anderson

1956   James David Anderson (1896-1957)

2007-2008   Sorn Estate – J. & W. Kay

West Town

1782-1792   Dalgain Estate

1882   Sorn Estate – William Weir

1900   Sorn Estate – John Harper Jr

1919   Sorn Estate – Andrew MacGregor

1941   Sorn Estate – Thomas Gibson

  -c.1984   Sorn Estate - Rutherford

c.1984-   George Henderson

Whiteflat

-1821   Auchinleck Estate

1821-1874   Auchinleck Estate – Mungo Bryson I (1794-1874)

1874-1921   Auchinleck Estate – Mungo Bryson II (1833-1923)

1921-1923   Mungo Bryson II (1833-1923)

1923-1936   Mungo Bryson III (1870-1936)

1936-*1941*	William Hastie Bryson
2007	Mungo Bryson IV

Woodhead

1882	Gilmilnscroft Estate – William Retson
1900-1919	Gilmilnscroft Estate – James Retson

BIBLIOGRAPHY

Archaeological and Historical Collections, Volumes 2 (1880), 3 (1894), 7 (1894), etc., Ayrshire and Galloway Archaeological Association, Edinburgh.

Borland, Maureen, *Shared Lives: Alexander Stephen, shipbuilder & James Templeton, carpet maker,* Maureen Borland, Kilmarnock, 2006.

Bunting, Mary (Editor), *The Busy Wee Toon where the Drum aye gaed roon, At half-past five in the morning – A Collection of Verses from Catrine and Sorn,* Catrine, Sorn & District Local History Group, Catrine, 1988.

Dalziel, Robert & Harrison, Terry, *200 Years of Catrine and Sorn Parish: A Cotton Tale,* Countryside Publications, Chorley, 1987.

Discovery & Excavation Scotland, various volumes, including 1991 and 1998.

Fasti Ecclesiae Scoticanae, (Volumes 3, 8, 9, 10), Church of Scotland, Edinburgh, 1920, 1950, 1961 and 1981 respectively.

Faulds, John C. S., *Sorn Primary School*, Privately Printed, Sorn, 2000.

Fisher, Allan, *Map of Lands of Daldillan ... surveyed in 1782,* located in Sorn Castle, 1782.

Fowler, James J., *The Presbytery of Ayr – its Schools and Schoolmasters*, in *Ayrshire Archaeological and Natural History Society Collections* (Volume 6, 1958-60), Ayr, 1961.

Fairbairn, Archibald, *Notes on Excavations of Prehistoric and Later Sites at Muirkirk, Ayrshire, 1913-1927*, in *Proceedings of the Society of Antiquaries of Scotland*, Volume 61, Society of Antiquaries of Scotland, Edinburgh, 1927.

Guide and Directory to Mauchline, Catrine, Sorn and Surrounding Districts, Mauchline, 1903.

Important Early, Classic and Military Motor Vehicles, Motorcycles and Automobilia, (Sale catalogue), Sotheby's, London, 1988.

Jamieson, Mary and Janet, *Auchencloigh W.R.I. 1921-1991*, A.W.R.I., Auchencloigh, 1991.

Killan, Gerald, *David Boyle, from Artisan to Archaeologist*, University of Toronto Press, Toronto, 1983.

Letters of John Graham of Claverhouse, edited by Andrew Murray Scott, in *Miscellany of the Scottish History Society*, Vol. 11, Scottish History Society, Edinburgh, 1990.

Lindsay, John, *View of the Coinage of Scotland*, Philip John Crowe, Cork, 1845.

McClure, David, *Tolls and Tacksmen*, Ayrshire Archaeological and Natural History Society, Ayr, 1994.

MacIlvean, John Gardiner, *The Birth of Football in the Burns Country*, MacIlvean, Cumnock, 1982.

MacIlvean, John G., *Catrine Church History*, unpublished manuscript, c. 2001.

MacIntosh, John, *The Poets of Ayrshire*, Thomas Hunter, Dumfries, 1910.

MacKenzie, Ross, *A Scottish Renaissance Household – Sir William Hamilton and Newton Castle in 1559*, Ayrshire Archaeological and Natural History Society, Ayr, 1990.

MacMichael, George, *Notes on the Way through Ayrshire*, Hugh Henry, Ayr, n.d.

Mair, James, *Cessnock, an Ayrshire estate in the age of improvement*, Ayrshire Archaeological and Natural History Society, Ayr, 1996.

Muir, Olive, *Emblem of Peace*, John Miller, Glasgow, 1935.

New Statistical Account of Scotland, William Blackwood, Edinburgh, 1842.

Paterson, James, *History of the County of Ayr, with a Genealogical Account of the Families of Ayrshire*, (2 vols.) John Dick, Ayr, 1847 and 1852.

Pigot, J., *National Commercial Directory of the Whole of Scotland*, J. Pigot & Co., London, 1837.

Pitcairn, Robert, *Ancient Criminal Trials in Scotland 1488-1624*, Bannatyne Club, Edinburgh, 1829-31.

Pollok, Robert, *The Persecuted Family – a tale of the village of Sorn and the Covenanters*, H. S. Nisbet, Mauchline, 1861.

Proceedings of the Society of Antiquaries of Scotland, Edinburgh, Vol. 20 – 1885-6, Vol. 32 – 1897-8, Vol. 61 – 1926-7, Vol. 77 – 1942-3, Vol. 114 – 1984.

Ranken, George, *Bush Essays*, Adam & Charles Black, Edinburgh, 1872.
The Land Law of the Future, Sydney, 1877.
The Federal Geography of British Australasia, Turner & Henderson, Sydney, 1891.
Wyndabyne, a Record of By-Gone Times in Australia, related by Reginald Craufurd, Remington & Co., London, 1892.

Ranken, Hew Blackwood, *Our First Sixty Years and a Bit Before*, Privately Published, Ballarat, 1985.

Register of the Great Seal of Scotland, 11 vols., Clark Constable, Edinburgh, 1984.

Regulations of the Parish of Sorn Mort-Safe Society, James Mathie, Kilmarnock, 1827.

Robertson, George, *A Genealogical Account of the Principal Families in Ayrshire*, E. MacQuistan, Irvine, 1824.

Sanderson, Margaret H. B., *The Mauchline Account Books of Melrose Abbey 1527-1528*, Ayrshire Archaeological and Natural History Society, Ayr, 1975.

Seretis, Kyle, and Poller, Tessa, *Gilmilnscroft Colliery and Glenlogan Ironstone Works Survey Project, Sorn, East Ayrshire, Data Structure Report, Project No. 1624,* Glasgow University Archaeological Research Division, Glasgow, 2005.

Slater, Isaac, *Royal National Commercial Directory and Topography of Scotland,* Isaac Slater, Manchester & London, 1867.

Smith, John, *Prehistoric Man in Ayrshire,* Elliot Stock, London, 1895.

Sorn Parochial Board and Parish Council, Minute Books, Account Books and other Records, Ayrshire Archives, Ayr.

Statistical Account of Scotland – Parish of Sorn, Edinburgh, 1796.

Steven, Helen J., *Sorn Parish – its History and Associations,* Dunlop & Drennan, Kilmarnock, 1898.

Strawhorn, John, & Boyd, William, *The Third Statistical Account of Scotland: Ayrshire,* Oliver & Boyd, Edinburgh, 1951.

Timperley, Loretta R. (ed.), *A Directory of Landownership in Scotland, c. 1770,* Scottish Record Society, New Series 5, Edinburgh, 1976.

Todd, Adam Brown, *Homes, Haunts and Battlefields of the Covenanters,* James Gemmell, Edinburgh, 1888.

The Poetical Works of A. B. Todd with Autobiography, Oliphant, Anderson & Ferrier, Edinburgh, 1906.

Covenanting Pilgrimages and Studies, Oliphant, Anderson & Ferrier, Edinbugh, 1911.

Warrick, Rev John, *The History of Old Cumnock,* Alexander Gardner, Paisley, 1899.

Weis, Charles MacC., & Pottle, Frederick A., *Boswell in Extremes, 1776-1778,* William Heinemann, London, 1971.

Wight, Andrew, *Present State of Husbandry in Scotland* (Two volumes), William Creech, Edinburgh, 1778 and 1784.

Wilson, Rhona, *Old Catrine and Sorn,* Richard Stenlake, Cumnock, 1997.

Wright, John, *The Whole Poetical Works of John Wright,* MacCormick & Gemmell, Ayr, 1843.

INDEX

Figures in **bold** type refer to illustrations